Praise for *The Shape of Sound*

'I devoured this in a day, fascinated, enlightened, moved.'
Helen Garner

'Powerfully written—books like this restore the world.'
Sarah Krasnostein

'Every now and then you come across a book that really makes you see your world anew. In the case of *The Shape of Sound*, Murphy has allowed me to hear something new. More than a memoir, this book reveals both glorious and shocking things about sound and society that I'd never even realised I didn't know. Murphy revels in words, finding the most extraordinary ways to render the body and mind as sometimes warring, sometimes synchronous. This book is special: it offers us a unique and committed voice, sure of the right things while also unsure of the right things. I challenge anyone to come away from reading *The Shape of Sound* without at least a handful of revelations. Mark the name Fiona Murphy.'
Bri Lee, author of *Eggshell Skull*

'Fiona Murphy is a spectacular writer. Her memoir about keeping a medical secret close, then celebrating disability, Deaf identity and community, highlights the need to remove barriers to access and inclusion. *The Shape of Sound* is brilliant.'
Carly Findlay, author of *Say Hello*

'*The Shape of Sound* is about coming of age, and coming to terms with the unseen and unspoken forces that impinge upon a life lived in a disabled or different body. In this utterly gripping book, Murphy writes with candour and elegance, as she challenges how the reader sees the world.'
Fiona Wright, author of *The World Was Whole*

'Fiona Murphy investigates the social, environmental, economical and political impacts of deafness and disability with rigour, yet without ever losing a pervading humanity. *The Shape of Sound* is an impressive accomplishment, equally industrious and delicate, and an exciting addition to Australian disability literature.'
Kylie Maslen, author of *Show Me Where it Hurts*

'In *The Shape of Sound* a young Deaf woman navigates the corrosive impact of ableism. With precise and elegant prose, Fiona Murphy chronicles the vigilance needed to exist in a world designed for hearing people and how this attentiveness, while debilitating, translates to a keen sensitivity. Through her intelligent observations, her persistence and strength, she highlights the importance of writing in helping her to inhabit her Deaf self. It is a beautifully crafted memoir, enriched by thoughtful rendering of the gifts of a life without sound.' **Jessica White, author of *Hearing Maud***

'*The Shape of Sound* is an exquisite, eloquent and poetic memoir. Fiona Murphy draws the reader into a different sensory world, and provides a devastating critique of a society that all too often punishes disability. A damn fine read.' **Astrid Edwards, host of *Anonymous Was a Woman* and *The Garret: Writers on Writing***

'I have been waiting for Fiona Murphy's debut: a memoir about the lived experience of deafness and a developing understanding of disability as cultural identity. There is no reading *The Shape of Sound* without wishing that every Australian would read it too.' **Sam Twyford-Moore, author of *The Rapids***

'Full of heart and delving into what it means to inhabit flesh, blood, sound and movement, *The Shape of Sound* is definitely a book I will return to over the years, and gain more from with each read. A brilliant debut.' **Katerina Bryant, author of *Hysteria***

'"Deaf people feel and see sound: the entire body becomes a receptor," Fiona Murphy writes in *The Shape of Sound*. You will feel and see this book. Every page vibrates with poetry and shines with brilliance. Murphy's gorgeous prose is a doorway to a new world—and we readers are lucky to have her as a guide.'
Sarah Sentilles, author of *Draw Your Weapons*

'*The Shape of Sound* is a game-changer, a book that challenges assumptions not only about what it means to be deaf, but what it takes to truly listen, communicate and connect. Fiona Murphy's writing is both powerful and poetic, her writing about the body visceral, candid and often exquisite.' Angela Savage, author of *Mother of Pearl*

'Fiona Murphy's writing—on the cost of concealment, the exclusion of others, and the mysteries and miracles of the human body—is so astute, generous and perceptive. There's such wisdom here about what we can all learn in the quiet by paying attention.'
Benjamin Law, writer and broadcaster

'Beautifully written, honest and heartfelt, this is the book I needed years ago, when I was grappling with my own sense of self as a disabled person. As a musician, I was enthralled by how Fiona experiences music, and I marvelled in her journey to true self-acceptance.' Eliza Hull, musician, writer and disability advocate

'This book is an act of resistance. In her raw and unflinchingly honest memoir, Murphy tells the story of how she overcame shame and secrecy to claim her Deaf identity. An outstanding work and a must-read.' Jax Jacki Brown, disability activist and writer

Fiona Murphy is a Deaf poet and essayist. Her work has been published in *Kill Your Darlings*, *Overland*, *Griffith Review* and the *Big Issue*, among other publications. In 2019, she was awarded the *Overland* Fair Australia Essay Prize and the Monash Undergraduate Creative Writing Prize. In 2018, she was shortlisted for the Richell Prize and highly commended by the Wheeler Centre Next Chapter program. Fiona lives in the Blue Mountains, NSW. *The Shape of Sound* is her first book.

The Shape of Sound

a memoir

Fiona Murphy

TEXT PUBLISHING MELBOURNE AUSTRALIA

textpublishing.com.au

The Text Publishing Company
Swann House, 22 William Street, Melbourne Victoria 3000, Australia

The Text Publishing Company (UK) Ltd
130 Wood Street, London EC2V 6DL, United Kingdom

Published by The Text Publishing Company, 2021

Cover design by Chong W.H.
Cover photograph by Fred Kroh
Page design by Rachel Aitken
Typeset in Granjon by J&M Typesetting

Printed and bound in Australia by Griffin Press, part of Ovato, an accredited ISO/NZS 14001:2004 Environmental Management System printer.

ISBN: 9781922330512 (paperback)
ISBN: 9781925923919 (ebook)

A catalogue record for this book is available from the National Library of Australia.

This book is printed on paper certified against the Forest Stewardship Council® Standards. Griffin Press holds FSC chain-of-custody certification SGS-COC-005088. FSC promotes environmentally responsible, socially beneficial and economically viable management of the world's forests.

My memoir is as true as I can recall. The names and identifying characteristics of some people have been changed to respect their privacy.

Identity is a fluid concept and a personal choice. Lowercase deaf refers to deafness as a medical condition. It does not indicate the degree of hearing loss an individual may have. Some people with hearing loss may prefer to use the term 'hard of hearing'. Uppercase Deaf refers to people who identify as culturally Deaf and may use sign language. Given the ongoing suppression of sign-language education, not all Deaf people are fluent signers or even have access to the Deaf community. Again, this word does not indicate the degree of hearing loss an individual may have.

In music, the lifespan of a sound is described in the following sequence: attack, decay, sustain and release.

Contents

Prelude   1

In waves   2

ATTACK

In words   6

Buttons   20

In secret   24

In corners   39

On lips   56

In sound   65

Flight   82

DECAY

On scars   86

In jest   100

Handshape   117

Orientation   138

Mother tongue   148

Pain points   162

SUSTAIN

On topics of conversation   180

Reasonable adjustments   182

Care work   195

In circles   200

On learning   215

RELEASE

The smallest bone to pick   220

In company   237

Location   242

In parallel   251

In marginalia   253

Expression   260

Different sounds of blue   263

Shapelessness   278

Works cited   283

Acknowledgements   297

Prelude

The body is a disjointed poem of mixed metaphors and similes. The spinal cord lashes out in a wild tangle—cauda equina—the horse's tail. Blood flows through the heart's atrium, the communal space in ancient Roman houses where the hearth burned hot and bright. In the wrist lie two rows of irregular bones, including the lunate, scaphoid and hamate—or the crescent moon, the boat and the hook. The ear cradles the smallest bones in the human body—the malleus, incus and stapes—all three can sit together on your fingertip like a speck of dust. Lean in close and you'll see their quiet, decisive strength: the hammer, anvil and stirrup. In motion they beat and thump the eardrum. In stillness their story continues, nevertheless.

In waves

My deafness became unmissable when I was learning to swim. Every week, from when I was five until I was seven, Mum took me to swimming lessons at the local community centre in Villawood, Western Sydney. At just twenty-five metres long, the indoor swimming pool was usually crammed with bodies, and the chlorinated air was stifling.

I would bob along by the edge, never wanting to be more than an arm's length from safety. The swimming instructor gathered her handful of students into the shallow end, where our feet could almost touch the tiles on the bottom. Her torso rose high out of the water, so, even now, I can't picture her face. She taught us how to kick off from the wall and rocket forwards, our arms and legs stretched long. Mostly, I just remember hopping on the spot, trying to keep my feet in contact with the tiles.

Eventually the instructor approached Mum and said that I seemed to be having trouble hearing, that I rarely followed her instructions and was either in distress or drifting aimlessly through each lesson.

•

Over two decades on, my body is still not calm in water. I'm proficient at swimming, but I feel unanchored and exposed—and my deafness remains unmissable.

Sound travels in waves. More often than not, when people actually hear sound it's at the moment of impact: when waves collide with the ear drum. This is the noisiest, most insistent part of sound. But what about before then? What about the build-up of all that energy and motion? Silence can be just as chaotic and momentous.

Sound is more than noise. In the same way as no one ever thinks of the sea as being simply the shoreline. The sea is wider, deeper, more complex than waves whumping against rock or sand. So why are sound waves only ever talked about as noise?

The prevailing assumption is that deaf people hear nothing, that they don't experience sound at all. Silence is often described as thick, blanketing, golden, constricting, suffocating, oppressive, impenetrable. These are the words I use when I talk about sound.

I feel sound rolling over my skin. I see it shimmer off other faces. I taste it in my mouth. Sometimes, it is all too much. I grab onto walls, back myself into corners and try not to be pulled under.

ATTACK

In words

I was born in 1988, three days before the First Fleet Re-enactment
Voyage sailed into Sydney Harbour, marking two hundred years
since Invasion Day. As Mum was labouring in Bankstown hospital
with her last child, the doctor suggested that she hold on, try to
coincide my birth with the birth of the nation. She thought he was
a fool.

By the age of five, I could rattle off the alphabet with singsong ease.
I'd rove around the house annoying my two brothers and sister by
reciting the letters as fast as possible. Quicker and quicker, until the
letters stuck together.

In Year One at Burwood Public School, in Sydney's inner west, we
were taught to keep our copybooks neat and tidy with the day's date
recorded in the top right-hand corner, followed by a heading in
capital letters. Towards the middle of that year, our teacher started
giving out demerit points if we were messy or careless. The tip of
my pencil hovered uncertainly in the air whenever she reeled off

instructions. My copybook stayed neat, as most pages were left blank.

We would also get demerit points if we didn't put our hand up before asking a question, or if we were caught talking when we should have been working. The points were tallied on a large poster. Three demerits and you'd have to pick up rubbish in the playground. Not wanting to risk getting into trouble, I stayed quiet whenever we had to pull out our copybooks. I'd crane my neck, looking around the table to decipher what everyone was writing. If I couldn't figure it out, I'd draw pictures or arrange my pencils in neat rows, waiting for lunchtime.

In Year Two, instead of pictures on the classroom walls, there were charts of fractions and long words. And no crates of soft toys or building blocks. We sat at our desks for most of the day, only allowed to play during lunch break. Flecks of rubber lay scattered across my desk as I erased mistake after mistake.

At the back of the classroom there was a box of large cards. During reading-time, we had to select a card. Each one contained a short story, two or three paragraphs long, and sometimes a picture as well. There were questions on the card and we had to write the answers in our copybooks. Unable to read anything other than my name, I would trace my finger over the curved marks that looked like hooks.

A few weeks into the school year, Mum took me into the city. As the train carried us through endless suburbs, she told me that I was going to play a few games and then an audiologist would check my ears. Years later, I found out that my teacher, having noticed my blank copybook, suggested I be tested for a learning disorder. This, as well as my swimming instructor's concerns about my hearing, prompted Mum to book an appointment with a child-development clinic.

After I'd spent the morning stacking wooden blocks and colouring in puzzles, Mum and I went out for lunch at a cafe. When we returned to the clinic, we were directed to a different office. The audiologist told me to sit inside a large box in the corner of the room. He put a set of headphones on me.

'Now, Fiona, pay attention and just press the button in front of you whenever you hear something,' he explained, before shutting the door of the box. The walls were covered in thick grey fabric that was supposed to trap all the noises inside. I wriggled with unease. I hated being the centre of attention.

The headphones squeezed my skull. I jabbed the button each time I heard a beep. The rest of the time I was bored. Finally, the audiologist let me out of the box and showed us a graph with two lines, one for each ear. The results for my right ear spanned the page, dots roaming through the full decibel scale. The results for my left ear sat on a straight line.

'Fiona is profoundly deaf in her left ear, and not all in her right,' the audiologist told Mum.

'Do you remember things suddenly becoming softer, Fiona? Quieter?'

'No.'

'Do you remember any loud noises? Any sudden pain?'

'No.'

'Do you remember ever feeling really dizzy?'

'Nope.'

He asked Mum if my behaviour had changed at all. Had I become more withdrawn? Mum said no. She told him that I was alert and inquisitive, and that I played well with my siblings.

'Well then, it's likely that she was born deaf,' he said. 'We'll do a few tests to make sure we haven't missed anything.'

I was told to lie absolutely still during the brain scan, even if I felt *really* scared. The machine made loud clanking noises. Lights flashed. I remember squeezing my eyes shut, then worrying if this meant the doctors wouldn't be able to see inside my skull.

Everything was where it should be inside my brain and my left ear.

'It looks all completely *normal*,' said the audiologist. 'Except, of course, nothing works.'

'Is there anything we should do? Hearing aids?' asked Mum.

'There aren't any hearing aids powerful enough for her left ear. Most deaf children have difficulty learning to read. All the sounds get muddled up. Fiona will just have to work hard to match letters with their sounds.'

'How?'

'With lots of practice. Besides, she seems to be doing alright.' Then he smiled at me. I grinned back.

Coincidently, my school had a small disability class, called a support unit, which had several deaf students. I had never spoken to any of them. I couldn't even recall seeing them in the playground. They only seemed to appear at school assemblies, a clutch of them standing off to one side of the enormous shade sail. Their classroom was in the old section of the school, where the windows were set so high not even adults could peek in. It seemed like a separate, faraway place. I refused to leave my class; I did not know those kids.

Despite the diagnosis, nothing seemed to change, the world was no louder or softer. But I was painfully aware that my ears somehow made me slower, less capable than my classmates. I began to notice how their pencils swept across their copybook pages. They could string together sentences and jot down answers during spelling bees. I remembered the audiologist saying that I had to work harder. I would tuck my pencil tightly into the web of my hand, trying to steady its tremble, as my copybook dampened from my sweat.

Together Mum and I would chant: *Ch, ch, ch, bah, bah, bah, rah, rah, rah.*

'No, no, Fifi. It's *RRR-ah! RRR-ah! RRR-ah!*' Mum would say, tapping the flash card.

Mum realised that I'd memorised all the early readers and had been dutifully parroting them to her whenever she asked me to read. I sat in her lap in an armchair as we worked through a large stack of flashcards; I could feel the sounds vibrating through her chest. I tried again, conscious of the air rolling in my mouth. Whenever I got stuck, instead of raising her voice, Mum tapped, clicked or clapped the sound. If I was still unsure, she would get me to watch her face. After a while, I got tired, irritated, and turned feral, kicking and whining. Mum persisted, stroking my hair, settling me down.

Letters stood in stern unmoving lines. I pressed myself into her body as she read. Slowly, the sounds started to feel physical, each with a distinct way of moving or tasting.

B: buzzes lightly on the lips. Say it slowly and you can make a swarm of bees.

R: the tongue rolls like a ladle scooping ice cream. Sweet.

P: the bottom lip drops low like an oven door swinging open, releasing a puff of warm air.

T: the tongue rises, its tip touching the roof of the mouth. And when paired with H, the tongue thickens and thumps.

F: all teeth and fizz. Bright, light, fruity. Fee-OH-nə!

Night after night, we sat together while my siblings played or watched television in another room. I grew to hate that armchair with its brown-and-mustard-striped upholstery and hard wooden arm rests. I used to chew my dinner slowly to delay the start of the reading lesson.

At bedtime, my siblings and I would paw at our books, trying to pick one for Dad to read. Our illustrated copy of *Ancient Greek Myths* had to be duct-taped together. We never got bored with stories about ships crossing oceans; long-haired sirens singing on rocks; one-eyed giants and gruesome battles; or the enormous wooden horse.

By the end of Year Three, my literacy skills were still well below average, but my teacher told Mum that he was impressed by my 'stickability'. I asked her what he meant. 'Sticking with something is a good thing,' she explained. From then on, whenever I got overwhelmed or frustrated, I told myself that I had stickability. This habit has persisted into adulthood. No other word gives me the same surge of energy and will—not stubborn, motivated, diligent, or persistent—no, I stick, stick, stick.

The following year, at the beginning of Year Four, the school advised Mum that I needed to make big improvements if I wanted to stay in the mainstream class. The thought of being in a special-ed class, where the kids looked and moved so differently from everyone else, was terrifying. The word 'special' didn't seem exciting or fun. My after-school lessons in the brown-and-mustard armchair became more important than ever.

A few weeks later, Mum had a chance encounter with an elderly gentleman who was wearing hearing glasses. She went through the Yellow Pages and found the telephone number of an audiologist in Sydney who made them.

We took the train into the city again.

'These glasses will help you hear,' the audiologist said, as he handed me a set of thick black frames.

Back then, in 1997, most people, including Mel B of the Spice Girls, wore glasses with thin wire frames. I held the bulky hearing glasses gingerly, afraid I might drop them. Unlike glasses that helped people to see more clearly, these frames had buttons and a dial. The thought of making the world louder was exciting. But was it worth it if I had to wear these ugly glasses? The audiologist must have noticed me frowning.

'I know they look big, but the frames need to be thick enough to contain all the wires that will transmit sound from the left to the right side of your head.'

'Go on, put them on. I'm sure you'll look fine.' Mum nudged me gently.

I tucked my hair out of the way and slid the glasses on. The lenses were clear plastic, so the office didn't shift and blur like the classroom did when I tried on my friend Jennifer's glasses.

'Now, make sure the tube is inside your ear,' he instructed.

I felt along the arm of the glasses, pinched the tube and pushed it in tight. It felt like an earplug. I could hear crackling in my right ear, like a poorly tuned transistor radio.

'How does it sound?' Mum asked.

I turned towards her in surprise. 'Your voice is so loud.'

'I bet you can't wait to wear them at school,' the audiologist said.

I spent the weekend standing in front of the bathroom mirror. My new glasses overwhelmed my face. They made me look serious, like my idea of an accountant or a school principal. I flashed my teeth at the mirror again and again, trying to get used to the feeling of my cheeks pushing my glasses upwards as I smiled.

Even though the weather was mild, on the way to school my face was hot and sweaty and my lenses kept fogging up. I took the glasses off and wiped them with the corner of my school shirt.

'Careful, you might scratch them,' Mum said, glancing from the road to me. 'Use that black cloth from your glasses case.'

As I polished the lenses, my hands shook. Most of my classmates didn't know I was deaf.

Three years earlier, when I had told a handful of friends, they lined up and screamed into my ear. Outnumbered and not wanting to disappoint anyone, I let them do it again and again. My compulsion to please everyone intensified. The same girls would order me to tie their shoelaces; hold their spot in the canteen line; fill up their water bottles; throw their apple cores or banana peels in the bin. I followed their instructions quickly and without complaint. Eventually, I realised that if I were alone no one could order me around. I began to spend lunchtimes collecting flowers or swinging upside down from a set of parallel bars. By Year Four, I was used to my own company. I became nervous when playing in large groups. It would be another twenty years before I read that in order to achieve social acceptance, 'deaf girls in mainstream education compensated [for their] lack of [conversational] improvisation with higher levels of prosocial behavior, agreeableness, monitoring, and pragmatic skills'. At nine years old, I just knew it was essential to avoid disappointing others, even if this meant I would have to experience discomfort.

I kept polishing the lenses and thinking about the day ahead. Today my deafness would become as visible as my frizzy hair and freckles. I worried that someone would yank them off and scream into my ear. Perhaps nobody would notice the buttons and batteries? And if they did, maybe I could say that spies like James Bond wear these glasses? As we neared the school, I slid them on and took a deep breath, squeezing my hands into fists to stop them from shaking.

'Are your glasses switched on?' Mum asked as she parked.

'Yup.' Reluctantly, I opened the car door and made my way towards the school gate.

'They look huge.' A classmate pointed at my glasses.

I glanced down and pretended to organise my pencil case.

'Seats, everyone. Pens and paper out, it's test time.' Ms Hull rapped on her desk.

Everyone dived into their seats. My glasses amplified the rustling of copybooks and unzipping of pencil cases. I wanted to turn down the volume, but I didn't want anyone to see the hearing aids.

'Everyone ready?' Ms Hull started each day with a spelling test. During the school holidays she travelled to Asia and Africa, climbed mountains and hiked through rainforest. I wished she would tell us those stories instead of testing our spelling.

'Okay, the first word is "fridge",' she announced. As she was exceptionally tall and straight-spined, her voice normally wafted above my head. Today, it sounded loud and clear in my right ear.

My chest expanded with hope. Maybe these glasses would make me as smart as everyone else.

For the next ten minutes, my head bobbed up and down as Ms Hull read out the list of words. I studied her face as she spoke. When I got stuck, I silently mouthed the word, trying to break it into syllables. As I chewed on each sound, I fell behind.

'All right, pencils down,' said Ms Hull. 'Ready to swap copybooks?' She picked up a piece of chalk.

Apart from a few attempts written in small, cramped letters, my page was mostly blank.

I pushed the copybook towards my neighbour, my eyes downcast. As Ms Hull wrote the words on the blackboard, my shame felt heavy and immense. The glasses hadn't made me any smarter at all.

By the end of the school day, my ears ached. Not from the sounds travelling through the plastic frames, but from the weight of the glasses. The tops of my ears were red and tender.

I was responsible for maintaining my glasses. It required a steady pincer grip to slot the round batteries into the back of each arm. The plastic tube that sat in my right ear would become clogged with bright yellow wax. I used a small brush to clean it out. The lenses collected fingerprints. I enjoyed running a soft cloth over them. Each night I placed the glasses in a large black case, making sure that the tube, cleaning implements and a spare set of batteries were nestled inside before snapping it shut, my face and ears finally free.

'Break it down.' Mum pointed at the page.

We were sitting at the kitchen table. At nine, I was now too old to sit on her lap. I was squinting, trying to picture the word 'calculate'. Unsure how to spell it, I let out a heavy sigh. As I grew older,

I realised that Mum had been fitting my reading lessons around nursing shifts, cooking, cleaning, grocery-shopping and looking after my siblings. Understanding how busy Mum was helped me temper my tantrums.

Dad worked six days a week in construction; he left the house before dawn and got the train home in time for dinner. After training as a bricklayer in Ireland, he had worked in England and Germany before migrating to Australia. Now he was studying to become a crane diver. He used to do his homework after dinner. Sometimes he'd explain that he was learning how to calculate the 'safe working loads' for each lift—so that the crane would not topple over or the chains snap.

'Studying hard is important. It will set you up for life,' he'd say. I took his advice seriously and began to think of school like a job. Sometimes I daydreamed about what life would be like once I finished school. Each Sunday, Dad would buy the newspapers. Together we leafed through them. I was drawn to the travel section, with its colourful photographs of the ocean, deserts and rainforests. I cut out articles of all the places I wanted to visit. I folded up the unread articles and stowed them in an old biscuit tin I kept under my bed. I imagined that, once I had finished school, I would open the tin, unfold the hundreds of newspaper clippings and be free to go anywhere I liked.

Mum nudged me, bringing my attention back to my homework. 'Give it a go. Everything is made up of tiny parts. Say it with me: *cal-cu-late*.' She tapped the table. I copied her. Then wrote down calqlate.

We kept practising until it was time to set the table for dinner.

'The next word is "recycle",' announced Ms Hull. 'Re-*cy*-cle.'

I lightly tapped out the word on the edge of my desk, then scrawled my answer with quick, assured strokes. Afterwards, I looked at the page in wonder, taking in all the big ticks.

The feeling didn't last long. The tests got harder. Words lengthened. I watched everyone else, convinced they were leaps and bounds ahead of me. At home, Mum continued to shepherd me to the kitchen table. Sometimes I could hear my siblings charging through the house or whooping from the backyard.

Mum reminded me that letters transform when coupled together. As she cut vegetables, she recited words beginning with 'a': apple sauce, alright, architecture, aspire, avocado.

'But how will I remember everything?' I whined.

'You have to treat each word as an individual—consider it closely and carefully. We all have our own quirks, letters included.'

My siblings and I started taekwondo at the Bankstown Police Citizens Youth Club. Twice a week we tightened our belts over our white starched uniforms. I left my glasses at home; I didn't like how they fogged up and bounced on the bridge of my nose. Our instructor taught us that observation was our best defence, that we had to stay alert. With time, he said, we'd learn how to read body language.

We stood in rows to practise kicking and punching; we moved slowly, perfecting our technique. With time, we did indeed quicken our pace and progressed to shadow-boxing, shuffling around, punching our shadows, ducking when they tried to kick back.

After each class, we zoomed around the basketball court. As I watched the ball, I lost track of the voices around me. I jogged backwards, then sidestepped along the edges of the court, trying to keep everything in sight. Trying to stay alert.

•

I hadn't worn my glasses over the summer and felt uneasy and conspicuous as I put them on for the first day of Year Five. On top of that, my body had started to change. Shorts were more difficult to pull up: my legs had thickened around my sides and bottom. I was growing hips. I felt heavy and flat-footed at taekwondo.

After shadow-boxing, we advanced to sparring with one another and wore mouthguards to protect our teeth. I learned to hold my fists on either side of my chin, tuck my elbows in and always stay on my toes.

'You should see a kick coming from your opponent's hip. If you watch their feet, it's already far too late!' our instructor yelled as we fought. 'Read their body language! Keep moving. Keep side-on, otherwise you'll be an open target.' He slapped his belly. 'It's all about perfecting the basics, then using them in combinations, kick-jab-hook. Get the rhythm. One! Two! Three!'

In taekwondo the emphasis is on clean, decisive kicks. I found the repetition and patterns of movements comforting. When we fought, the aim was to attack and retreat, attack and retreat.

'Knowing when to retreat is important,' said our instructor. 'It allows you to conserve your energy, decide what to do next. But remember, even in retreat you must always keep your guard up.'

I followed a similar pattern at school. In class, I attacked my work with gusto: studying the body language of my teacher and classmates; forcing myself to keep moving through writing tasks, even when I felt overwhelmed; raising my hand whenever the teacher asked the class questions. I was alert, energetic.

Each lunchtime, I retreated to the library. At first, I'd sink into a soft chair and just sit in the cool, silent space. Then I began to flick through books. Over time, I worked my way through shelf after shelf. Reading distracted me from thoughts of starting high school; the growing pains of puberty; the worry of mishearing my teacher or classmates. With my elbows tucked in, chin down, I used books as a shield.

I spent so much time in the school library that the librarian gave me a badge: library monitor. It was my job to hush others, to safeguard the silence. I did so with rude authority.

Buttons

The accordion is not a shy instrument, neither in sound nor temperament. It asks you to hold it close, though never to hug it. The bellows, when pulled in and out, can easily catch on clothes. My button accordion had a deep golden belly, its pleats made of a stiff papery material. Not long ago, when I began to play the opening notes of an Irish reel, a guttural wail poured out. A pained sound. The bellows had split. A tear. A wound.

My accordion is old—second, third or maybe even fourth-hand. Its origins are unknown. My parents bought it the first time they took me Home. They had been living in Australia since the 1980s. After having four children in four years, it took them until 1997 to save enough money to fly us all to Ireland. Once there, they tried to find ways to make our memories of Home brighter, longer lasting. At the beginning of the trip they bought us each a tin whistle: mass-manufactured and portable. We played the whistles as we drove through the countryside visiting relatives, each note strident. After a few days, two of the whistles were dented from sword fighting and produced harsh, lisping sounds.

BUTTONS

During the last week of the holiday, in a moment of unprecedented extravagance, Mum and Dad bought a handful of second-hand instruments: a fiddle, a banjo, an accordion and a bodhrán. The man in the music store reassured them that the instruments, though worn or marked, were of 'the finest quality'. Antiques even. They believed him. Especially as, apart from blowing on the tin whistles, none of us had ever done anything more musical than clap our hands.

When we returned to Sydney, my sister claimed the fiddle. One brother claimed the banjo. The other stuck with the tin whistle before eventually graduating to the flute. As the youngest, I let them determine the pecking order and weaselled away to a quiet corner; my obsession with reading was just starting to take hold.

Along with the bodhrán, the accordion sat in the lounge room untouched. Its rusty chrome chest plate and round white buttons were eye-catching. Its square bulk was intimidating. More than year later, when I was ten, I finally plucked up the courage to approach it. I looped the leather strap around my right shoulder. The instrument sat squarely on my lap. No matter how I pecked at the buttons, or pulled at the bellows, the accordion produced loud, reliable sounds. I could feel the music vibrating through my chest. Maybe I'm a natural? I thought.

'Not so loud!' my sister yelled from our bedroom.

'Go play that thing in the garage!' one brother snapped.

I squeezed the bellows in, dragged them out, again and again, drowning any opposition with clear, assertive notes. I felt bolder than ever before. Unlike schoolwork, learning the accordion felt playful. I laughed at my mistakes and felt a swell of pride when I managed to play a handful of notes correctly. The feeling of delight returned the next day. Soon I was in the habit of dropping my schoolbag by the door and looping the accordion's leather strap over my shoulder. I taught myself songs from a music book and Mum bought me a video of other accordion players. I loved watching their fingers charging up and down the buttons.

As my own fingers got stronger, they too began to race up and down the rows of buttons. Like many beginners, I thought speed equated to skill. I revved my way through reels, jigs and polkas, playing at such a clip that the notes blurred, morphing into something beyond music: pure joy to me, noisemaking to others. I didn't care. I was the one making the noise.

Eventually, once I began to play with other musicians—first my siblings and then, years later, with strangers—I learned that slowing down and staying in tempo with others made you a more skilful musician. Even so, over twenty years on, I still felt a rush of pleasure from any sound produced by my accordion, as though it was gifting me its attention. That is, until it groaned in pain.

I examined the bellows closely. There were a series of fine cracks and a long tear. I felt foolish: I had never stopped to think about the health of my ageing accordion. If I'd had keener hearing, would I have detected the sound deteriorating? Perhaps the instrument started to wheeze long before the paper pleats gave way. But playing the accordion had never been about the actual sound of music; it was the *feeling* of music beneath my fingers that I relished.

Other accordion players suggested it would be cheaper and far easier to replace the instrument rather than get it mended. Each time I picked up another accordion, however, I lost confidence and coordination. The feeling in my chest was no longer full and comforting. Whereas the buttons on my old accordion were loose in their sockets and clacked when touched, the buttons on new accordions felt springy, almost too willing to call out each of my fumbling errors. The firmness of new bellows made songs sound stiff and cool; it was not the warm, buttery sound from my old bellows.

Brain Eno often got musicians to play different instruments from the ones they had been trained to play—wind musicians might have been asked to beat on drums, string musicians might have had to lay down their bows and blow—Eno wanted to shake them free of any habits, awaken their physicality.

I didn't buy a new accordion. I was nostalgic, resistant to change. More than anything, in my late twenties, I wanted to recreate what it felt like when I first drowned the house with waves of big, bold music.

In secret

We talk about secrets as if they are physical things. They are a burden we carry. They sit heavily on our consciousness. These metaphors, it turns out, have real-world properties: secrets literally weigh bodies down. Researchers have found that individuals with secrets move differently—perceive hills to be steeper, distances further—compared to those without secrets. I think about how my body has spent years living in this skewed state of reality. Even though I was born deaf, the sensations of heaviness and discomfort only started when, one by one, my classmates cupped their hands around my left ear, their breath hot as they screamed, testing if I had told them the truth. It was then, at six years old, that I started to consider the truth a threatening thing.

Sefton High School in Western Sydney offered the possibility of a new start. Apart from my siblings, no one at the school knew that I was deaf. I refused to wear my hearing glasses. I wanted to appear normal.

Although it was a public school, entry was competitive. Each year, half of the Year Seven cohort were accepted if they passed the selective school test—a statewide examination to identify high-achieving students. The other half were admitted if they lived in the surrounding suburbs. Although I'd failed the test, I was accepted into the community stream.

To signal how a student was admitted, each Year Seven class was named after one of the letters in the school's name. The S, E and F classes were selective and the T, O and N classes were community. According to playground rumour, the classes were ranked, 7S consisting of the smartest kids and 7N, my class, the least capable kids. Whether this was true or not, I believed it. I was certain I was the dumbest student in my grade, if not the entire school.

Despite wanting to distance myself from the label 'deaf and dumb', sometime during the first week, I slipped up.

I was sitting in a circle with a group of girls. One of them asked me a question, but I only realised I was being addressed when my neighbour nudged me and said: 'Well, what do you reckon?'

Flustered, I blurted out an apology.

'Sorry, I'm deaf in my left ear,' I explained. 'What did you say?'

'Like, completely?' asked a girl sitting across from me.

'Yeah.'

'What happened?' asked another, her high ponytail bobbing as she leaned into the circle.

'Dunno. The doctor thinks I might've been born like this.'

'Weird.' The word echoed round the circle, the girls suddenly animated by my revelation.

'Yeah, stupid deaf ear,' I said, hoping to hurry the talk onto another topic.

This, however, was a mistake. My deafness was not forgotten. The next time I misheard something, someone called out—'Deaf

Fi!' I blinked hard. Everyone in the group was laughing at the play on words: deafy. A rough laugh escaped from my throat.

The next time I misheard, there was another round of laughter and I realised that I had set the tone: my deafness had become a running gag.

It was during the first week of high school that I discovered I had a deaf accent. My classmates and teachers asked me where I came from. Each time I said Bankstown, they shook their heads and said: but where were you born? America? Canada? A group of boys taunted me every day, telling me to go back to America. Or they'd ask me—why do you speak like that? I explained that my parents were Irish. But you don't sound Irish, they countered. It was the same when my sister's friends, in the year above me, asked why I sounded different from her—my explanation that I inherited my accent just didn't make sense.

I remembered back to those long afternoons of sitting on Mum's lap, my back pressed into her chest as she read out each phonetics flashcard, her voice rumbling through my ribs. The idea of elements of her accent imprinting on my body would have been comforting, if it were not for the daily teasing. My peculiar accent only made my deafness seem more marked, more obvious. Words started to feel uncertain in my mouth. Having no deaf friends, I didn't know that deaf accents are common. Instead, I felt like a misfit whenever people pointed out that I sounded nothing like my family.

It occurred to me that people had been commenting on how I spoke for years. They said I was either too loud or too soft, that my laugh was too disruptive, a shriek or a cackle. Even when I tried to adjust my voice levels, I would get the volume wrong. The year before high school, in 1999, my siblings and I had auditioned for a youth choir. There was a call-out to schools across New South Wales for children to sing in the opening and closing ceremonies of the Sydney Olympic Games. Surprisingly, we all got in.

For the next twelve months, around fifty of us congregated in a local school hall. We were told that choirs of a similar size were meeting in schools across the state, and that we would join together for the Olympics to become a sea of voices. Each week we worked our way through the choir songbook. We were divided into sections—soprano, alto, tenor, bass. I didn't get tired of telling people that I was *an alto*; it sounded so professional, so musical.

We were taught that the throat is made of muscle. It must be warmed up and cooled down. We learned how to breathe—using our diaphragms to pull air deep into our lungs—but discreetly, so we didn't 'gulp like fish' mid-song. Maintaining bright, show-business smiles, we followed the conductor's hand, alert to each flick of her baton. We stood in a neat arc formation, the tallest in the back and the shortest in the front. I was in the front row. When we sang, waves of sound soared and rolled across the hall. We were spectacular. Or at least, every parent said so.

After a few months of rehearsals, the conductor announced that she would select a dozen students to audition for a solo. As we sang a medley of songs, she walked around the room, leaning in to listen to our individual voices. I watched as she tapped on shoulders. After the second chorus, I received a tap.

When it was my turn to audition, I stepped onto the stage and the pianist smiled, before beginning to play the national anthem, a song that we had practised most weeks. I started to sing. After a few bars, the pianist glanced at me, her fingers picking up speed. Breathless, I tried to follow along. I gulped some air halfway through singing *Aus-traaaa-lia*. The conductor gestured for me to sing louder, then winced as I did. My throat felt raw and strained from the effort. After a few more bars, the pianist stopped. She held her hands up as if surrendering.

'Look, I don't know what tempo or even pitch you're aiming for.'

I wasn't sure what to say. Singing had never felt so confusing.

'That's okay, we'll give it another shot,' said the conductor. 'Maybe go down an octave. Are you okay to start again, Fiona?'

I nodded vigorously, before standing up tall, like we had been taught. Throughout the song I watched the pianist grimacing. My voice felt thin. I braced my stomach, trying to give each note more strength. The conductor stepped back a little. Afterwards she simply said: 'Your voice is better suited in a crowd.'

I didn't feel embarrassed, because I agreed with her. Singing made sense when I stood shoulder-to-shoulder with others. When the auditions were over, we returned to choir practice. Once I was nestled back into the group of altos, my body relaxed, filling with air and strength.

When I thought about the audition, I began to understand my confusion and disorientation. Without feeling the air shift and the vibration of each note resonating through the bodies of all the other singers, I was lost. Floundering, my voice had wobbled from high to low, loud to soft.

At school, I became weary of speaking. I tried to keep my voice on a tight leash. Even so, I didn't know when it was booming or retreating. Sentences would trail off, until words left unspoken sat deep inside of me. Up until then, I thought that hearing loss only meant that I was dumber than other people. I was oblivious that deafness affected *how* I sounded. My lack of awareness made sense: I had never heard my own voice.

Unable to control my deaf accent, I persisted in trying to persuade people it was a quirk of inheritance. I needed to make sure that as few people as possible knew I was deaf. I entered a mode of doublethink: trying to figure out what was normal behaviour and what was deaf behaviour. I dissociated from conversations, mentally scurrying back to survey the scene, checking if I was passing as normal.

Over the next few weeks, I formed a rigid set of rules: never ask anyone to repeat themselves; never ask anyone to speak up; never request to move closer to a conversation, even if it meant missing out on what was said. And the most important rule: never show any effort or confusion. I had seen enough films to recognise the troubled look of deaf characters, their expressions exaggerated and clownish to the point of comedy. Not wanting to be mocked or laughed at, I thought about my face a lot. I practised hiding my fierce mental focus behind a soft, neutral expression. In the playground I aimed to look cheerful and unconcerned. Discomfort was tucked into the corners of my mouth. This became easier when I had to start wearing prescription glasses. Behind the wiry frames, I could blink away any confusion I felt.

The average person has thirteen secrets. This conveniently ominous number was determined by a trio of researchers from Columbia University, who analysed some 13,000 secrets and compiled their findings in the paper 'The Experience of Secrecy'. It is a spectacularly dense read. Their research methodology alone stretches over a dozen pages, plotting how they attempted to circumnavigate their subjects' desire for concealment.

Analysing secrets is an inherently difficult task. Previous researchers relied on secrecy-assignment manipulation, the process of asking test subjects to conceal information within laboratory settings. A sort of manufactured secret. The trio from Columbia ruled out this approach as it 'seem[ed] risky to assume that the effect of withholding the word "mountain" from others within a social interaction is no different than the effect of choosing to keep one's infidelity a secret from a spouse.' Mountain. What a gentle, inoffensive word. Withholding it would be like a word game, an act of artful, if not *playful*, trickery. A true secret elicits in the keeper a certain constricting alertness that cannot be assigned or manipulated into being. You don't so much keep a secret as it keeps you, holding you in tight-chested suspense.

So how did these researchers harvest so many secrets? They did what any good friend would do—they didn't press for details. Using succinct surveys written in plain English on anonymous online forums, they allowed individuals to reveal only as much as they wanted. After all, the act of concealment is a desire for self-preservation. As one of the researchers wrote: 'To have a secret from others is to create an alternate world, one to which others don't have complete access.'

An errant word has the potential to elicit terror in the secret-keeper. The thought of others accessing my alternate world was destabilising. On the rare occasion when deafness or hearing loss was mentioned in school, I would seize up, as if holding my breath would somehow make me smaller and undetectable. With each passing school term, my fear of being found out intensified. Thinking about deafness, even when alone, felt too risky.

It would be disingenuous if I didn't admit that, at times, this deception gave me a thrill. I congratulated myself on the skill I had for passing as normal, and on my strength for not breaking any of my rules, even when I felt lost in a rush of noise. In fact, the more I hid my deafness, the more it felt like I had beaten it.

By Year Nine, I was only intermittently teased for having an accent, and I began to find my footing in conversations. Having always had boisterous conversations with my family, I no longer wanted to be a bystander at school. I was tired of catching onto the thread of half-heard sentences. I started to treat conversations like a game: I strove to make people laugh. I used sarcasm, irony and puns, enjoying the slipperiness of the words, feeling victorious each time I elicited a laugh, even if it was at someone else's expense. Leaping from one non sequitur to the next, I began to feel that I was wittier than others. I was irritated by how *lazy* people were in their thinking, so linear and literal. Each time I felt great satisfaction after another string of wordplays or loud laughter, I'd tell myself that it wasn't vanity, it was necessity.

Of course, even with intense effort and an insufferable ego, it was impossible to fully conceal my deafness. High school conversations were oblique and elusive with subtext. Information was traded behind cupped hands and directed deep into an ear. After a few instances of people trying to whisper into my deaf ear, I told everyone self-righteously that I hated gossip. I made a point of walking away when the conversation shifted to soft, secretive asides.

Friendships are forged and deepened with the exchange of personal histories. We *need* secrets; they act as offerings, means of establishing a shared trust. Revealing attractions, ambitions and desires creates intimacy. Even extinguished secrets—the sort that no longer spark fear if revealed—allow friendships to thrive. Despite their lack of potency, the things that we *used* to hide can be just as revealing as the secrets we maintain.

Many people use high school as a way of discovering their

interests, experimenting with new friendships, fashion and infatuations. To me, school still felt like a job. Each day, I ate lunch with the same group of people. I was preoccupied with the effort of not revealing anything personal—not even my interest in music or martial arts—as if it might expose my deafness. I rarely saw any of my classmates outside school, not even during the holidays.

Yet when I was alone, my body still reacted acutely, with sweat and spasms, whenever I imagined having to reveal my hearing loss. According to 'The Experience of Secrecy', we are most frequently reminded of our secrets during dull, unguarded moments—standing at the sink doing the dishes, coasting through the supermarket aisles, waiting for the lights to turn green, or trying to hustle a fitted sheet over the last corner of a mattress. As soon as you relax, your mind roves through areas of thought typically corralled into some dark corner.

Given that people spend between a third and half of their waking hours entertaining off-task thoughts, it's possible some might feel haunted by their secrets. This is an act not so much of self-pity as of self-regulation. The more you try to suppress a thought, the more your mind will spontaneously dredge it up and remind you of its existence: *Hey, don't worry. Your secret is still sealed away. Here, let me show you where you locked it up.* 'The ironic process of mental control' is how scientists have dubbed this perpetual haunting of oneself.

Whenever I was alone, I would check and double-check the list of people who knew about my hearing loss. I reviewed how I had explained my accent, as well as the excuses for why I would often mishear things (blocked ears, endless head colds, a habit of day-dreaming).

Keeping a secret means living in a state of exhaustion. Numerous studies have found that secretive people tend to experience more physical and psychological pain than others. My secret ensnared me. Most days, my body was visited by a quiet, tedious panic.

Lunchtimes were a riot of noise, hundreds of conversations ricocheting off concrete and glass. The school library was unappealing: its small selection of books and lack of rules to safeguard silence meant it drew a crowd who preferred playing computer games to reading. As a way of escaping the playground, I joined an environmental club called Streamwatch, part of a network of civilian scientists who monitored the city's waterways. My sister had told me about the club, which happened to consist of her friends. Once a week, a geography teacher would chaperone a group of eight to ten students to the creek that ran behind the school.

Enclosed by the chain-link fence from the neighbouring industrial estate, it felt like our private place. We'd peel back the wire, crawl through, then slide down the sandy escarpment. Using nets attached to retractable poles, we fished out rubbish. Within a few minutes, we'd always have a large garbage bag filled with tinnies and chip packets.

We also collected samples from the stormwater drain and ran water-quality tests, recording the data with steady focus, before sending it to Sydney Water. As we worked, ducks paddled cautiously alongside us. We did such a rigorous job that we won a state environmental award.

I looked forward to Wednesdays. It was only in those quiet moments, occupied by the task at hand, that I felt safely anchored inside my body.

Once people reveal their secrets, they move as if a weight has been lifted off their shoulders. I used to wonder what it would be like to be unburdened, to feel light and at ease, to be open about my deafness. Declarative rather than reticent. It wasn't a daydream, all soft and yearning, but rather a thought experiment, a rigorous weighing up of possibilities and probabilities. An experiment that was always aborted. Within moments of letting my secret loose, I would panic and quickly seal it up it again.

My secret felt like a splinter. Doctors describe splinters as a foreign body, which, unless extracted, will remain unabsorbed for the rest of someone's life. My body grew around my secret; consequently my fears of exposure shaped me. That's what fear does: it fortifies. It slows the transmission of trust. It disrupts the body's intrinsic rhythms with a surge of adrenaline: fight, flight or freeze. I learned to ignore this deep, troubling state of discord.

As I neared graduation, I looked forward to starting university. I figured that 2006 would be another new beginning. Only this time I vowed not to tell anyone about my deafness.

I spent hours flicking through the New South Wales University Admissions guide; it had been dog-eared and highlighted by my siblings. My brothers were both studying accounting and my sister was studying exercise and sports science. Having been picked last for every sports team, I couldn't imagine spending three years studying exercise science. I didn't waste a moment considering accounting.

I tried to imagine what it would be like to study subjects I hadn't known existed—sociology, kinesiology, human resources. I ran the idea of studying psychology past my family over dinner, and was surprised when they said I'd never shown any interest in listening to people talking about their emotions. I hadn't realised how obviously uncomfortable that kind of intimacy made me. I tried not to think about all the times I had abandoned conversations as soon as they felt too personal, too revealing.

Returning to the manual, I looked for careers that valued logic and reason. I happened upon urban ecology, which seemed like an ideal choice. I mentioned it at dinner.

'Is it like a town planning?' asked Mum.

'No, more like studying the impact of buildings.'

'Like sewerage? Or power grids?' asked Dad.

'No, it's studying how birds and trees cope in cities.'

'Is that a real job?' Mum raised an eyebrow.

My parents have always worked with their hands. They prize practicality and suggested I study physiotherapy. 'You'll have a steady job, earn good money, learn *proper* skills, and be able to work anywhere.'

'Besides,' added Mum, 'there'll always be injured people.'

After growing up in rural Ireland, where 'everyone was poor, so we didn't know any different', and living through economic declines in England and Australia, they were adamant that my siblings and I strive for recession-proof jobs.

'You need to make yourself useful. Think about what you'd learn to do with your hands.' Mum said.

'Nobody will ever be able to take that away from you,' Dad added.

Even my sister was convinced. By the end of 2005, she had combined her studies in Exercise and Sports Science with a Master of Nursing. I put physiotherapy as my first preference. Partly to appease my parents. It also meant that, if I got accepted, I would be attending the same campus as my sister. We still shared a bedroom, but I missed seeing her at school.

Strangers would often remark—*I can tell you are sisters*. Many would ask—*are you twins?* In my final weeks of high school, one of my sister's former teachers approached me:

'I had no idea there were two of you. I thought you were the same person.' She laughed, adding, 'I always wondered how strange it was to see her so often in the playground and hallways. She always seemed to be everywhere at once.'

Regardless of these regular comments, I couldn't see our similarities. I had always wanted to be more like her. She was decisive, forthright and sociable, whereas I tended to be overly analytical, cautious and introverted. She could study while watching films; I needed complete silence. Everything seemed to come so quickly, so easily to her.

Without consciously realising it, I always followed her lead—picking the same school subjects, sports and clubs. While many of our interests overlapped, I also trusted her judgement implicitly. My decision to pick a degree at the same university she was attending felt both comforting and inevitable.

The Sydney University course guidelines had a caveat: all prospective physiotherapy students must be comfortable with disrobing as well as touching and being touched by others. The near nudity didn't faze me. I was more unnerved by the vagueness of the second part of the caveat: you may only enrol if you are physically able to engage in all the tasks. Would I need to tell the university about my hearing loss? I wasn't even sure what physiotherapists did besides massage muscles. Too afraid to contact the university, I tried to think through the issue logically. I had dozens of debates with myself:

You got through high school. How different could uni could be?

But isn't deafness classified as a disability? So, wouldn't that mean I have a disability?

No, no, definitely not. You're not one of those special ed kids.

But my audiogram clearly shows that I have a deficit. What if I am disabled?

Don't use that word! You've come too far to give up now.

Although I left physiotherapy as my first preference, I decided it was unlikely I would receive an offer of enrolment as the entrance mark usually wavered between 95 and 99 points. And I had been cheerfully told by teachers not to expect too much of myself—to cast my net wide and apply for courses with 'realistic' entrance marks. So I rounded out my application by selecting every environmental ecology degree on offer.

After my final exams, I spent time imagining that future: quiet days of walking alongside waterways, auditing the health of trees and analysing the impact of concrete or steel.

The emptiness of the long summer days unsettled me. Jogging through the streets of Bankstown, arms pumping, cheeks puffed, I felt as if it was the first time I was moving without any sense of direction.

My body hollowed when I sat at the family computer and read my score: 96.95 points. For twelve years I had always expected to be pulled out of mainstream classes for being deaf and dumb. Instead of the score validating my diligent and obsessive approach to study, I felt grim with exhaustion. I wanted to forget the years of studying every night and every weekend. Even at seventeen, I could tell that I had wasted my youth.

•

On a hot afternoon in January 2006, I accepted the offer of a place in physiotherapy at Sydney University. I decided, somewhat superstitiously, that it was meant to be. At no point did I ask myself: is this what I want to do?

Not long afterwards, I got a job as a physiotherapy assistant in a small rehabilitation hospital. For the rest of the summer, between folding towels and assisting patients with knee replacements into the hydrotherapy pool, I worried about the university's caveat. Was I breaking the rules by enrolling in the degree?

I watched the physiotherapists speaking gently but clearly to the patients, ensuring that they understood the instructions. Most of the patients were elderly and wore hearing aids. I began to think that I might be able to do this job.

At lunchtime I studied my sister's anatomy textbook. She had recently stopped eating lamb as 'it looked too much like human flesh'. I wanted to get a head start on some of the basics, but soon enough I was hooked. Every fact felt instantly meaningful. I learned that the hip is a 'ball and socket' joint and that there are twenty-six bones in the foot. I traced my finger over the diagrams of bones as if I was flicking through an old family photo album.

Whenever I went running, I thought about how my muscles were contracting, pushing blood to my heart. How my lungs were expanding, oxygenating my blood. With each stride, I thought about my gluteal muscles wrapping around my hips and pelvis. Being able to visualise the insides of a body felt thrilling, powerful.

As the summer came to an end, I bought notebooks and pens, wrote my name on each cover in neat lettering. Another new beginning. What was another four years of keeping my deafness a secret? Could I even call it a secret? Wasn't it really just a lie?

No, this was nothing more than another act of necessity.

In corners

When I began studying anatomy, I was daunted by the extent of the new vocabulary. I had to reconfigure the human body into a multitude of small elements, each with a specific name. Even seemingly insignificant corners and bumps of bones had names. In time, these landmarks became more obvious, once I understood their purpose. I was learning the geography of bones: the rough patches where muscles latch on, the notches and shallow indents that serve as passageways for blood vessels and nerves to crisscross the body. But until that knowledge cohered inside my own body—so that whenever I palpated warm skin, I could picture what lay beneath—I was bewildered as I waded through lists of names.

As most anatomical terms come from Latin and Ancient Greek, it was comforting to think about the syllabus as a language, rather than as lists of obscure words. Through exhausting repetition, I learned the new combinations of letters and sounds by rote. Eventually, they folded into my memory and replaced the language I used to know for the body—collarbone to clavicle, shoulder blade to scapula, shinbone to tibia, and so on. It took me longer still, years in fact, to realise that these words in their original form were names for simple, everyday objects. Clavicle, for instance, comes from the classical Latin word *clavicula*, which means 'small key, bolt'. This long thin bone performs an elegant twist whenever the arm lifts, like a key turning in a lock. The scapula is a flattish bone with a pointed tip. Its name is derived from *skap*, 'to cut, scrape'. Not only does the shoulder blade resemble a shovel, but it's thought that the scapulas of animals were once used as such, blades for cutting and scraping the earth. Then there's the shinbone. A long, straight bone, *tibia* means a pipe or flute. And, for a time, these wind instruments were also made from bone.

But the early anatomists' nomenclature came undone when they got to a portion of the hip bone. Since the curved and somewhat knobbly bone does not resemble any known object, they called it the *innominate*, Latin for 'not named'.

Once we know the origins of these words, the boundaries between our bodies and the world become permeable. Just as our bodies are named after commonplace items, our built world has taken on anatomical terms. A building can have good bones, there is the heart of a house, roads are the arteries of a city. In considering the poetics of space, or more specifically the form and function of buildings, the French philosopher Gaston Bachelard used a touchstone phrase: 'I am the space where I am.' Perhaps there are no real boundaries at all.

The languages of buildings and bodies are so intertwined they are almost circular. How we understand the world is through our bodies and how we understand our bodies is through the world. When the bones of the body meet one another, side by side or end to end, they 'articulate', from the Latin word *articulatus* ('separated into joints'). The commonplace meaning of articulate, beyond the body, is clear, distinct speech. As if each word in a sentence has been separated into joints. When the bones of a building meet one another, sturdy and upright and angled for loadbearing, they are called joints. And it is in these narrow spaces where walls meet, say in the corner booth of a cafe or backed up against the wall of a bar, that sound, at least for me, becomes articulate—the walls do the work of funnelling voices towards me, allowing speech to become distinct and clear. I am the space where I am: on the edges, cornered.

'We shape our buildings and afterwards our buildings shape us.' When Winston Churchill said this in 1943, he was being more literal than poetic. He was arguing that the British parliamentary Commons Chamber be restored to an 'adversarial rectangular pattern' after it had been destroyed during the Blitz. At the time, Churchill was countering calls for a sweeping circular or horseshoe arrangement favoured by other legislative assemblies. During the debate, Churchill went so far as to suggest that the original shape of the Chamber was 'responsible' for the British two-party system; maintaining the narrow, tightly cornered space would therefore be essential for retaining parliamentary democracy. His argument was met with overwhelming support in a free vote and Sir Giles Gilbert Scott, whose projects included the red telephone box, was the architect tasked with the job. Today, some seventy years after the Commons Chamber was reopened in 1950, the parliamentary website states that 'the confrontational design helps to keep debates lively and robust but also intimate'.

I think about the buildings that have shaped me, the places that have caused my body to bend and shrink, to surreptitiously separate myself from crowds and head for the margins of a room.

Even when I try to resist tucking myself into a corner, my body still buckles. Candid photographs, after parties or nights out, reveal my body contorted in angles of effort, my lips folded into a grim line, my arms nested together as if holding myself firm. In these photographs I see a shell of a thing, alert and watching.

I try to imagine what it would be like if all buildings were designed to keep conversations lively and robust. Buildings where I wouldn't need to press myself into walls to avoid sinking in the swell of sound. Large public spaces that felt intimate by design. Just imagine the ease and democracy of it all.

'When you're speaking to a patient who is deaf or hard of hearing, make sure you're facing them,' explained the educator before she clicked to the next slide.

The hospital's disability-awareness training was optional, and even though it was a medium-sized suburban hospital with 450 beds and hundreds of staff members, only a handful of people showed up. Sitting next to another physiotherapist from the 2010 new-graduate program, I pretended not to notice that he was nodding off. Apart from when we scoffed our lunch, this was our only chance to sit down. Every day we raced from ward to ward, trying to work our way through the list of patients, knowing that tomorrow the list would be boosted by new referrals.

'And, before starting your consult, please turn down the volume on their television sets, to reduce the background noise.'

I'd already been turning off television sets before commencing a physiotherapy session—for my own benefit. But even with the television off, I still had to lean in when the patient spoke. Often there were other televisions blaring nearby, machine alarm systems going off, medication trolleys rattling past. Once home, it took until bedtime, or even longer, for me to unwind after being coiled tight in focused listening.

'Try not to yell or exaggerate your words. Most deaf people rely on reading lips, and yelling will distort your facial features.'

I shifted uncomfortably in my chair, unsettled by my jealousy. I wished my colleagues would look at me while talking; speak slowly and clearly; ensure their faces weren't shrouded in shadow or backlit; flag down my attention with a wave before starting a conversation; allow me to sit or stand on their left side so I could hear them. But none of my colleagues knew that I was deaf. In this building, my place of work, I hid any difference or discomfort.

Although I felt uncomfortable talking about my own body, it was my job to ask people about their bodies. With only a thin curtain closed for privacy, I asked patients in four-bed rooms to disclose intimate details. How do you sleep, eat, use the toilet? Do you need assistance to shower or get dressed? Is there someone who can take care of you once you go home?

The process of gathering someone's personal history is a chance for patients to express themselves before the objective examination, which includes assessments such as gait speed, flexibility, strength and endurance.

We were told not to get 'bogged down' in personal histories. We were taught how to extract useful information by asking direct questions. Whenever a patient had difficulty recounting their medical information—muddling up timelines of their symptoms and previous treatments—they were labelled poor historians. Their version of their story had to be treated with suspicion.

The months passed and I felt a sense of pride as I got faster at collecting personal histories. I tweezered out key information with close-ended questions—yes or no. I learned to do this by watching doctors. They would swan onto the ward, ask each patient two or three quick questions, then leave. Following the hospital's guidelines, I documented succinct summaries of the patients' personal histories, while my objective assessments were long and dense with detail.

Every three months I rotated to a different section of the hospital. For the first few weeks of each rotation, I felt as if I was starting a completely new job. After work I read through my textbooks, refreshing my memory of anatomy and biochemistry, knowing that any mistake I made could have dire outcomes for my patients.

It was the end of spring when I began my final rotation of the new-graduate program in the hospital's stroke ward. The impact of a bleed in the brain can be so vast that it might take days, if not weeks, to arrive at a clear prognosis. Some say strokes should be renamed 'brain attacks', so that they are taken as seriously as heart attacks.

As most stroke patients experience various losses of strength, speech, vision, memory, sensation and cognition, we worked as a multidisciplinary team—occupational therapists, doctors, speech therapists, dieticians, social workers—to figure out how our patients would navigate the 'real world'. From accessing their home, shopping centres and public transport to having a shower, getting dressed and eating meals.

At university I did a subject called 'An Introduction to Sociology'. I learned that our health and wellbeing are significantly impacted by our cities, suburbs and even streetscapes. For example, individuals who live in neighbourhoods without footpaths often experience higher rates of diabetes, depression and hypertension—they may not have the space or incentive to exercise safely. The lecturer explained the social model of disability, listing examples of how poor design can be disabling, but the information came across as dry and theoretical. Only now, as I worked with my patients, did I understand how the built environment could restrict a person's life. Most of my patients barely maintained their balance when walking across the gym's smooth floor—walking on a nature strip or even across the sloping hospital car park would have been out of the question.

After work, I began to pay attention: I noticed the cracks in footpaths; the lack of ramps to mount kerbs; bus stops without benches; buildings without elevators or escalators. I felt ashamed that I had never looked, *really* looked, at the world in this way before.

I remembered how we had spent a university tutorial learning how to use wheelchairs, wheeling ourselves around the campus car park for half an hour, before giving up when our arms got tired. Now, almost three years on, it occurred to me that we practised in the car park because the rest of the campus was largely inaccessible to wheelchairs. Given the university's caveat, I wondered how many people couldn't enrol in medicine or allied health degrees because they were unable to hide their disabilities. At first I felt angry. But then immensely relieved that I could pass as non-disabled.

Knowing that we couldn't rebuild the world, the team worked hard to get each patient strong, balanced and mobile. In the rehabilitation gym, we created exercise circuits. During the Commonwealth Games, we hosted our own sports carnival, awarding ribbons and a podium finish to whoever completed the highest number of repetitions for each exercise: tapping toes on a ten-centimetre high step; standing up and sitting down; picking up a Styrofoam cup without crushing it; walking laps of the gym. We were determined to get our patients home. Whenever exercises were performed in a sloppy or incorrect manner, we called it 'cheating'. Cheating wasn't allowed. Patients were instructed to repeat the exercise until they got it right.

If a patient's recovery plateaued, family conferences were called, contingency plans made. As a team, we needed to work out ways to safely discharge patients, prescribing equipment and home modifications. Every so often, returning to the 'real world' was impossible. The only places designed to cater for patients with complex care needs were aged-care facilities—with their wide corridors, raised toilet seats, grab rails, and wide turning arcs to steer the bulky mechanical lifting equipment. Nobody wanted to go there.

Towards the end of my new-graduate year, I had a meeting with one of my supervisors. He asked me how I was doing.

'Well, I keep showing up, which I suppose means I'm doing okay.' Tears fell quickly. My response shocked us both. I admitted to feeling stressed about managing my patient load. He offered advice about work flow and how to prioritise my patient list. In the end, he said, 'You're doing okay. You're confident and have the skills to back it up. You really just need to get better at asking for help.'

Once home, eyes still red, I began to treat my own personal history—that I was fine and coping well—with suspicion.

On busy days at the hospital, I began to notice that I automatically worked through my lunch breaks rather than ask for help with my case load. If I did eat, I chewed mechanically, before rushing back to the ward. I only stopped to go to the bathroom when it became an urgent need.

Yet whenever I saw that my colleagues were busy, I readily offered to assist, even if my own schedule was tight. It was easy and immensely satisfying. But I felt selfish and burdensome if I considered asking for help.

When did I begin to equate asking for help with failure? I attempted to plot out my personal history, asking myself the same direct questions I asked my patients: What was the mechanism of injury? When did the symptoms start? Have you sought treatment? What makes the pain better? What makes it worse?

Yet even when thinking hard, I couldn't construct a clear timeline. I couldn't detect any obvious patterns in my internal resistance. I focused instead on counting the days until I didn't have to return to the hospital. Perhaps, with a fresh start, I could begin again.

Shortly after the end of my new-graduate year, I flew to London. A few months later my oldest brother joined me, and we began the six-month journey back to Sydney in a large diesel truck. The couple who owned the truck called themselves overlanders and were members of a small community who drive around the world. They enjoyed driving slowly through countries, rather than flying over them. They opted for rough backroads over smooth highways. Once through Europe, we passed into Asia. From Turkey we drove through Iran, onwards to the Himalayas and across the Tibetan Plateau, passing from country to country until we reached Indonesia. From there we flew to Darwin, switched to a van, before driving to Sydney via Adelaide.

During those months looking out the truck window, I thought about how my body changed while working in the hospital. First I became slim, then drastically too thin; my period became irregular, before disappearing for months at a stretch. Because of stress fractures in my feet, I walked slowly and off-kilter. I understood that my body was fracturing with stress, but, at that stage, I didn't have a language to express pain in a way that wasn't biomechanical.

Pain experts call the brain a key part of the body's danger transmission system. The brain creates signals—sensations of burning, biting, stabbing, shooting, lacerating—that we feel in our bodies, as an indication that something is awry. Our brain is seeking our attention, calling us to act and protect ourselves from danger. I thought of my pain as a physical fault, the consequence of poor posture, muscle weakness, lousy running technique. Not once did I think to question my newfound compulsion to run ten kilometres, through dark streets before work each day, or my need to double this distance each weekend, only stopping when numb with lactic acid.

To avoid campsite fees on our overland trip, we camped on the shoulders of roads, paddocks, beaches, deserts, mountain plateaus— anywhere farmers were unlikely to herd us on in the middle of the night. Together we picked the best place to build a fire and the most private area for pissing. If we were lucky, there were shrubs or trees. In the desert, we simply walked into the darkness, squatted down and switched off our head torches.

Before pitching my tent, I examined the lay of the land, checking for rocks and dips. I estimated the path of the sun and the angle of the wind. My tent had pliable poles that formed a neat dome. I loved every inch of it. I even loved stooping to enter through the flyscreen and sitting down to get dressed.

Awake by first light, I was filled with a gentle joy. I lay still, without any compulsion to run.

For as long as I can remember I've woken up early. I suspect this habit developed as a result of growing up in a large family in a small home. With six of us and three bedrooms, sharing space was a given. I have a fond and vivid memory: I am eleven years old. I pad up the hallway, through the kitchen and towards the deep-cushioned armchair. Hours pass; my head is in my book. By midmorning, bedroom doors will swing open. The house will become cluttered with conversation. But until then, as my eyes dash from line to line on the page, the house feels enormous, the silence soft and spacious.

It was only once I returned to my family home that I realised how much I missed crawling into my tent and lying alone in the quiet dome.

After landing a job at an inner-city physiotherapy clinic, treating office workers who called themselves 'weekend warriors' because they played contact sports, I moved into a share house in Sydney's inner west with a friend from uni and two of her friends. It was a three-storey terrace, with black mould in the bathroom and a temperamental stove. My room was classified as a study by the real-estate agent. I could touch the opposing walls with arms outstretched and had to shuffle sideways past the single bed dominating the floor space, but the room still felt immense, because it was entirely mine.

Every few weeks we hosted house parties. The concrete back-yard would be filled with tea candles in old pesto jars and overturned milk crates. The kitchen, small and sticky, became the dancefloor. We'd pick themes, depending on the season or whatever props we thrifted from hard rubbish day—spring fling; alpine lodge; island holiday; hipster or bogan; Eurovision; Halloween. On the weekends that we weren't hosting a party, we'd go to others in the neighbourhood. Friends in a nearby share house once trucked in sand and turned their backyard into a beach. Another time they created a sideshow carnival. They worked in the film industry and spent weeks constructing set pieces: a kissing booth, a wheel of fortune, a feats-of-strength machine.

During the week, I slipped back into a strict schedule of rising hours before work in order to run. I craved this stretch of time. Before six in the morning, the skies were only for the bats and the birds. As the sun rose, a steady stream of planes began to fly low overhead, only stopping at eleven at night. I adjusted to the staccato flow of conversation, affectionally called the Marrickville Moment and Petersham Pause after the neighbouring suburbs beneath the flight path.

At work, I listened attentively as people described their pain. Away from the thin curtains and crowded hospital rooms, the questions didn't seem as invasive. And without the relentless demand to discharge patients as quickly as possible in order to free up a bed, I found myself becoming more engaged in each patient's story. My questions softened, and were now more open-ended.

Located at the bottom of an apartment complex, the clinic was a small space with no natural light. The walls were painted grey, the same colour as the floors, furnishings and all our treatment towels. My boss burned essential oils and played CDs of gentle instrumental music featuring hand-drumming and bells. Patients occasionally referred to the space as having a 'womb-like' quality. While it was quieter than the hospital, I had back-to-back appointments, so time management was still essential. My work involved talk and treatment, collecting symptoms and stories, while my patients lay face down. I had to crouch in an effort to hear them, their faces pressed through the hole in the plinth.

For each treatment technique, I devised ways to work around my deafness. So much of physiotherapy involves positioning yourself behind or alongside a person, looking at the curve of their body, not at their face. If a patient was sitting or standing, I learned to angle a full-length mirror to catch their reflection. Unlike my colleagues, I didn't play music in my treatment room. And I left the overhead fan switched off, unless it was an exceptionally hot day.

At night I went to the pub. I drank, talked, laughed until my throat hurt. My days and nights were full. The sharp blue mornings were empty and mine. Only when my old injuries flared up—the dull ache in the midsection of my foot; the click in my right hip; the searing sciatica—did I realise that my morning routine had always been one of retreat. A moment to suspend my thinking. To be all muscle and hot breath. I ran through the pain, convincing myself that as long as my period didn't disappear, I was okay.

Even though I have now lived for years with fewer people and in a series of larger rooms, I still rise early. Mornings feel fresh with potential. My mind feels vigorous and wanders, unrushed and unencumbered. It is in these moments that I feel like I can *think*, rather than react or recoil.

Living in the city and working in a job that required intense listening meant that my days and my body were always hedged in by the demands of sharing a soundscape with others. By night-fall, after hours of keen focus, my body felt flattened, my thoughts tangled.

It took me until my late twenties to recognise how, or even when, I become fatigued. It isn't heavy limbs and wide-mouth yawning. It is a hard-edged sensation of effort. My body exhibits the long list of symptoms of sensory overload: I become wide-eyed and riled up; relentlessly chatty yet speaking in increasingly chipped or incomplete sentences; restless and short-tempered, although completely indecisive; my heart thrums too quickly, streams of sweat run down my arms and legs.

Until I spent those six months living in a tent, I thought it was normal to wake up feeling rested, then slowly become scattered and borderline incomprehensible by nightfall.

While I'm getting better at recognising this frenetic version of myself, paying attention to when my skull begins to tighten with tension, I still need practice at taking myself home to rest. But, even if I try, I can't avoid the noise of the day. When I enter a room, I do a quick, almost unconscious audit of the space. The walls and ceilings, the position of chairs and tables, the lighting and ambient sound-scape. I look for exits, or bathrooms I can head to if I need respite.

I spent most of my Year Twelve formal in the bathroom. At the time I didn't understand why my skin suddenly felt too small or my head so full, but I could only exhale when there was a door and several walls separating me from the thump of 2005's Top 40 hits.

Now, whenever I can, I avoid places that trigger sensory over-load—cafes, bars, shopping centres, cinemas, stadium concerts, sporting events, protests, and city streets. The ordinariness of this list makes me realise how few places there are where I feel at ease. And just how small my world is becoming.

There is something about Churchill's argument about buildings and bodies that tugs at me. His argument is flawed, even faintly ridiculous, but it makes sense to my body, a deaf body. Churchill appeared to be passionately arguing for clear communication rather than for the safeguarding of democracy. Historically, democracy has flourished in the round: large assemblies of people able to converge and see one another. The design of the Commons Chamber has been described as 'not especially large—68 feet by 45 feet at the ground floor level; tiny in comparison with the dim perspectives of the Hall of Representatives at Washington (93 feet by 139 feet)', and it is exclusionary, even for elected members of parliament, as it contains only 427 seats for 646 MPs.

Churchill was against giving 'every Member, not only a seat to sit in' but 'a desk to write at, with a lid to bang'. He argued that the Chamber was empty most of the time, only filling up during a vote. In those instances, having members spilling into the aisles would, in his view, create a 'sense of crowd and urgency'.

'Having dwelt and served for more than forty years in the late Chamber, and having derived fiery great pleasure and advantage therefrom, I, naturally, should like to see it restored in all essentials to its old form, convenience and dignity.' Churchill's speech during the debate in October 1943 focused on his own physical experience in the building, an experience that happened to include hearing loss.

By December of that year, his physician, Dr Charles Wilson, noted that the Prime Minister was having difficulty hearing on the telephone. Perhaps Churchill's arguments for retaining a 'confrontational design' were motivated by wanting to retain the historical ties to British democracy, but it seems no mere coincidence that his recommendations benefited someone who was hard of hearing.

And yet Churchill made no mention of his hearing loss in any of his published works. I think of my own way of assessing spaces. The dread I feel when entering a wide-set room with high sweeping ceilings, where sound swooshes upwards and out of reach. The Commons Chamber is narrow—you can see the faces of your opposition only 'two sword lengths away', which is conveniently well suited for reading lips.

This degree of proximity wasn't welcomed by everyone. One opponent to the confrontational design argued: 'I have often felt that it might be better if Ministers and ex-Ministers did not have to sit and look at each other, almost like dogs on a leash, and that controversy would not be so violent.'

Whether or not Churchill was motivated by his hearing loss isn't really the point—it is who decides how buildings are designed that is relevant. These decisions happen behind closed doors; they are conversations of power, the outcomes of which literally shape what happens to our society and our bodies.

In my new-graduate year, I began to realise that cities aren't designed for disability. Millions of bodies have to work around the 'normal' design. It has taken a number of years for the penny to drop: this includes me. Yet I always prided myself on passing as normal, at whatever cost.

'While hearing and able-bodied children are encouraged to dream big, deaf and disabled children are conditioned to strive for invisibility, aspire for normalcy,' writes Sara Nović in *Between the Lines: Disability Invisibility in literature*.

If I choose not to talk about my deafness, I will always be the space where I am: orbiting the able world.

French philosopher Maurice Merleau-Ponty captures the interplay between people and space by suggesting that we are 'the flesh of the world' (*la chair du monde*). We become part of the space and the space becomes part of us—'All flesh, and even that of the world, radiates beyond itself.'

My body shapes the world as much as it is pressed out of shape by it; it is both complicit and conditioned by race, gender, sexuality and class. While I am weighed down by secrets and shame, I have passing privilege. Even now, years on, I instinctively hide my deafness, assimilating into the narrow definition of normal. I greedily cling to this power, this control.

•

In the years that followed the rebuilding of the Commons Chamber, a 'wiring mechanism' was installed around the perimeter of the room, which Churchill also had installed in his home. Some have suggested that it was an early hearing conduction loop—to direct sound towards hearing aids. This is, however, unlikely as, according to Dr Wilson, 'efforts to get Winston to use a hearing aid have come to nothing; he would not persevere with any instrument'. Others have speculated that the system might have involved a microphone and speaker to amplify voices. The lack of specific detail about how Churchill coped with his hearing loss is not a coincidence: any mention of his deafness was omitted from his official biographies.

The desire to conceal or minimise one's disability is still not unusual among people in positions of power. Knowing that other people, including world leaders, have feared being discounted by their disability gives me an odd comfort. I'm not hyperbolic. I'm afraid.

On lips

'Midnight Special or Earl's?' Kate asked me as we passed one another in the kitchen.

'How about the Courthouse or the Vic?'

'We might not get a table. Besides, the drinks are better at Earl's.'

'Cool. Leave here at nine-thirty?'

'Perfect.'

She had moved into the Stanmore share house in early 2013. By now, we'd been living together for almost eighteen months. Within weeks she had gone from being a stranger found on Flatmate Finder to my closest friend.

We were in a continuous stream of chatter about politics, feminism, climate change, music and literature. We talked as we pegged out laundry; on the stairway landing, cups of tea in hand; in front of the fridge; at the supermarket; over dinner at the kitchen table or pub. Our sense of humour was specific and absurd. We would parody ourselves, doing anything to make each other laugh. Best of all, we both readily admitted whenever we were clueless or unsure about something. There was never any pretension or pride in our conversations. We were amassing a prolific store of shared memories and in-jokes.

Trusting someone who wasn't family felt thrilling and wholly new. At twenty-four years old, I could see how much I had previously withheld myself from the possibilities of this kind of friendship. I began to try harder not to be so hesitant, so closed off. Over the next year, a series of friendships shifted from casual to caring: I would text almost daily with different friends, as well as catch up a couple of times a week, trading thoughts, feelings and the details of our days.

Despite beginning to feel more secure in several friendships, I made sure never to mention my deafness. I didn't want to risk placing any strain on them. In loud cafes and bars, I listened closely even when my head would start to pound and sweat rolled down my back. I wanted to be a *good* friend. Someone who could always be relied upon and who didn't disappoint.

By 2014, I had left the womb-like physiotherapy clinic. Now I worked weekends at a small inner-city hospital. During the week, I worked full-time at a busy Pilates studio located in a heritage building that had once been a chocolate factory. Lofty ceilings, thick stone walls. The air was cool even in the middle of summer. Dozens of people passed through the doors each day. As an instructor, I was always 'on the floor', surrounded by bodies that were bending, stretching, pivoting. Between adjusting equipment, demonstrating exercises and calling out instructions, there were always lots of conversations. The atmosphere was one of community and goodwill. Friendships were forged in the studio and people attended one another's weddings and children's birthday parties. During repetitions of abdominal crunches we would chat about our week. I tried hard to remember the incidental facts about my students' lives—their family arrangements, hobbies, ambitions, conflicts, travel plans—a scaffold that allowed me to 'tune into' conversations.

Most nights, after finishing a late shift, I would meet up with my friends in pubs or bars around the inner west. I performed the same trick—memorising and tracking conversations. Although I was exhausted, I kept pushing myself to keep up with lots of friends. There were countless moments that filled me with joy: chatting on a bench, coffee in hand; lunges and squats after running up and down the hills at Sydney Park; playing pub trivia on wet nights, when the overflowing streets kept everyone but us diehards away; browsing through Elizabeth's Books, trading opinions about the ones we'd read; stocking up on dips from Sultan's Table before picnicking on a scarf in Newtown Park; strolling through the Art Gallery of New South Wales, silently pointing out the paintings that caught our attention; sinking into the couches at Lazy Bones while listening to bluegrass or jazz bands; roller skating around Summer Hill's skate park, dodging kids on scooters; walking into the city, taking the long way through back streets, just so we could talk for longer. I felt so lucky, so grateful, to have so many wonderful friends. Life was fun, full. Until it started to feel like a grind, again.

It turns out I had told Kate about my hearing loss. Recently, I asked her during a phone call if she could remember when or how I disclosed my deafness.

'You told me on the day I moved in. You mentioned it in such an offhand way that I forgot almost immediately.'

I was shocked that I had mentioned it, especially so early in a friendship. But Kate had been a stranger at that point, so I guess I didn't see it as a risk.

'I feel bad that I forgot about it. But you were always making other people feel so at ease, even complete randoms. You acted so carefree, so unflappable. It took me ages to understand how hard you must have been working.'

She went quiet for a moment, then her voice cracked: 'That's why I was so confused when things started changing. I thought I must have done something terrible to upset you.'

It may seem naive, but it was only in my mid-twenties that I realised, devastatingly, that some people don't actually listen when others talk. They just wait to speak.

Simone Weil compared attention to prayer—rare, pure, full of generosity and desire. To me, paying attention had always felt inevitable. In packed pubs, I would lean forward, ear first, angling my head in time with the conversation. Watching lips and eyebrows closely. Whenever words slipped past me, I'd hide my confusion by switching the topic of conversation or buying another drink. Later, I would leave the pub alone, rubbing my back, my muscles ropy from hours of obedient focus.

When I was well rested, my brain felt muscular, reflexive and swift. Adjusting to the cadence of a new voice was a fantastic challenge, a sensuous thrill. But increasingly, as I juggled two jobs and a busy social life, I was having to grapple to keep up in every conversation. More and more, whenever I went out, I felt as if I was being sidelined, spoken over or simply ignored.

Once I grasped that not everyone was attentive when I spoke, I felt pathetic for not recognising it sooner. I decided to stop trying so hard to be a *good* listener. Instead, I wanted to only give as much as I got. Yet, even fierce with resolve, my body still leaned towards conversations, no matter how dull or inane. I couldn't understand why I was so weak-willed.

Instead of turning down invites, I began to leave earlier than most, often disappearing without saying goodnight. Swaying from the ebb of wine, I'd crawl into bed and switch on my lamp to tear through books. I started to crave these moments of silence, the unguarded ease of it. Reading allowed me to home in on a single voice, rather than scanning dozens of faces in dark, crowded rooms, desperately trying to untangle the hard knot of conversation.

By the end of 2014, I rarely joined our close group when they went drinking. I didn't want anyone to see me frazzled and cranky from fatigue. I made excuses: I'm too tired; I have an early shift tomorrow morning; sorry, I'm saving for my next trip overseas.

Over the previous months, Kate had often asked me what was wrong. I denied that anything had changed. I was cold and detached. We began to bicker over small things. Our old joke of parodying ourselves became a mean way of mocking one another. One night, at the beginning of 2015, while walking home from the pub, we had a row on Stanmore Road. Kate had pointed out that I had been acting differently for months and she was unsure if we were even friends anymore. Standing under a street light, I screamed: 'You don't understand!'

'Then tell me!' Kate screamed back.

'You never listen when I talk!'

'That's absolute bullshit! Do you realise how much effort I put into this friendship? I am constantly asking you: how are you feeling? Yet, you never open up.'

'But you don't listen!' I howled. 'Whenever we're out you're always on your phone or looking around the bar for someone better to talk to.'

'I like people watching!' she yelled. 'And just because I'm

looking at my phone doesn't mean I'm not listening to you!'

I didn't believe her.

Not long after my argument with Kate, I noticed that I would often stop speaking whenever someone looked away from me, only resuming the conversation once they had turned back to me. I had been treating every interaction as though the other person were also deaf. This felt like a startling insight to have at twenty-seven years old.

I never learned how to read lips. At least not consciously. That weekend I tested myself. Sitting with friends at the pub, I followed the flow of the conversation. I took off my glasses. Faces softened. Words blurred. The conversation churned around me. I squinted hard, but the room remained a whitewash of noise. After a few moments, I slid my glasses back on. As faces came into focus, so too did the conversation.

For the rest of the night, I noticed that I used my whole body to listen—eyes watching, skin feeling, muscles tensing. My head swung from left to right as I watched sounds ripple across faces— sometimes words were clear, distinct; at other times they remained indecipherable. I later learned that, in the field of sound research, this is called 'glimpsed speech'.

I hadn't realised how much I used my eyes in order to hear. Small, confusing moments now began to make sense. As a phys- iotherapy student, I was allowed to observe a few orthopaedic surgeries. We were told that seeing a body sliced opened, bones sawed, a new joint cemented in place, would teach us empathy. It would allow us to understand, in rich, visceral detail, the pain and discomfort each patient experienced when wheeled onto the orthopaedic ward to recover. As observers, another student and I were directed to stand at the top of the operating table, where there was a ventilator and a heart-rate monitor. The patient's head rested just in front of our bellies. We peered over the green sterile sheeting that had been strung up to protect the patient's face during the operation. As I stood on my tiptoes I imagined the horror of overbalancing and toppling onto the patient or knocking over the ventilator. I was glad my surgical mask hid my nerves.

Two surgeons, one on either side, dug into the patient with their scalpels. When my fellow student elbowed me hard in the ribs I looked up, followed her gaze: the surgeon on the left, a mask covering his mouth and nose, was narrowing his eyes at me. I stood in silence, unable to figure out what I had done wrong. I found out later that he had been angrily demanding why I hadn't bothered to answer his questions—questions I hadn't heard.

I continued to notice how I would parse faces—instinctively seeking lips, eyes, cheeks—gathering enough clues to guess what someone was saying.

Homonyms (the bark on a tree or the sound of a dog; lie down here or lie to me) and homophones (pear/pair, ring/wring) are just some of the traps for lip-readers. Lips, teeth and tongue move in the same manner yet deliver completely different meanings. Conversations are clotted with context because words shape-shift in definition, depending on the sentence.

I realised just how particular I was about words; my default mode is still to question their sound, spelling and even their etymology. At times, this can make me insufferable, prone to getting bogged down in details and holding people to their word—even recounting conversations, phrase for phrase, back to friends or family weeks, if not years after the fact.

I've been told that my memory for conversations can make people uncomfortable. I never used to drink much, especially at parties and large gatherings; I tried my best to stay switched on, only going home when people's words became washed-out with alcohol.

When I was twenty-two, one of my aunts said, 'Don't make it so obvious that you are sober, alert and watching. Nobody will ever trust you if they know you'll recall everything in the morning.'

Not wanting to make others feel uncomfortable, I learned to hide my ways of intently listening during conversations. I leaned backwards to lengthen my sweep of a scene, then twisted in towards sound; mine was a body that monitored the tone and timbre of voices, calculating how they would react with surrounding surfaces—the ping of steel, the refraction of glass, the soft soak of timber, the kindness of carpet to soften hard edges; a body that harboured a hope for familiar topics so I could piece together the fragments of half-caught syllables; a body that was always alert and guessing; a body that appeared to ease, tipsy and laughing; a body that could pass, blend in and be trusted.

And then I learned that my heart had been neglected.

I stumbled across a hearing-aid advertisement that made a distressing claim: because of the left ear's proximity to the heart, research had 'proven' that it allowed us to listen to its rhythms and concerns:

> Those with greater hearing loss in the left ear may find themselves less able to understand their spouse's moods or arguments, while those with greater hearing loss in the right ear may seem to lose some of their logical reasoning abilities...For those of you with hearing loss in your left

ear, you may want to do your marriage a favour and look into getting an Audicus hearing aid.

I immediately started digging into scientific databases to disprove the ad. There was some flimsy research that differentiated the function of each ear—experiments conducted in noisy Italian nightclubs, with researchers asking for cigarettes and observing whether revellers offered their left or right ear to a stranger. Other studies described a 'left ear advantage': subjects demonstrated a stronger recollection of emotive words when they were played into their left ear compared to when they were played into their right ear. It was suggested that this is why mothers tended to cradle babies on their left side. And why people have been observed switching the telephone receiver to their left ear during emotional conversations then back to their right ear during more logical interactions.

I picked apart these studies, determined to find fault in the methodology of each one. After hours spent cross-referencing journal articles, in a moment of panic I worried that my hunger for empirical data was proof that my brain relied on logic alone. Maybe I couldn't hear what my heart wanted? If others could hear when their hearts swelled or bruised, was I missing out? Desperate to further disprove the studies, I downloaded multiple dating apps and went on a flurry of first dates, and the occasional second or third date. Soon I got tired of it all and stopped. Exhausted and, I think, heart-sore.

In sound

'Why now?' the audiologist asked after I sat down.

'I've heard the technology has changed a lot,' I replied.

She nodded as she delicately measured my ears. 'Your ears are the size of a child's. I'll have to order the smallest pair.'

Two weeks before the appointment I had typed 'one deaf ear' into Google. I'd recently met several people with hearing aids who were ecstatic about them.

'It's just like before,' they said. 'Actually, probably even better than before.'

Better. Better. Better. The beat of *better* drummed in my head. Had a new type of hearing aid been invented? Something smaller, faster, slicker, something that could make me better?

The search engine suggested that instead of 'one deaf ear', I must be looking for 'unilateral deafness'. I casually scrolled down the search results, expecting to find brand names of hearing aids, but recoiled when I read the impact of unilateral deafness—irritability, social isolation, jumpiness, frequent headaches. One of the entries described people with unilateral deafness as often misdiagnosed with ADHD and suffering from 'chronic interpersonal communication difficulties', their body language and mannerisms 'awkward or unusual' as they stare at other people's mouths or tilt their head frequently in an almost 'bird-like' manner.

As I read through the list, each dot point collided with a memory: feeling frantic with confusion during conversations; becoming swamped with fatigue in a crowded room; the shrill headaches that took days to shake; the grip of tension I felt whenever I walked through crowds. I pictured my head bobbing along to conversations, pecking at words, without breaking eye contact.

Bile racing up my midline, I kept reading. People with unilateral deafness are often perceived as boorish, domineering, socially awkward and evasive. The descriptors seemed like neat euphemisms. Memories of being called cold, robotic, unrelenting, calculating and unfeeling reared up.

Unlike during my hypochondriac moments, I was now confronted by a clinical description. Why did I ever think that I could pass as hearing? My feelings of unease were no longer self-contained. I immediately booked an appointment at the closest audiology clinic, only a twenty-minute walk away. But I had to wait two weeks—before things could get *better*.

By then, the list had become a subsonic hum, reverberating through me each time I looked at someone's lips or tilted my head to hear better: *you are boorish, awkward, evasive.*

The beat of *better* changed to a dull drone—*broken, broken, broken.* During the fortnight before my appointment, I stared at advertisements for hearing aids. In one, the text beneath a photograph of a man holding the hand of a much younger woman said: *my midlife crisis is obvious, my hearing aid is not.* The technology was described as discreet. Perhaps my secret would be mine to keep.

The audiologist consulted my previous hearing tests.

'I'm sorry, but there are no hearing aids that will allow your left ear to work. However, you're an ideal candidate for a CROS aid,' she said. 'Contralateral Routing of Signals. The aid contains a microphone that captures sounds and feeds them to your right ear.'

She held up the device, a small plastic box with a transparent tube curving upwards. It looked innocuous enough, unlike the hearing glasses I wore in primary school.

'You'll feel as though you can hear from your left ear. It'll help you figure out where sounds are coming from without using your eyes.'

A memory of playing Marco Polo surfaced: an excruciating forty minutes at the Year Seven camp, when, with my eyes shut, I threw myself around the swimming pool yelling Marco! Marco! Marco! My feet and fingers reaching, reaching, reaching as I tried to chase the echoing responses of Polo! Polo! Polo! Eventually, just when I was too exhausted to call out anymore, someone swam into my outstretched hand.

The promise of precision was heart-quickening. Better. Better. Better. From my internet research, I realised how painfully obvious it was that ears were designed to work as a pair, a tightly synchronised tandem act. Locating sound—Polo! Polo! Polo!—happens with the ease of a card-trick sleight of hand. The blockish shape of the human skull means that one ear receives sound before the other. By analysing the time difference between the signals, the brain determines the location of the sound. Even with their eyes squeezed shut, my classmates were able to track the movements of everyone in the pool. My right ear had no point of reference to which it could orientate itself. Flinging myself around the pool, I just assumed that I was hopeless at water sports.

'So, once you switch this on, it'll get rid of your head shadow.'

The audiologist explained that sound waves thumped against the deaf side of my head. Some dissipated, rerouting and reaching my right ear; others were lost. I imagined the left side of my head as perpetually in darkness.

'This device will make sound three-dimensional,' she continued.

'Three-dimensional?'

'With only one ear, your brain simply doesn't receive enough information to properly process sounds, which is why the world sounds flat to you.'

'Flat?'

'Everything is at the same volume and intensity. There is no distinction between anything.'

She explained that ears are designed to home in on a single voice; all other noises, or 'interference'—vacuum cleaners, the drone of a microwave, the rush of water from a tap, the bleep of traffic lights, footsteps—are filtered out, allowing the brain to effortlessly amplify and focus on a speaker of their choice. Of course, most people don't realise their bodies can do this. It is spontaneous, this *ease* of entering a conversation. Someone like me, she said, doesn't have that luxury. My soundscape is flat and featureless.

My mouth slipped into a narrow jag. I thought of the countless nights spent listening to bands in dingy pubs. Music gigs were the only places I felt comfortable. It was too hard to talk in the noise; we just danced, tumbling around as if we were in the drum of a washing machine. During my early twenties, I wrote gig reviews for street press. I devoted hours to listening and thinking about music. I had assumed that being half-deaf just meant that I heard everything at half the volume. I felt sick at the revelation that sound could have a completely different shape. What had I been missing out on?

'Test them out for a fortnight and then let me know if you want to purchase a pair,' said the audiologist.

'Great.' I'd figure out a loan, pick up more shifts teaching Pilates, sell all my books or maybe some clothes, anything to rid myself of my flat world.

'It's okay if you don't like these hearing aids. Not many people born with hearing loss like yours feel comfortable using them.'

'Why?'

'They're used to how they operate in the world. You've had over two decades without binaural hearing. As soon as you slip these on, a number of things will happen to your brain.'

She went on to explain the process of 'summation'—the hearing aids would allow auditory information to pass between both hemi-spheres of my brain for the first time. 'Once both sides of your brain are communicating, sound will become approximately ten per cent louder, but also three-dimensional. Here, have a go.'

I took off my glasses and reached for the device, desperate for my brain to get as much information as possible, to let light into the dense shadowlands. My fingers trembled as I slipped an aid over each ear, fitting them snugly to the curves of cartilage. I slid the tube into my ear canal. Then I gently put my glasses back on. The tops of my ears felt crowded.

'Now, flick the switch.'

I fumbled, tugging my hair as I felt for the controls. Then I heard a few short notes, like the scales on a xylophone, ringing *inside* my left ear. I shivered with delight.

'Stay facing the desk.'

The audiologist walked behind me. I could hear water splashing on porcelain. The sound was anchored to the right side of the room. I heard her standing next to a sink. It felt as if a set of eyes had pushed through the back of my skull.

'Now, I'm going to switch on the air-conditioning unit.'

The office filled with the noise of the blasts of chilled air. I automatically tensed, ready to focus on what she would say next. White noise had always been like a snowstorm, impenetrable and disorientating: I'd never been able to hear conversations over the boil of a kettle or the buzz of a microwave.

'So, what do you think?'

Her voice swooped and dived, landing like a dart in my ear. I could hear each word with awesome clarity.

'It might seem a bit odd.' She had stepped closer. Her voice rose above the din and rushed to the foreground, spot lit and centre stage. The sounds of the running water and the air-conditioning unit, both distinct, had now faded. So this was what people meant by background noise? That sounds literally receded. No wonder people could sit and chat in busy restaurants, their brains unconsciously conducting the mess of sounds, seamlessly focusing in and out. Maybe I would no longer need to press my back against the wall in crowded rooms? I imagined myself casually picking any seat when dining with friends, without having to calculate how many people in the group would be sitting to my left.

'How is it?'

She had moved back towards the sink. My ears felt pert, attentively tracking her movements. The anticipation of not having to check over my shoulder whenever I heard footsteps in the dark already felt thrilling. Maybe I would be able to lower my guard? Perhaps I'd become less uptight? Yes, life was definitely going to get so much easier, so much better.

'Well, it's…'

That was odd.

'It's not bad. Kind of…'

It happened again. My head was filling up with my voice.

'So you like it?'

I simply nodded. My curls brushed against the hearing aids, creating a frisson of sound, high-pitched and screeching. I had never realised that hair could be so distracting.

'Fantastic.' She sat back in her chair. 'Guess I'll see you in two weeks.'

As I stepped out of the clinic, my ears felt hot and full. I paused by the door and wiggled the tube in my right ear, pulling it out before sliding back in.

The soundscape of the street came rushing towards me. From the left there was a *click-click-click* of heels on tiles. Behind that there was the *squeak-squelch-squeak-squelch* of running shoes. I turned and saw a woman walking, and about twenty metres away a young girl jogging. From behind a clipped hedge I could hear the *slap-slap, slap-slap* of thongs. Did walking always sound so loud? A sensation of claustrophobia crawled over me. Were there always this many people around?

I lingered by the clinic's front door. A siren wailed. Somewhere to the right of me there was an ambulance hurtling through side streets towards Royal Prince Alfred Hospital.

It was only ten per cent louder, I told myself. That wasn't very much, was it? After a few moments of lecturing myself, I stepped forward. Sounds clobbered me from all sides. I struggled to stay upright. I needed to get home.

When I heard the screech of brakes, I scrambled backwards, flinging myself against a wall. I watched a truck roll past, well within the lane markings and cruising at the speed limit, but it had sounded so close, as if had accidently mounted the kerb and was charging towards me. I felt like a child, completely ill-equipped to navigate traffic safely.

My eyes skittered back and forth. Checking my phone, I realised I'd only had the hearing aids on for ten minutes; taking them off now would be pathetic, cowardly. Pedestrians streamed past. They seemed so relaxed. Why weren't they choking on all this noise? My mouth felt full with the taste of every new sound.

I forced myself to start up the hill. After a few moments I turned into a laneway, the walls luminous with spray paint. There was a sour smell of piss and rotting garbage. Bin day. It would take longer to criss-cross through the laneways of Newtown, but I'd be able to avoid the lunchtime rush along King Street.

I walked quickly, arms swinging to propel myself along, but I soon discovered that every action had acoustic consequences. My clothes, previously inoffensive cotton blends, shrieked from the friction of my skin. I held my arms still. Eventually my shirt and pants softened with sweat, producing more of a whimpering sound. The heavy tread of my feet reverberated through my whole body. *Thud-thud-thud*. I slowed down, stepping on the concrete with more care.

Sounds from far beyond my line of sight continued to collide into me. The world wasn't just louder; it felt bigger, as if the landscape was being reconstructed, wider, deeper. My ears picked up the scrape of rubber on concrete a full minute before I saw a guy skating up a laneway. As he rolled past, the sound of the wheels was exquisitely painful. I felt guilty for the hours I'd spent skating around the backyard with my mates last summer after we found a collection of abandoned skateboards in a side street. The bald wheels tore across the concrete late into the night. I'd never considered how the sound must have travelled into the terraces on either side of us.

Exhausted, I cowered at a set of traffic lights. I was still only halfway home. My hands hovered over my ears. I could just take the things out. The *ratatata* of the lights changing to green sent me scampering across the street as if caught in a storm, my hands now covering my head.

Once home, I was blanketed in fatigue. I removed the hearing aids from my ears and the world softened with a sigh. As I pulled off my clothes, I spoke to myself, testing if my skull was free of my voice. Words tumbled out of my lips without echo. Falling into bed, I pressed my right ear into the pillow and silence slid over me like a cool, oily lotion.

I woke at dawn and switched off my alarm. After getting dressed in leggings and a light jumper, I gingerly hooked the hearing aids over each ear, debating whether to tie my hair up or leave it like a veil over my ears. I hadn't told my boss or any of my clients that I was deaf. Twisting my head from side to side in front of the mirror, I tried to gauge how noticeable the aids were. The tube, which ran from the top of the hearing aid, down the front of my ear, before sliding into the canal, looked so large and obvious. I played with my hair, pulling it up and down, before yanking it into a high ponytail when I realised I was running late.

I walked more slowly than usual, wobbly and off-centre, wondering how I would be able to teach Pilates today. Each exercise demanded smooth strength and control. Or flow, as I told my clients. My toes caught on the lip of the footpath. The boundaries of my body were blurring as the back streets of Stanmore became animated, sonically charged. The branches of trees thwacked in the wind. The hinges of a gate barked when its bleary-eyed owner pushed it open. I tried to ignore the thump of my feet as I picked up speed, noises hounding me like a pack of snarling dogs.

At the studio, I loosened my hair in order to hide the hearing aids. I smiled brightly as my clients arrived. The 7.30 a.m. classes were always chatty. Normally I joined in, asking questions about the clients' families, their work, their plans for the weekend, but that day I was still too unaccustomed to hearing the sound of my own voice. Instead, I swallowed my chatter, stretched out my hands and moved my body through each exercise, while grinning, grinning, grinning through the pain of learning how a dozen bodies sounded as they huffed through an hour of abdominal exercises.

Sound waves are continually crashing into our bodies. Even with noise-cancelling headphones, our skin soaks up sound. It is up to our brain to decide which noises are important and which ones to ignore. People with completely intact hearing learn from a young age how to unconsciously filter out unimportant noise—planes, traffic, their own breathing. Thanks to my new hearing aids, my brain was inundated with new information: my three housemates chatting in the kitchen; footsteps ascending the stairs; the calamity of bin day; clocks on walls and watches on wrists ticking out of time with each another; my body, rumbling, chewing, farting. Everything I had imagined doing over the next two weeks—watching bands play; taking a phone call on a train; lingering in a cafe during the lunchtime rush; drinking gin until everyone's lips became unreadable—now felt too frightening, too intensely sonic. A floodlight had been switched on inside my skull. Without my shadow, I felt stark and exposed.

•

Halfway through the first week, like a tired child I panicked and summoned tears. My mouth puckered and eyes blinked. After a few minutes of effort, my cheeks were still dry. With a final dry heave, I whimpered at my body's unwillingness to weep. I wanted to release the tension and tumult inside me, to prove to myself that it wasn't just in my head.

Ordinary, benign sounds undid me. A knife on burnt toast. The glug of someone drinking. A car's indicator clicking with harsh impatience. I missed the smooth, gentle nothingness in my left ear, and how, whenever I turned my head, silence spread like molasses. Even when I was standing still, I could now hear the air shifting around me, intrusive and lingering.

The Pilates studio was crowded that week. My muscles were twitching with nervous energy and I was moving indecisively. During each shift, I dropped equipment, tripped over exercise mats, lost track of my thoughts. My brain felt soggy, heavier, as if it was holding onto every sound. I reduced the scope of my movements to avoid any unnecessary noisemaking. I lightened my footfall, avoided talking, fidgeting, scratching.

Later, back in my darkened bedroom, I recalled my university lectures in neuroscience: the brain constructed like a layer cake, pulpy and dense. I found comfort in the clinical language used to describe the geography of the brain: golgi apparatus, myelin sheath, cerebellum, medulla oblongata, words that allowed me to detach and think of my body as a specimen. Contained. Not made unruly with sound.

The brain thrives on creating order. Our bodies are a series of finely tuned habit loops. Networks of neurons map our experiences of engaging with the world—how we walk, stand up, brush our teeth or hair. It is less taxing for the brain to launch the same sequence of movements. The most established path, the path of least resistance, is refined by repetition.

As my brain was now learning to hear with two ears, new pathways were being swiftly bulldozed into place. Areas of my brain previously never exposed to noise were now being flooded with sound waves. I reminded myself of this so I understood that the headaches and exhaustion I was feeling were real and for a reason. But a snarl, low and mean, also played on a loop: *just try harder.*

The sensation of disruption and disorder would continue for hours after I had taken off the hearing aids. As I lay in bed with a throbbing head, I asked myself: what damage have I done? My mind and body no longer felt familiar. More worryingly, they no longer felt like they were under my control.

Discomforted by the intensity of my reaction, I wondered if this was normal. I googled hearing aids. Each website emphasised the ease of the technology, how these devices offered people the chance to start 'living again'.

My bedroom door stayed shut. I stopped going out unless it was for work. More than anything, I wanted to go back to the steady predictability of sound, silence and shadow.

Walking home from work one night, a barrelling wind unsettled latched gates. Metal on metal. I added that to the inventory of sounds I now hated.

When my alarm went off, I stared at the black hearing-aids case, sitting like an anvil on my bedside table. There were six days left until my next appointment with the audiologist. I pushed my head hard into the pillow.

After a few moments, I dragged myself out of bed and put on my uniform, a polo top and slacks, while my housemates enjoyed a Sunday sleep-in. I debated whether or not to wear the hearing aids. With only a week to go, it felt pointless to give up now. Especially as my career involved coaching patients through the rehabilitation process, encouraging them to stay the course, to trust that things would get better. And yet I wondered if this trial was a mistake. It was throwing up more questions than answers. Eventually, I hooked the hearing aids over the back of each ear. I tensed as I heard the xylophone chime, signalling that the hearing aids were now communicating with each other. On the train to work, I was chaperoned by self-pity.

At work, I pulled off my latex gloves with a *thwack*, discarded them, then spun my hands under the tap. The motion detector was triggered. A laminated poster above me detailed the proper hand-washing technique. I'd seen the same poster, developed by the World Health Organization (WHO), thumbtacked above sinks in countless hospitals I'd visited as a clinician or patient. Today, feeling exhausted, my head was bowed as if in a moment of grace.

The water ran hot. I replicated the choreographed sequence, interlocking my fingers, reciting the alphabet as I worked soap into every crease of skin and nail. The WHO advises that this procedure should take the same amount of time as singing 'Happy Birthday' twice through. While practical, it makes hand-washing feel like a sad, lonesome ritual when repeated more than fifty times a day.

As I cued each letter of the alphabet to my breath, I was acutely aware of how my hearing aids were forcing my brain to manage thousands of micro-decisions, amplifying and telescoping in on sounds. I had never considered hearing as a particularly complex or interesting sense, but now I felt as if I'd lost control. Weren't these aids a good thing? Shouldn't I be grateful? I kept waiting for my new hearing to feel normal. But I was uncomfortable within my body. Being in a hospital didn't help.

The architecture of a hospital allows for ease of movement— hard floors, corridors wide enough for two gurneys to trundle side by side, thin curtains that can be quickly pulled around beds, centrally located nurses' stations with multiple entrances allowing healthcare workers to dash in and out to gather notes and take phone calls. In this place built for unfaltering movement, voices and patient call bells carry clearly across wards. It's no wonder that the most consistent complaint patients have at discharge is about the noise levels. It's true that patients can't sleep properly in these buildings. Often even their own bodies are amplified: an alarm system announces blood and oxygen levels. Alerts signal a kink in a line delivering fluid, or when blood desaturates, or when the heart ticks up a notch in rhythm.

As much as I enjoyed working in healthcare, I wondered what it would be like to work somewhere quiet. Maybe then I would have the energy and verve to live a fuller, more social life.

After drying my hands, I took off my right hearing aid. Then I pressed my index finger onto the soft cartilage flap, which acted like a poorly stitched suture. Sound seeped in: the constant whoosh of industrial air-conditioning, the hum of fluorescent lights, the clattering of trolleys burdened with bland lunches or freshly laundered linen, the mechanical wheeze of ventilators, the wet whelp of my patients trying to rid their lungs of phlegm. There was still another hour until lunch, when I could enjoy the quiet relief of reading. Thirty minutes to convalesce.

A beeping pierced my daydream. I looked around and saw the light flashing above bed eight. My patient's oxygen levels were dropping. I hooked the hearing aid over my ear, pulled on a pair of fresh gloves and returned to work.

My ears felt thin-skinned and raw, I left the hearing aids off for longer stretches of time. Even without them on, I was still easily startled by any noise, no matter how small. I had become sensitive, irritated by sound. It didn't take much—a conversation with a friend; a short walk; ordering a coffee—to push me into a state of sensory overload.

By the end of the trial, my head felt harrowed by sound. I handed back the aids to the audiologist, murmuring my thanks, then left her office, my shoulders hunched and my ears unadorned. I zigzagged through back streets, cutting a new route home, where I bolted a cup of tea before dragging myself to the Pilates studio, braced for six hours of polite chatter.

Within a few weeks of returning the hearing aids, I travelled to South America, then on to Europe. From February to June, wanting to feel carefree, I drank sickening amounts of alcohol, plunging into blackouts. During the day I drove my body to sweat—striding across windswept plains, climbing mountains, bike-riding, dancing. Whenever I was in a new city, I'd leave my friends and sit in the quiet splendour of a museum or gallery, unable to pay attention to anything at all.

I hoped that my sense of dislocation was some sort of homesickness. But once I landed back in Sydney, my skittishness intensified. I couldn't gauge the *real* volume of the streetscape. Even the most cheerless street corners triggered vivid sense memories. I fell towards silence. I wanted to scour the noise from my skin.

•

Six months after I had trialled the hearing aids, I nodded hello to the barista at my local cafe and slid into my usual seat, before noticing two women signing. They were sitting a couple of tables over. My curiosity transcending decency, I gaped at them. Their hands flew up and down, touching cheeks, ears, elbows. As they conversed, I kept my hands under the table, opening and closing them, and digging my nails into my palms to punish them.

I left the cafe feeling helpless, imagining a future when I'd be swaddled in only the memories of sound, unable to communicate. It wasn't hard to imagine; Dad had recently started struggling to follow conversations. His noise-induced hearing had steadily declined after years of working in construction.

That weekend I watched him trying to decode the family conversation as it travelled around the dinner table. Everyone was talking at once. The neighbour's dog was barking and the footy was blaring on the TV in the other room. He leaned back in his chair; the resignation evident on his face felt desperately familiar to me. He lowered his gaze and finished his meal without saying a word.

Later that night, I cajoled him into getting hearing aids, I assumed that because he had acquired hearing loss at a later age, he would have a better experience. I caught myself using phrases I'd read in hearing-aid advertisements: *it will make your life easier, more enjoyable.*

During the conversation I was fiercely jealous. Why couldn't I have an easy fix? Since returning to Australia, I'd stopped going out; my focus had shifted towards the future. I had read that almost fifty-eight per cent of people aged between sixty-one and seventy years have hearing loss. This jumps to seventy-four per cent in people aged over seventy. It seemed likely that I would acquire further hearing loss as I aged. Even if I lost only a small amount, would

I be able to maintain a job? Relationships? How would I keep up with conversations?

I hadn't realised just how much I was banking on the hearing aids as my backup plan. It was a terrible and formidable thought: *this is it, you better make the most of it.* I was filled with a sense of urgency.

I felt compelled to relocate, leave the inner west, to get away from the flight paths; the rumble of trucks up Enmore Road; the proximity of people; the routine of ducking into dark bars; the sheer slog of trying to keep up with conversations. I clicked open dozens of tabs, scanning job ads for occupations I knew nothing about. I imagined myself working in a quiet office. Carpeted floors. Soft furnishings. Meetings in boardrooms, with only one person speaking at a time. Hours of deep, reassuring silence, perhaps even solitude, during the workday.

I'm sure I would have reached this tipping point even without the hearing-aid trial. The decision to book an appointment with the audiologist didn't come out of nowhere. I can see now how my energy levels had been erratic throughout my twenties. How I was often sick, ploughed over by one infection after another, never quite recovering. How furious and frustrated I felt all the time. I suspect that, even without the hearing aids, I would have been overcome by the sudden urge to flee.

During those weeks of looking for a new career, a new life, I lashed out at my siblings over inconsequential things, brandishing the sort of rage I hid from friends, knowing it was ugly, mean and inexcusable. I was in a foul, unreconciled mood.

Flight

In mid-July 2015, I was working an evening shift at the Pilates studio. At nine o'clock, I said goodnight to each of my clients as they left the studio. I wiped down the exercise equipment, straightened up the towels and turned off the lights. After shrugging on my jacket, I locked the entrance. Once outside, I started the brisk walk home from Annandale to Stanmore. I enjoyed striding through the dark streets. It allowed me to unwind after being surrounded by people for hours. Without this, falling asleep felt impossible.

Less than twenty metres from the studio, I was grabbed from behind. A set of hands roamed my body. As they squeezed my buttocks, I found my voice and screamed. I twisted away and screeched: Fuck off!

The man let go and bolted across the road. Once he was out of sight, my body buckled. Alone in the dark and still a twenty-minute walk from home, I dialled my brother, who lived nearby. He immediately got in his car. I hurried towards busy, brightly lit Parramatta Road to meet him. As I waited, standing with my back pressed up against the green tiles of a pub, I could still feel the stranger's hands pawing at my body. My heartbeat was quick and anxious.

It wasn't the first time I'd been sexually assaulted or harassed by a stranger in a public space. I'd been groped or touched on public transport, in pubs and at music festivals. Each experience was irritating and unpleasant. But the shock and force of being grabbed on a quiet suburban street left me reeling. As I stood alone, waiting, the darkness now seemed like a dense, ominous space. Most of all, I was bitterly disappointed by my reaction. Instead of defending myself with fists and feet—punching and kicking—I had just screamed. For years, I had felt secure in my strength and ability to defend myself. Now I no longer trusted my body.

Apart from my brother and housemates, I told no one about the assault. And I didn't talk openly about the hearing aids either. I couldn't find the words to articulate the rage, shame and sadness that had surfaced during the past twelve months. Instead of trying to understand or dissect the source of my discomfort, I focused on submitting dozens of applications for jobs located out of Sydney.

I want a job with *responsibility*, I told my friends over drinks. I want my career to *progress*. For weeks, as I looked through job advertisements, I imagined wearing heels, tailored clothes, and I fantasised about painting my nails bold, lurid colours—nail polish is banned in all clinical work as it can colonise microorganisms. I imagined sitting at a desk, undisturbed by the beeps of heart-rate monitors and ventilators, in a job where I could just fire off emails, instead of having to talk to people for hours at a stretch.

In August 2015, I secured a job at a not-for-profit organisation that developed clinical guidelines for the safe use of medications. A job that required me to relocate to Melbourne. I was hoping for a new beginning.

I sent a text message to my family, telling them I was moving to Melbourne in September—for good. I didn't stop to think how unbelievably casual and hurtful this would be. In that moment, I thought of no one but myself, and nothing but flight.

In Melbourne, while sleeping on a friend's couch in the inner-city eastern suburb of Richmond, I hunted for a place of my own. I had narrowed my search for a share house to this area. The Yarra River was within walking distance and there were plenty of parks. After about ten days, I found a sundrenched flat perched on the rise of Richmond Hill. My new flatmate, Cassie, was softly spoken and focused on her work. She had moved down from the Sunshine Coast a year earlier to pursue a career as a software developer and admitted that she was still settling into the city. Cassie was keen to keep the flat a 'sanctuary', which meant that I would have to forewarn her if I wanted to invite people over. Every night and weekend, she played folk music albums on the living-room stereo while coding at the kitchen table.

The flat adjoined a laneway, a popular shortcut to the major retail strip, Bridge Road. Each morning, a parade of hot air balloons bobbed past the windows. During the day, voices rose high and clear into my bedroom. At night, footsteps echoed through the dark, but the noise didn't bother me. Once I had my right ear on my pillow, the world was silenced.

DECAY

On scars

My mother has the Hands of God. A patient christened her with the compliment. After work, still in her nursing uniform, she recounted the moment with a small proud smile. Years on, the epithet has been folded into our family story. Whenever her hands press onto a fevered forehead or reach up to tuck hair behind an ear, we remind her that she has the Hands of God. Sometimes, I wonder if this is why I have dedicated my life to learning how to use my hands in ways that are practical, considerate.

I was fifteen years old when I began to learn how to care for others. Twice a week, for the better part of a year, I attended after-school classes in Assistant Nursing. I learned how to make beds so that the sheets lay creaseless and the mouth of each pillowcase faced away from the door; to position someone with their pillows arranged to alleviate pain and ensure a deep sleep; to slide under-wear over hips; to buckle belts and button up shirts; to wipe the crust of sleep from eyes and shit from bottoms; to comb hair free of tangles, without tugging or yanking; to brush teeth either in my hand or in their mouth; to warm a dollop of moisturising cream by rubbing it first in my hands so it didn't feel like a cold slap; to spoon food so the metal edge of the cutlery didn't slice the roof of a mouth or clink on teeth; to gently scratch an itch; to prepare my hands for work, with nails trimmed, filed smooth and varnish free; to ask my hairdresser *please keep it long enough so I can tie it up*; to bend at my knees and hinge from my hips; and to always pause at a bedroom door after everything seemed to be done, and ask *is there anything else I can do?*

The job helped me pay my way through university. I woke before dawn to assist people out of bed and get them ready for the day. Each hygiene routine was unique to the client—a shower or sponge, a bar of soap or bodywash, a shave or a beard scrub—I learned to follow instructions, my hands becoming their hands. And then, for the rest of the day, I would go to class.

During the next four years of physiotherapy study, I learned new ways to heal people. I practised on members of my family; I would get them to lie on the couch or perch on a kitchen chair while I hovered over them, making bold attempts to straighten or twist joints, working my way through the syllabus systematically and with little explanation to my long-suffering family. I was more concerned with strengthening my hands than wasting time with words. Eventually, they would lever themselves upright and limp away, their fictitious ailments cured. Within a few weeks, they would flinch whenever I touched them.

By the time I graduated in 2009, my fingers had become strong and full of feeling. Years later, after almost a decade of clinical practice, I learned that my family had, for a time, nicknamed me the Hands of Torture. I was mortified, but I knew they were right. I also knew that my hands had matured since then. Over the years, I've held hundreds of warm bodies that were in pain. When I was a student, in order to counteract my nerves, my grip had been steely. As a clinician, my approach softened; I became nimble and responsive. With time, my confidence and expertise grew—no matter how uncomfortable I felt in my body following the hearing-aid trial and the assault, I still felt as if I had complete command of my hands.

And then, as is often the case, life got complicated.

It was late January 2016, a week after I had turned twenty-eight, when I broke my wrist. As I reached the crescendo of Stevie Wonder's 'Signed, Sealed, Delivered, I'm Yours', I slid on soap suds and landed with spectacular force on my left hand. Once I had unhooked myself from the edge of the bathtub, I saw that my left wrist was stuck at a sickening angle. I grabbed a towel and attempted to wrestle it over my legs and shoulders, my left arm folded into my midsection, crooked and powerless. After a few minutes, I leaned against the wall to recover, my skin still mostly wet.

I was flying to Sydney that afternoon to celebrate my birthday with friends and family. I was convinced that I just needed to get to hospital, have a plaster put on, and everything would be fine. Gingerly supporting my wrist through the pain, I pulled on some loose clothing and set off for the Epworth Hospital. The ten-minute walk took twenty, my arm slung across my chest, my hair dripping down my back.

After being triaged, I sat on a hospital trolley waiting to be reviewed by a doctor. I texted the friends I'd planned to meet for drinks that night. You can sign my plaster, I typed, then added a series of cheerful emojis.

As I lay alone in the small hospital cubicle, I pictured what was happening inside my body. My wrist was hot and throbbing. The fracture would have filled with blood carrying immune cells, neutrophils and macrophages, which would now be feasting on the dead bone in my wrist. Clever body, I thought.

An hour later, I was exhausted, fed up with my body.

'I need to refer you an orthopaedic surgeon,' announced the emergency-room doctor, after examining me.

'Surgery? I figured I'd just need a plaster.'

She pointed to the X-ray pinned to a lightbox, where my wrist bones were glowing.

'You've got a compression fracture. The bones have been crushed and pushed out of place. Your wrist needs to be cleaned up before we put a cast on.' She moved towards the door. 'You can wait there for the surgical review.'

'But I've got a flight this arvo.'

She turned around.

'I won't make it, will I?'

'No chance.'

The orthopaedic surgeon arrived an hour later and explained how he would reorganise the archipelago of fractured bones with pins and a plate. He could fit me in on his surgical list tomorrow afternoon.

'Do you want to stay the night? Or would you rather go home?'

'Home, please.'

I walked back to the flat with my arm coddled in a blue sling. Waiting for Cassie to come home, I sat on the couch for hours, bruised and bone-weary, my scalp itchy and my hair still caked with shampoo.

Later that week, my head cradled in a hard-plastic basin, I enjoyed the sensation of two hands working my hair clean. I left the hair salon with a bare neck, my curls cropped short. It looked drastic but felt sensible. Unfortunately, even at just two inches long, my hair was still hard to manage. Showering had become a tense and tuneless task. The base of the bathtub was now covered in a thick non-slip mat. An ugly but necessary purchase, one that didn't completely dull my apprehension. I stood braced, holding my left hand aloft as if in a salute, as I gave my hair a rough scrub.

I developed a one-armed choreography to cook meals and make my bed. I adjusted my wardrobe, eschewing button-up blouses for baggy shirts; zipped up jeans for elasticated pants; lace-up shoes for slip-on sandals. Everything was loose and unflattering.

At work I typed with one hand. It was slow and tedious. Within a week of starting the job I wondered if I had made a mistake. I was used to working collaboratively. In my new position, a series of line managers were required to approve even the most minute task; the lack of autonomy was stifling. I realised that my definition of *progress* was really just financial remuneration. By entering a new industry, however, I was starting again. My income had dropped steeply and any career advancement would require further university study. The most unexpected realisation was that I missed working with my hands.

But now, while I sat at my desk nursing my splinted arm, I was astonished by my good fortune. Notwithstanding all the shortcomings of my new job, the ability to continue working while healing felt like a deep, unending luxury. It also meant that, for short periods each day, as I sat at my desk crosschecking spreadsheets, I could forget that I was injured.

On the weekends, I slouched around the streets of Richmond under a large sunhat, following the same route every time as if in a holding pattern. I thought about the small threads of bone cells latching onto the steel plate in my wrist, and how after a bone breaks it becomes temporarily thicker. As I walked, a spool of thoughts beginning with 'when I' unravelled with each step: when I get better, I will start going out; when I have more energy, I will get a new hobby; when I'm mended, I will start exercising again; when I can use both hands, all will be well.

A colleague, noticing my interest in books, invited me to join the office book club. She emailed me almost daily, letting me know about upcoming author talks and theatre productions. I began to visit book shops and libraries that she recommended.

Keen to fill my evenings after work, I enrolled in a ten-week creative-writing class. Once a week, the teacher encouraged the class to write 'freely' and 'without worry'. At first my sentences splintered with self-consciousness.

'There are no right or wrong answers,' she explained to us. 'Write whatever comes to mind, even if you think it's absolute rubbish. You can always polish it later. Just remember that you can't edit a blank page.'

It was freeing to think of writing as an iterative process: mess and playfulness were encouraged, everything could be revisited and refined. The classes became the highlight of my week.

On the nights I didn't have a writing class, I scrolled through job sites. I decided to think of 2016 as a sort of gap year, before returning to physiotherapy when my wrist was strong. I applied for a job in Ulaanbaatar as a disability policy adviser, promoting access and inclusion across Mongolia. The deployment date was June. Applicants were warned that they must be able to endure physical hardships due to extremes in the weather, be willing to travel long distances, and to work autonomously. People with experience of disability, including 'lived experience', were encouraged to apply.

As I wrote my cover letter, I contemplated whether I should mention my hearing loss. Was I deaf enough to be counted as disabled? Or would the recruiters consider me too deaf and discount my application? I spent hours drafting the letter, imagining my body into the role. Unable to determine if my deafness would be considered an asset or liability, I omitted it from my application.

It was a cold evening in early April, during the final class of the creative-writing course, when the tendon of my left thumb snapped. It wasn't audible, or even painful. My thumb simply flopped down. Despite intense, wilful effort, I was unable to lift it.

While my classmates continued to write, I placed my hand on my lap and my thumb lay powerless. That night, we'd been encouraged to invite friends and family to watch us perform pieces we'd written. Without either close friends or family to invite, I had come alone. I sat quietly, assessing my thumb. After a few moments of flicking it back and forth, I tucked my hand into my pocket and kept it there for the rest of the evening. At home, a wave of exhaustion pulled me to sleep. It had only been a month since I had stopped wearing the wrist splint and got back into the rhythm of using two hands. Another injury was too much to think about.

One of the screws in my wrist had severed the tendon to my thumb—extensor pollicus longus (EPL), the tendon that holds the thumb straight and long. It helps pulls the thumb towards the index finger, allowing the joint to be opposable—to grab, pinch and grip. According to some scientists, this ability allowed humans to achieve dominance over all other species.

I was referred to an orthopaedic surgeon who specialised in the fine mechanics of the hand. He explained that there was no way of stitching the frayed ends of the tendon back together. I would need a tendon transferred from my index finger to my thumb.

'If I don't get the length of the tendon right, your thumb could end up sticking out like this,' the surgeon said, making an L shape. The 'loser' sign.

I nodded, saving my emotions for the toilet cubicle.

'Your brain will need to readjust and learn how to send signals to the new tendon. You'll have to work hard to regain the use of your thumb. Your result is dependent on your rehabilitation,' he said, neatly sidestepping my concerns about whether I would be able to work as a physiotherapist again.

'The earliest we can book you in for surgery is the end of June.'

'June? But that's almost three months away.'

'Your bones need time to strengthen before I can remove the hardware holding everything together. It'll be alright, there's no more damage you can do. Just be careful you don't catch it on anything,' he said, before turning towards his computer screen.

I left the surgeon's office with a smile plastered to my face. I wanted to be a good patient, polite and compliant. I intended to release my emotions later, once I was alone. But the tram was too crowded, the local park full of small children playing. And Cassie was camped out in the living room, coding. The bathroom was too small and still made me nervous. I went to bed swallowing tears, my gut roiling.

A few days later, an email landed in my inbox, congratulating me on progressing to the next round for the role of disability policy adviser in Mongolia. I would have to sit a psychometric test to determine whether I was mentally resilient—was I available sometime next week? With one hand, I typed up a response, withdrawing my application. As I pressed send my heart clenched.

When a friend, a sports physiotherapist, saw my thumb she gagged and turned away.

'It looks dead. Nah, I can't look at it, it's making me sick.'

Others simply averted their eyes. Even I couldn't bear to look at my thumb, hanging like a fallen flag. I began to position my left hand out of sight, tucked into pockets or nestled into my lap. I told myself this was safer and made it easier to avoid catching my thumb on furniture and tangling it in my clothes. And yet I knew that was not the whole truth. I simply couldn't bear to look at my thumb: it provoked an intensity of feeling I could barely comprehend. My whole body felt unmoored by a strange, disorientating grief, which wasn't helped by knowing that the longer my thumb dangled unused, the quicker it would fade from my muscle memory.

Lately, I had begun to think that I was lucky to have been born deaf—I had never had to adjust to my body. If anything, the experience of having my hearing 'restored' was more disruptive than I had anticipated—the swift reorganisation of my brain's neural pathways had made me feel strange and uneasy in my skin. A period of sadness followed, so protracted that it felt as if it was my new identity. Not even tears could soften my dense sadness. Though perhaps they would have if I had cried more. I can only remember two instances, some twelve months apart, when I released a long, wet howl. My confusion kept me dry-eyed and strung out. It was as if the hearing aids had rewired my body. Having just regained a sense of normality within my body, I worried that this injury might push me into another period of wild unease.

I remembered one of my anatomy lecturers explaining the

brain's motor cortex as she walked around the lecture theatre. 'Each part of the body is mapped to the motor cortex. The body is basically designed to carry the brain around.' Without any motor messages from my brain to my left thumb, this section of my map was fading. It was a hollowing feeling.

The amount of brain space devoted to each body part is based on the complexity of the part's movements. We ask a lot of our hands. They move in unison to clap, and each finger acts as an assertive individual while touch-typing. Whereas elbows and toes and ribs have much smaller repertoires of movement, thus requiring less space in the motor cortex. How our brains perceive our bodies is vastly different from how we see ourselves reflected in the mirror. While studying neuroscience, partly to procrastinate and partly out of morbid curiosity, I used to examine small figurines called homunculi, three-dimensional models of the brain's map. Now these gangly creatures haunted me. Each homunculus had a heavyset jaw with lush, pillowy lips, a torso that was a slender column and arms as thin as twigs. Their hands were at least five times the size of their body, so enormous, so fleshy and full that the figurine could not hold them up; instead they rested heavily on the ground.

Without my thumb as an anchor, I couldn't grip onto cutlery or hook around my waistband to pull up my pants. The longer I went without using my left thumb, the harder it would be to reclaim this space in my brain. It was not just a matter of regaining strength and flexibility, but also my sensitivity.

I had been accustomed to my hands knowing how to gain a patient's trust, and retain that trust while I gently crawled my fingers over their flesh with confidence and respect.

A colleague once described their hands as having ten eyes, each fingertip providing different and useful information. I had come to think of my hands in a similar way—but instead of eyes, they had ears, they listened. When I touched someone, my hands were asking and answering, acting and reacting, instructing and listening. I have learned that acts of care are finely calibrated through communication. I missed *feeling* a treatment have an effect—the soft sinking when a knot dissolved; the sudden freedom of a stiff joint moving; the light, feathery sensation of a nerve gliding smoothly through muscles.

The office job had given me the silence I had craved. But an errant decimal point or a clunky explanation could have fatal outcomes for the medication guidelines we were working on. The company had policies to ensure there was silence in the editorial department. Most of our communications happened via email. Any conversations, including telephone calls, were conducted in an adjacent space called the quiet room. But I hadn't realised how much I would miss the conversations between my hands and other bodies.

My training was not only to locate pain, but also to offer solutions and solace. I tried to think of what I would say to someone in my situation, the words of comfort I would use. But it was hard to think of kind words when I didn't know what the outcome of my injury would be. What if the tendon was too long or too short? Stitched too tightly? Or put under strain too soon? It could go snap, snap, snap and my hands would no longer be a pair.

Too anxious to read, I now spent most evenings sitting in my bedroom watching *Offspring*, a medical drama with storylines that often had swift and clear resolutions. It was also set in Melbourne, so I could convince myself that I was getting to know my new city.

'How's it all going?' Mum asked during one of her regular calls.

'Fine,' I said before quickly diverting the conversation. 'Work's busy. The mornings have been frosty.'

'I hope you're ordering takeaway. Or at least getting ready-made meals, something warm and hearty.'

'Sure thing,' I lied. Money was tight, I couldn't afford the extravagance. I had just received a $10,000 tax bill. The physiotherapy work I had done in Sydney for the past eighteen months had been freelance. My trip to South America had been funded by my misunderstanding of how taxation works for contractors. The tax office had placed me on a repayment plan. The first repayment wiped out the savings I had left after relocating to Melbourne. The next surgery and subsequent rehabilitation would put me even further into debt. I made do with snacking instead of going through the fraught process of buying or preparing meals. It helped that my appetite had dulled. Shrinking in size and confidence, I dragged myself through the cold Melbourne winter.

When talking to my family, I pretended that everything was fine. My voice hurt from the strain of trying to sound upbeat, so I began to avoid answering the phone, or I cut conversations short. At work, I ate lunch at my desk to avoid my colleagues' constant enquires about my hand and my general wellbeing.

In June, my sister flew down from Tamworth in New South Wales to help me after the second surgery. Her sensible, clear-eyed attitude made it difficult to pretend that everything had been fine. While I recovered from the surgery, she stocked my freezer with home-cooked meals.

'Okay, are you ready to start?' My hand therapist asked me.

We were both looking at my thumb, sitting at a right angle from my hand. I'd been waiting eight weeks for this moment.

'Just try to bring your thumb and index finger together.'

'I am.' Sweat pooled in my arm pits, the muscles of my left arm contracted as I tried to move my thumb, which remained straight and immobile.

'Keep looking at it, keep touching it. You need to remind your brain that you have a thumb.'

To ensure a scar heals you must touch it. If you don't, it can become sensitive even years after an operation, spiking with pins and needles. There is only a small window of time when you can calm the nerves and soften stitched skin.

It was July when I was finally allowed to touch the scars on my wrist, six months after breaking it. The night after my first visit to the hand therapist, I tentatively applied pressure to my thumb in a slow, circular motion. It was numb, almost wooden. Would it ever feel like a part of my body again? I pressed down hard, harder than I would have for a patient. My skin went red from the blood rush. I kept trying to knead feeling into the stiff, useless digit.

One scar ran down the inside of my wrist in a clean line. On the top was another shorter one, a deep groove. A small nick of a scar was at the base of my index finger, and one more wobbled along the base of my thumb. Each scar indicated where the surgeons had entered my left hand, the points of contact between bone and steel. Although I had touched many scars on my patients, I was reluctant to touch my own, for reasons I still find difficult to articulate. Instead, during that bitterly cold July of 2016, I kept my scars covered and only occasionally touched them.

After a few weeks of dismal effort, my hand therapist chastised me. 'Your scars are still thick.' She warned me that I needed to really 'dig in and break up the scar tissue', otherwise the tendons and nerves running down my left forearm and towards my fingers would become rigid and immobile.

'Of course, I don't need to tell you that,' she said.

She knew I was a physiotherapist, and we both knew that if, I didn't fully commit to the rehabilitation process, my left hand might not grab and grasp and pinch and pull and grip like it did before, or even at all. We both knew what that would mean for my career. And yet the scars left me dazed and idle with shock.

'You need to massage them for at least ten minutes, three times a day,' she insisted.

I nodded and agreed that I should be more diligent. That night I studied my scars, trying to imagine my body belonged to someone else, hoping I could assume the role of a clinician, alert with compassion, yet motivated for a good result, ready to dig in with firm, unflinching hands. Within moments, I had rolled down my sleeve and turned on another episode of *Offspring*.

In jest

A scar can take up to a year to mature. That's the word doctors use: *mature*. In the time it took for my scars to become softer and more elastic, my grip on my secret loosened. In July 2017, twelve months after the surgery on my thumb, I talked openly about my deafness on stage in front of a packed theatre.

It's hard not to think about this metaphorically: it took a physical fracture to highlight the internal fracture of my identity. Half-hearing and half-deaf. Physical healing allowed for psychic healing to occur. A fusing of identity.

This account is too linear in action and consequence. And yet I sometimes find myself connecting the events of my life, as if there were some obvious trajectory. A certain perspective, a specific telling of the facts, gives me the kind of cold comfort that comes from desperately wanting to retain a level of control or certainty. Or is it simply another way of telling myself, superstitiously, that everything happens for a reason? In reality, this story is only linear in time; for the rest, it is made messy by the cyclical pulse of shame and fear.

•

In September 2016, an email had landed in my inbox offering me a place in a free comedy-writing workshop. What luck, I thought. I needed a laugh. Melbourne University was setting up a research project, asking the question: can comedy be used to empower women with disabilities?

It felt like months since I had laughed freely, unconsciously. By now I had equipment to strengthen my hands: putty, elastic bands, lengths of thick, bendy plastic that came in several colours. Acts of daily living had become part of my exercise routine: I practised picking up paper clips; folding laundry with all my fingers pinching and gathering the corners of shirts and towels; typing with all my fingers; washing my hair slowly and with each fingertip; carrying an empty mug. I was clumsy, uncoordinated and prone to cheating.

During my convalescence, I had been trying to find the words to describe my experience of trialling hearing aids. I'm not sure what prompted me to stop writing stories and start writing about myself. It was a compulsion, a distraction from my current situation. The writing process felt like dry-retching. I hocked up the same few words page after page—thud, footsteps, scratch, trapped, echo— each reverberating with a shocking reminder of sound.

'I don't know if I am helping or harming myself by writing this essay,' I admitted to Kate after weeks of trying to arrange my thoughts on the page. She had witnessed me retract, turn inwards, during the trial. Our friendship had faltered after I left Sydney. Instead of talking several times a week, in 2016 we spoke at most once a month. Eventually, after she came to Melbourne for a weekend in early 2017, we continued to ring weekly and talk for hours.

'Perhaps you should just stop?'

I was glad we were speaking over the phone; my face was tender from crying.

'I want to, but I just...' I swallowed a surge of emotion, then asked her about her cat.

A few weeks later, I submitted the essay to a literary magazine. I hated the process of dredging up memories, but the act of framing my feelings with punctuation felt galvanising, even if it didn't resolve any issues for me. And knowing that the essay would sit unread in the magazine's slush pile for months felt like a way of suspending all my thoughts about the trial. Now, as I followed the email's instructions for enrolling in the workshop, I could begin to focus on writing for a laugh.

The workshops began in late October, when the sky was still low and grey. Four guide dogs, each wearing a florescent coat and harness, lay in the centre of our circle of twenty participants. After the team of researchers introduced themselves, we all signed waivers. While the course facilitator, the Comedian, introduced herself, we smiled faintly, comforted by her rolling laugh. Occasionally, if someone strolled through the auditorium's double doors, one of the dogs scampered up to its owner; otherwise they rested their heads on their paws.

The head of the research team explained that we were part of 'a researcher incubator, which houses projects that both promote the craft of comedy and investigate comedy as an instrument to advance human rights agendas'. The entire project would be filmed for research purposes. As she talked a man roved the room, a large black camera hoisted onto his shoulder. I kept my head down.

And then it clicked: comedy. Of course, that meant stand-up. I should have realised it sooner. Over the next five weeks we each had to develop a comedy routine to perform in front of an audience. When signing up for the workshop, I had assumed it would focus on the craft of writing and would help my short stories become lighter, more buoyant.

'The best performer on the night will go on to receive mentoring and have a chance to tell their jokes, their stories about disability, at the international comedy festival.' The researcher smiled before bringing her palms together. The group applauded. My hands were slippery.

As a woman reversed her mobility scooter away from the microphone stand, everyone clapped. We had to introduce ourselves as if we were opening our comedy set.

None of us had done comedy before, so we'd been given a prompt—'I know what you're thinking'—which I later discovered is a classic opening line used by budding comedians. The Comedian explained that we often laugh at things that are true. It's about the moment of recognition. But to get there requires a strategy; it is too confronting to look at the truth square in the eye. Comedy is created by misdirection: a sequence, a set-up and a pay-off. Sure, you can take a shortcut—it's easy to coax a quick laugh by saying something shocking—but we were told that the best laughs, the ones that last the longest, come from carefully calculated friction.

When I stood behind the microphone, I was almost hugging myself.

'You'll have to figure out a way of explaining what your disability is, otherwise the audience will be confused,' the Comedian said.

I let my arms hang by my sides as if welcoming courage into my body. When none came, I folded my arms, once again forming a tight barrier of flesh and bone. 'I know what you're thinking...'

I looked around the room, then down at my feet. My eyes stung. Before they could brim, I bit the corner of my bottom lip. The pain was a quick distraction. Lifting my head, I trained my eyes on the opposite wall.

'I know what you're thinking…who's this fraud? Why is she performing comedy at a disability show?'

I took a deep breath. 'Feel free to heckle, I won't hear you. I'm deaf.'

In the second workshop, the Comedian dissected the anatomy of a joke on a whiteboard. Each joke is essentially a story with a beginning, middle and end. I tried to follow closely, but my mind wandered. Over the past week I had become fixated on the prompt 'I know what you're thinking'. Whenever I tried to think about how to finish the sentence, I became tense, guarded.

The Comedian stepped away from the whiteboard and explained the importance of leaving room in our set for the audience to laugh. Jotting this down in my notebook helped me to focus, and concealed my face as the camera panned across the room.

What is my story? I wrote in my notebook.

'There are no wrong answers. I just want you all to start thinking "funny",' said a follow-up email. I was still stuck on the opening line: if I said I was half-deaf, would they heckle and ask, 'What does half-deaf even mean?' If I said I was deaf, would they heckle and say. 'You don't sound deaf! Where are your hearing aids?!'

These were questions that I had been asked by strangers. It had always been easier just to avoid mentioning my hearing loss. But now, compelled to complete the homework task, I would need to figure out how to describe myself—truthfully.

Could I even call myself deaf, given that I could hear? I felt as if I resided in a serrated in-between place: half-hearing and half-deaf. Instead of two halves making a whole, each half rubbed up against and eroded the other.

I began to feel jealous of people without any hearing at all. It seemed easier to be either one or the other, hearing or deaf. Did being half-deaf even count as being disabled? Now that I had to think openly about how I defined myself, I dreaded being laughed at or told to leave the workshop. Entering a place of truth meant exposing myself to a horrifying lack of certainty. It seemed safer to stay within the unshifting story that I was 'normal'.

'But you've done so well. Why are you giving up now?'

I stood on the corner of Victoria and Swanston streets, my phone pressed to my ear. The footpath was crowded with office workers and university students.

'Fifi, are you still there?' Mum asked.

'Yeah.'

'Well?'

'I just thought...that maybe...'

She waited for me to continue. Her words had rattled me. Why was I giving up on keeping my hearing loss a secret? Eventually she cleared her throat.

'Just drop out of the workshop. You've done so well to overcome your deafness. Don't you realise that by talking about it, you'll only make life harder for yourself?'

The theme for week three was 'writing from pain'. I ignored the preparatory email and focused solely on showing up. I had spent the last few days replaying my conversation with Mum, which had gone exactly as I anticipated: we had agreed that my speaking openly about being deaf would be self-pitying and troublesome.

While my family had always readily accommodated my deafness, our narrative had always been that I had beaten it by learning how to read. My grades were proof of this. All week I asked myself: why was I now so desperate to give up my secret?

Once in the workshop room, I grasped one hand in the other, pinching myself to stay calm. I avoided looking at the microphone—as if this would stop me from being called upon to practise jokes—and focused on the guide dogs: all long hair, soft paws and tails that swished along the wooded floor.

Had I asked myself the questions in the preparatory email, I might have begun to recognise how much pain there was sitting deep within my body:

1. Do I want to write from pain or about painful experiences?
2. If yes, am I sufficiently 'over it' to joke about it? Will it hurt me to make jokes about it?
3. Can I make it funny? It is not enough in this context that it be *important*—in a comedy show, there must be humour.

I realise now, some four years on, that the Comedian had asked each participant exactly how they told their stories. And how other people—friends, family, doctors, strangers—*wanted* to hear their stories. She understood what many of us didn't: that we were struggling to find a language for our bodies that wasn't diagnostic and solemn. She pointed out that most of us had been describing our bodies as a set of symptoms, limitations and malfunctions. As important as this was, it mostly added up to specific clinical information, the sort that medical teams tended to focus on. 'But is this *really* your whole story?' asked the Comedian.

The page of my notebook with the question—*what is my story?*—stayed blank. Although I had collected hundreds of personal histories, I floundered when asked to tell my own.

I'd learned to be careful about which words to use when talking with patients. My approach softened after I read a study that demonstrated how words can rub and burn just as much as they can soothe. Test subjects lying in an MRI machine were read metaphorical and literal descriptions—the operation went smoothly (the operation went successfully), his manners are coarse (his manners are rude), she is a bit edgy (she is a bit nervous)—each phrase recited in a neutral tone with minimum inflection. The results were conclusive: textured metaphors caused the brain to react as if it was being touched.

The words often associated with injuries—wear and tear, frozen, burning, stabbing, shooting, lacerating—are brutal. Although I've used them habitually, I have found them difficult to wring from my tongue. These words are embedded in our vernacular and shape our understanding and experience of pain.

I had always diligently analysed how I spoke with patients, but I had never stopped to analyse the words that are often used to describe hearing loss. In the workshop, I sat with my notebook and wrote down some of the frequently used phrases—stone deaf; deaf as a post; deaf as an adder—realising finally that it was little wonder I sometimes felt cold, dense and unhuman.

I was still having trouble writing my introduction. In the fourth workshop, the Comedian suggested I just keep it simple. As most of the participants had asked if I was from Canada or America, she suggested I create a series of jokes based on my accent. Later, she sent me a short draft script of how I might introduce myself:

> Hi, so I know some of you are probably thinking, 'She doesn't sound like she's from around here…' You're right, I'm from Sydney. You know Sydney, it's this really great place with a giant bridge and…sunshine.
>
> But yes, I know my accent sounds a bit unusual for some of you. No, I'm not Canadian. I'm not American (thank God—that he's not my president either). I'm deaf. I learned to lip-read from my Irish parents and ended up with a Canadian accent.
>
> Yes, you heard that right: I am a deaf Australian (*do Aussie accent*) with Irish parents (*do Irish accent*) and a Canadian accent. I'm like magic, eh? (*in Canadian accent*).

I appreciated the gesture. It was kind, helpful. I liked how cheeky and forthright it sounded. Even though Cassie wasn't home, I closed my bedroom door and tried practising the different accents, hoping to bring the script to life. But despite my forced enthusiasm, the words tasted like cardboard.

Each workshop the jokes got funnier—occasionally gloriously lewd—and our laughter was raucous, unrestrained, as people began to share stories filtered free of medical jargon.

My own writing was stilted with anxiety. The performance was scheduled for December. I continued to drag words out of myself in a slow, painful process of recollection. Yet nothing seemed useful, or even close to resembling how people generally talked and thought about deafness. My life had few overlaps with Helen Keller's, the only *real* deaf story I'd ever read.

Eventually I remembered my primary school's sign-language choir. They performed in Auslan, Australian Sign Language. I joined when I was nine years old, attracted by the startlingly white gloves. The choir wore all black, so their hands seemed illuminated. Thrilled by the theatrics, my whole body trembled with excitement.

Rehearsals were held in the school's disability unit, housed away from all the *normal* classrooms. I had never been in there before; it was the place for special-ed kids. During the first rehearsal, the teacher's hands took us through the song word by word. Then we practised with music. As we signed, the teacher lifted and lowered her right hand to demonstrate the beat of the music. My hands seemed slow. When the teacher turned to write on the board, I looked at the kids with bulky hearing aids. Without instruction, their hands slid softly into shapes, both smooth and exact. I realised I had just been plodding along to the music. With a leap of optimistic logic, my hopeless signing confirmed that I wasn't really deaf. I didn't belong in this space, and after one performance I left the choir.

Was there a joke in this? Something about my obsession with the gloves? My general enthusiasm? My awkwardness? My inability to use sign language? But each time I tried to make the memory into a light-hearted story, I faltered.

After the workshops finished in November, we were sent a questionnaire, which I can remember reading at work. I kept the email open for hours, returning to it every so often to add a few lines. It felt transgressive to think about my deafness while surrounded by my unknowing colleagues in the open-plan office. This was perhaps the most time I had spent trying to make sense of my feelings during the research project.

What was the most important thing you learned from doing the workshops?

I've learnt that the sky isn't going to fall in if I tell people I am deaf. That may sound like an exaggeration, but this entire process has been a huge reckoning with all the invisible scripts I've had in my head about disability and my identity. I've always felt guilty and ashamed if I have to ask people to repeat themselves. Now I feel more confident explaining that I am hard of hearing—you'd think I would already be able to do that, given that I have been deaf my whole life—but at least I'm finally starting to get the hang of it.

These workshops have been one of the hardest things I have done. I'm so happy that I've done them. Exhausted but thrilled. Thank you.

In many ways this was true. And in other ways it didn't even come close to the truth.

Due to unforeseen circumstances, the researchers delayed the final performance. They said it would happen sometime in early 2017. We were encouraged to keep developing our routines. Over the summer, I didn't write any jokes. I had received an email from the literary magazine: they wanted to publish my essay. I was surprised. The comedy workshops had distracted me from all thoughts about the essay.

I hadn't told my parents about the essay. I wondered if I should withdraw it and just follow their advice to stay discreet. After a few hours of indecision, I accepted the offer of publication. As I pressed send, I thought—fuck it, nobody is going to read it anyway.

That night I couldn't eat. I felt sick with regret.

When the editorial notes arrived, the editor gently inquired whether I had intended to capitalise Deaf, and provided a link from Deaf Australia, which explained 'the guidelines around terminology'. When capitalised, Deaf refers to individuals who use sign language and identify as culturally Deaf. When it appears in lower case, deaf is used for anyone with hearing loss who considers it in the same way medicine does—a deficit.

Two definitions? The word I was so fearful of having associated with my body became instantly more complex, more intimidating. I closed the email, burning with the humiliation of being caught off guard. It was obvious that I didn't even know the basics about deafness.

One afternoon, while marooned on the couch, I caught a Victorian Emergency Services press conference. The speaker was flanked by an Auslan interpreter—their presence was so novel that it later became a national news story. I watched the interpreter's dexterous, almost muscular fingers map out the advancing fire front. I was engulfed by jealously.

It had been seven months since the tendon transfer. Even after coaxing my fingers through a series of daily stretches, my left hand still felt foreign. I had to remind myself that it was attached to my body.

I was transfixed, staring at the interpreter, his hands flexing and extending. I felt another wave of powerful emotion, but this time it was more than jealousy—it was something closer to rage, which lingered unresolved. I had no understanding of why I was so confused and angry at myself.

Since receiving the editor's email, I kept thinking about deaf terminology. Upper case or lower case? Each was charged with meaning. As a thought experiment, I placed my body into each letter, trying it on for size. The capital D seemed so tender and so expansive, reaching up and out. The lower-case d sulked low, protecting its small round body behind a high straight wall. It was clear which one I was. That night, I emailed the editor to say that I wanted to keep the word in lower case.

After my essay was published in March, friends and acquaintances discovered that I was deaf. Many expressed their surprise. Some asked questions, which I felt ill-equipped to answer, now that I was aware deafness had its own terminology with political and cultural implications. I cut the conversations short, pretending I had somewhere to be. I was abrupt, possibly rude, and definitely terrified.

I was now relieved that the comedy show had been postponed. I imagined the researchers analysing the footage from the workshop, deeming me ignorant and culturally insensitive. I even considered dropping out of the program. But I knew this could adversely affect the study's data set and final result. And I didn't want to be part of that grim statistic: 'attrition'.

Besides, the workshops had inspired some of the participants to pursue comedy and they had been attending open-mic nights. I didn't want to jeopardise the program's funding. I resolved to try harder to feel empowered.

•

By the middle of autumn, there had been no updates from the research team. I comforted myself with the thought that the comedy show would probably never happen. My focus returned entirely to my hands. After months of rehabilitation, I still needed to be alert to what the hand therapist called my 'monkey grip' habit (picking objects up with only my index and middle fingers). My opposable grip was stiff and forced. Holding a mug of tea with my left hand was still dangerous.

Having seen Auslan interpreters at every weekly update throughout Victoria's 2016–17 fire season, my initial unease and jealously settled. When I saw another Auslan interpreter at a panel event at a literary festival, I was struck by the flexibility of her hands. Now curious, I found an evening beginner class starting in August. I pictured my hands moving purposefully, fluently. It seemed unlikely that I could return to manual therapy, the most 'hands-on' speciality in physiotherapy. But perhaps I could use my hands in different ways—maybe even become an Auslan interpreter?

In the days that followed, my thoughts returned again and again to the image of my hands as limber and strong. A feeling of lightness rose in me for the first time in twelve months. It was a while before I recognised it as hope.

At the beginning of winter, we were told that the show had been scheduled for July. Instead of writing jokes, I imagined all the ways the audience could heckle me: 'You're a fake! A fraud!'

Unless plotted out on an audiogram, my deafness was invisible. For the first time, I wished I wore hearing aids.

The need for physical proof wasn't limited to my deafness. In the months since I had begun to disclose my deafness, a sense of uncertainty had seeped through all my interactions. I felt the need to substantiate every story, even when people hadn't asked for it. Worried I might be considered unreliable, or untrustworthy, I discredited my own thoughts with phrases such as: I think; might; perhaps; maybe; possibly.

I wondered if this yearning for proof was stronger in me than it was in others. After my hand operations, I had been advised to rub vitamin E oil into my skin to help erase the scars. I didn't bother. Instead, I worried about what was happening beneath my skin, the ways in which my bones and tendons were stitching together. Now, almost a year on, I gained solace from the collection of scars on my left hand. They offered evidence that the fear I had felt about losing my thumb had been real and not just heightened emotion or hyperbole. It was deeply reassuring to look at my hand and think—yes, this really did happen to my body.

Will I always live with underlying uncertainty? Both within myself as well as with others' uncertainty about me? Even after some acquaintances had read my essay, they still said, 'No, that can't be true, you can't be deaf.'

In the week before the show, I barely slept. I lay awake in a sweat, in spite of the dense cold in our unheated flat.

It was too difficult not to tell my new flatmates that I was preparing for a comedy show. My mood had been so low, so frazzled, that I wasn't surprised when they asked what was wrong. I had moved into the North Melbourne flat a month earlier. Unlike my previous share house, this new living situation immediately felt homely; it reminded me of living in Stanmore.

'Comedy? Go on, tell us a joke!' said Alison.

'Do your whole set!' Megan shouted, as she threw herself onto the couch, gesturing towards the middle of the lounge room.

'I haven't written it yet.'

'God, no wonder you're so stressed.' Alison clucked her tongue sympathetically.

I wondered if I should explain the real reason I was on edge. Neither of them knew about my hearing loss.

Megan shuffled sideways, making room for Alison on the couch. I was the only one left standing, as they waited for me to start a practice run.

'Well, it's just that…it's so easy to procrastinate, right?' I forced myself to laugh. Not willing to give up my secret just yet, I fobbed off their requests to perform.

The microphone was spotlit. I stood in front of the crowd, who were sitting in tiered rows, their faces shadowed beyond the stage lights. My left hand was covered in handwriting, panicked prompts to help me remember a series of jokes I had cobbled together only two hours earlier. I hadn't timed my set, so I talked slowly, hoping to pad out the jokes with meaningful pauses. My voice felt like a handful of gravel; each word was delivered with a hard edge that allowed me to control my nervous tremor. It also allowed me to pretend I was someone else. Someone braver, tougher.

After a series of jokes about moving to Melbourne, I headed into deaf-related topics:

Lip-reading has been called a series of sensible guesses. Without my glasses, my hearing drops. I recently read a statistic that people with glasses are twelve per cent less attractive on dating apps. Sounds a bit rough, eh? [wiggle glasses up and down]

But it levels the playing field. Truly.

Whenever I wear my glasses, I also think most dates are twelve per cent less attractive because I can actually see what they are saying.

Later that night, the Comedian said that I looked completely at ease on stage. As if I had been performing for the past decade. She told her followers on social media that I could be the love child of Mel Buttle and Judith Lucy. I was shocked at how well I hid my terror, even while it filled me with nausea.

The day after the show, I felt weak and ill; it took me hours to get out of bed. I drank lurid drinks teeming with electrolytes. That night, I rang Kate and updated her about the show. Afterwards she said, 'There is nothing more exhausting than a vulnerability hangover.' Was that what honesty felt like? How would I cope revealing my deafness from day to day if the consequences were so obliterating?

Handshape

Keen to get the first pick of the seats in the classroom, I arrived early. The desks were arranged in a horseshoe shape to allow us to talk as a group, signing across the open space. I selected a seat that kept my back to the wall of windows. The room overlooked the Fitzroy Gardens, where office workers were powerwalking past the bare trees. Sitting there meant that my right ear was angled towards the front of the room, where the teacher would be standing.

I pulled off my beanie, then pushed up my sleeve so I could massage the scar running down the inside of my wrist. It still felt thick. Recently, during the final consultation with my orthopaedic surgeon, the tendon transfer was deemed a success. And yet I still hadn't regained the freedom of movement I once had. My thumb stuck out at an awkward angle, immobile unless cajoled. When I rolled my wrist clockwise, it clicked and jammed. It seemed impossible that I would ever return to working with my hands.

Introductory Auslan level one and level two was offered as either a weekend intensive, or as a weekly class over ten weeks. I had enrolled in the slow stream option, hoping that my left hand would be stronger after five months of signing.

I let my scars rest and flicked through the course manual, a dictionary of sorts. Beneath each word was a photograph of a person demonstrating the sign. I copied a few signs, my hands stowed shyly under the desk.

There were nine other students: a clutch of teenagers, wearing overalls and Doc Martins; a couple, whose heads lightly touched as they whispered; a few men and women in business attire, who carefully set out stationery on their desks. The atmosphere was buzzing with nervous anticipation and enthusiasm.

A woman with short curly hair stood in front of the whiteboard. She adjusted her scarf before rapping on her desk. Everyone turned to face her. Waving hello, she smiled, then moved her hands up and down quickly, flexing and turning her fingers. A man's voice said, 'Hello, welcome to Auslan level one.'

I scanned the room, searching for the source of the voice. Standing at the back of the room, a young man had his hands folded behind his back. Tall, his hair neatly combed, he wore a white button-up shirt. He stared intently at the teacher. As she signed, he spoke.

'I'm your teacher and this is my interpreter. You might have noticed that I am deaf.' She pointed to an ear and smiled. 'For the next ten weeks I'll teach you how to sign.'

As she pointed out the fire exits, the evacuation points and toilets, my confidence ballooned. I made links between her signs and the English equivalents: *door* looked like the same gesture you'd make to open or close one; *stairs* were two fingers representing legs, walking up and down. After so many years of watching people closely in order to lip-read, would I have a slight advantage when it came to learning sign language? I felt a small glow of pride. It was a new and strange feeling thinking of deafness as advantageous.

'This will be the only class with an interpreter. For the next nine weeks it'll be just us,' our teacher announced. A few people looked worried.

For the first hour I copied her hand movements earnestly. We started by saying *hello, how are you?* Around the room we went, waving and pressing our hands to our chests, bringing them forward, two thumbs up. We only knew how to response with *good* (a single thumbs-up), which we said again and again, smiling at our own eager attempts to communicate.

In the second hour, after a cup of tea, our teacher demonstrated a series of signs: *who, what, when, where,* and so on. As my hands boldly copied hers, the teacher approached my desk and signed *no.* She tensed her hands, fingers pressed together, then angled her arms up and down, as if hacking the air. Was this the sign for robot? But why was the teacher dancing? I glanced down and flicked through the manual. Seeing my confusion, she waved at me to stop. 'Soften your hands, try to be less jagged,' she said in a high, thin voice. So I was the robot.

Once back home, I felt lit up. It had felt good to use my hands and work my brain. I relayed the class to my housemates.

I signed a few phrases as Alison and Megan sat on the couch, the television blaring in the background.

'I learned the alphabet when I was in school!' Megan said. Her right index finger touched her left thumb. 'A.' She paused. 'Nah, that's all I can remember.'

'You've got so many random hobbies, Fiona. I've been thinking of taking up sewing again,' Alison said, as she picked up the TV remote and switched the channel—*The Bachelor* was starting. I

retreated to my bed with a cup of tea. I still hadn't told either of
them that I was deaf.

Sitting on my bed, I looked through the course manual again.
In the photographs each model wore a dark block-coloured top and
their hands hovered high and clear of their body. I lifted my own
hands, studied the models, and produced a few angular, self-conscious motions, as though my tone were agitated or stilted. Soon I
got lost in the spatial abstraction: which hand was the left one and
which the right? The manual was like a trick mirror, requiring a
sort of inversion.

'Auslan? But how on earth will you fit that in?'

'It's only once a week.'

'But you already do so much! Writing classes, book clubs, going
to the theatre, comedy shows, running, gym classes, concerts, art
exhibitions. And aren't you also volunteering with some charity?'

'It's fine, Mum. I like to be busy. Besides, it could be good.'

'Good? For what?'

'For my hand. All the movements will make it stronger. More
flexible.'

'But won't it be too much stress for the tendon? You really
should just rest your thumb, at least for a full year. You shouldn't
risk it. Imagine what would happened if it snapped again?'

'Mum, I'm a physio. I know what I'm doing.'

'You won't be a physio if it snaps!'

'I'll take it slowly.'

'You always say that, then you push yourself to exhaustion.
Maybe just try to relax, okay?'

Eventually we hung up, both frustrated.

•

The classroom was quiet without the interpreter. We'd been instructed to limit our speaking in English as much as possible. Although buoyed by a week of practice, I realised that, without the interpreter, I needed to concentrate hard to keep up. Our teacher tried to communicate everything in sign, but whenever she saw us struggling, she spoke, or wrote on the whiteboard. If we copied our teacher standing in front of the class we would sign everything backwards. To communicate via sign language requires the skill of 'mental rotation'—that is, the ability to reorientate yourself in space without moving. During the class, it felt as though I was reading from right to left, unable to reverse the signs in my head. I found myself twisting to face in the same direction as the teacher.

We began by practising fingerspelling. In Auslan there is a dominant hand, either left or right; in our class there was only one left-hander. The rest of us initiated most signs with our right hand. As we practised the alphabet, our teacher told us to think of our right hand as a piece of chalk and our left hand as a piece of slate— the functions never switched. The right hand moved more, as it illustrated signs on and around the left hand.

Enthusiastically, I signed the alphabet, then I spelled my name, occupation, followed by each item that sat on my desk. Once more, my teacher told me gently to 'be less forceful'. After she'd walked away, I looked at my hands helplessly.

Years of steady, controlled movements in physiotherapy meant it was difficult now to make my body move more casually. Whenever I assessed other people's bodies, I would also assess my own, ensuring that I avoided injuring myself—repetitive strain to wrists and thumbs, and stiff necks and backs are typical aliments among physiotherapists. Even now that I worked in an office job, my habit of assessing and managing my posture remained ingrained. Every hour or so, I moved through a series of stretches at my desk.

Truthfully, this cautious self-awareness started long before university. As a teenager, having received compliments about my ability to dance, I thought it would be fun to learn jazz dance. Throughout the lesson the instructor chided me: 'Stop *thinking* so much and just move!' I didn't return to the class, preferring instead to let loose at music gigs and festivals. It wasn't until I was in my early twenties that I tried another dance class—Ceroc class, a form of jive and swing dancing that one of my brothers had been doing for years. The instructor told me to 'move with the music' and 'stop fighting myself'. Music usually made me feel warm and limber, but now I was stiff-limbed and self-conscious, desperate to follow every instruction as perfectly as possible.

As the Auslan teacher introduced the next activity, it struck me that I was still 'fighting myself', tensing up by overthinking every movement.

Walking to the tram stop, on the way to my third Auslan class, a memory from three months earlier occupied me:

'I spent half the time looking at the Auslan interpreter. You know, trying to figure out what they were saying,' my friend confessed as we left the Malthouse Theatre. We folded our arms and turned our backs to the biting wind. I braced myself: was this the ideal moment to reveal my deafness?

In the lead-up to the comedy show I had hoped to be more open about my hearing loss. I'd found that the most nerve-racking conversations had been with friends. I worried that they would feel I had never trusted them enough to tell them, and that they would lose their trust in me.

I stayed quiet, waiting for her to continue. When I'd treated patients who were deaf or hard of hearing, their families often expressed irritation at their loved one's 'unwillingness to pay attention' or 'refusal to wear hearing aids'. I'd learnt to expect disparaging comments about hearing loss, even from kind people.

'It was beautiful, wasn't it?' my friend said.

I nodded in agreement.

Standing at the side of stage, the interpreter had effortlessly embodied the entire cast's lines. In the dark theatre, I'd sat in a complex silence, fixated on her signing, trying to suppress a kind of furious fatigue. As my friend talked about the performance, the set, the characters' motivations, the lighting, I focused on my breath: inhale and release. She didn't mention the Auslan interpreter again. Feeling as if I'd missed an opportunity to confide in her, I launched into pithy opinions about the plot, before saying goodnight.

It was only when I reached my tram stop, absorbed in my thoughts and slightly out of breath, my blouse lined with sweat, that I realised I'd been charging through the streets at a reckless pace.

Three months on, my hands aching from the effort of signing, I was coming closer to decoding the feelings I had while watching the interpreter at the theatre and at the press conferences.

For years, I had felt an apartness when surrounded by people; there was always a void I needed to cross in order to connect. In my twenties, I had become increasingly vexed by the effort I had to invest in every conversation—effort that I shrouded in secrecy, prioritising the comfort of others, never wanting to burden anyone by asking them to repeat or rearrange themselves so I could see their face.

Until that night at the theatre, the sight of Auslan interpreters had always provoked anger in me. I realise now, of course, that it was my way of masking a deeper, more persistent loneliness and self-hatred, a desperate need to belong, and a fear about my future.

Our teacher told us about SignBank, an online Auslan dictionary, where you can look up words and watch short video clips of people signing. I created a shortcut to the website on my desktop, and clicked on it during my work day in the office, typing in random words that I had failed to express in conversations with friends over the years. I hoped that signing these words would make me feel confident about revealing my deafness. From the Auslan dictionary:

Feeling (noun)

1. The vague idea that something is probably the case, but without being sure. English = impression.
2. Your emotions, attitudes or physical sensations that you experience. English = feelings.

I wrote a brief description to help me remember the sign: run the third finger of your right hand up the right side of your chest. Allow your face to be lit with the emotion you wish to convey— happiness, confusion, dismay.

In the next class, we were instructed to ask each other our ages. I considered lying. I was twenty-nine, only a few months away from turning thirty. But it was not my age that I wanted to hide, it was my hands. They failed to follow my commands.

Just like the written letter, the number nine is both round and straight. Our teacher talked us through the sign.

'Point your right hand towards the left, with your palm facing you. Create a pistol shape—right thumb hooked, and the rest of your fingers thrust straight out. Then tuck your little finger into your palm.'

My little finger flung itself outwards like a petulant child, again and again, insisting on being with the other fingers. I had to coax it back into position. Most of my classmates seemed to have the same trouble. Some held their little finger in place with their 'subordinate' hand. Others tolerated their little finger pointing to their chest instead of folding into the palm of their 'dominant' hand. Both positions were wrong, the equivalent of mispronouncing or misspelling a word, something we were only just beginning to appreciate. Our teacher reminded us every lesson that our hands must clearly produce each sign if we wanted other people to understand us. We must never be sloppy or careless. And so we mostly avoided the number nine whenever we could.

Other numbers are less physically demanding to sign. The number thirty is a simple gliding movement. First you form the number three, which is the same shape as the scout's honour. Then you sweep your hand forward.

My classmate signed—*you, how old?*

I opened and closed my right hand indecisively. Then I answered the question slowly and truthfully. My right hand cramped during the tram ride back to North Melbourne.

At home, while waiting for the kettle to boil, I kept practising signing numbers. To make it more meaningful, I tried to sign my phone number and realised that I didn't know the sign for *zero*. I tried to figure it out on the spot, shifting my hand into different positions. Later, when I looked it up, I learned that the sign was the right hand curved into a claw-like shape. An open circle. The handshape made sense when I saw it in context, although it looked nothing like my guesses. I felt ashamed that I still thought I could figure out a language by guesswork.

·

In my attempt to memorise the Auslan alphabet, I took to spelling all sorts of things: labels of food packaging, kitchen utensils, to-do lists. Most of all, I signed my own name over and over again, like a child caught in the delight of finding something that belongs just to them.

By week five of the course, we spent most of the lesson standing up, rotating partners and signing simple sentences like: *Where do you live? How many siblings do you have?* It became obvious that, even though I had been practising at home, I hadn't committed many signs to memory. I kept referring to the manual. The teacher paced around the room, rescuing us from tangles and reminding me in particular to loosen up. My body was stiff, slowed down by down the desire to get everything right

'How have you been?'

I swivelled around and watched my colleague Vanessa propel herself towards me in her office chair.

'Great. I went to a sign-language class last night.'

'Nice one! I learned some sign when I was working in Vanuatu.' She pointed to her chest. 'My—' She stopped to think, before flicking her hand up and down several times. 'My name is Vanessa, how are you?'

'In Auslan it looks like this—' I started to introduce myself.

'Wait, isn't sign language the same everywhere?'

'No, there are hundreds of sign languages.'

'Seems a bit silly. Wouldn't it be easier to just have one?'

I wasn't sure how to respond in a tactful way. The question had previously passed through my mind, but now, having learnt about sign language, it seemed ridiculous that there would be a universal language. Each country, even region, has its own language, many of the signs imbued with a particular sense of place and history. I had just learnt, for example, that *morning* is the same motion as tucking a folded newspaper under your arm. I could have told her that I had learnt from my textbook that sign languages are not based on spoken languages and were not invented by hearing people. Each language was developed by communities of deaf people scattered all over the world; signed languages therefore have the same complexity and expressive capacity as spoken languages.

But instead of giving Vanessa a lecture, I shrugged. 'I think it's kind of cool.'

The trams were delayed. I arrived to my sixth Auslan class flustered and hungry. Tying my hair back into a bun, I stifled a yawn. Work had been busy; all I wanted was to spend the night on the couch, but if I missed a class I'd fall behind. Our teacher demonstrated how to sign different types of food. My signing was stroppy. It was harder to hide my feelings in Auslan than in English.

Tired (adjective)

1. The feeling that you want to rest and sleep. English = tiredness, weariness, fatigue.
2. The feeling that you want to stop doing something because you have lost interest and enthusiasm. English = weariness.

Point your right fingers to your chest. Exhale and allow your hand to flop downwards like the motion of a body folding with fatigue.

The words in the manual were arranged thematically. Every evening I studied a new section. I had once read that studying before going to sleep accelerates the process of learning, that the unconscious brain has a better chance of consolidating knowledge when it is not disturbed. I had attempted to learn the ukulele this way, plucking strings at midnight, waking in the morning with the hope that a kind of synthesis had occurred. If I'd stuck with the plan for more than a fortnight, I might know if that theory worked.

Week by week, sitting up in bed, the manual propped on my lap, I began to accumulate discrete lists of words for greetings, animals, weather, sports and hobbies. I knew I should temper my enthusiasm. After all, my teacher continually encouraged us to revise words we'd been taught in class. But I couldn't help forging ahead, hoping that the head start would help me relax and loosen up.

Unfortunately, I wasn't sure if I was forming the signs correctly. Each photograph in the manual was a clean take: the models stood under bright lights that levelled out shadows, so there was no depth, texture or momentum. More complex signs, such as *washing machine*, *budget* and *relationship*, shifted in orientation and hand-shape, requiring two frames to explain the sequence of actions. But even then, the pictorial instructions had been abridged to fit the manual's page layout. It would take more than a dozen frames to render these signs comprehensively.

During an interview about the craft of documentary film-making, Ken Burns said: 'All filmmaking is a still photograph [taken] twenty-four times a second. The limitations of our human form create what is called "persistence of vision". So we're actually looking at twenty-four still photographs at 1/48th of a second each, followed by 1/48th of a second of black, twenty-four times.'

Our brains fill in the gaps, creating a sense of movement—persistence of vision—from moments of stillness. As I sat at home, staring at my Auslan manual, I knew there was potential in these inert photographs—I imagined the models' hands moving in all directions. With so little information, it was like staring at a set of schematics; I needed to see the creases and edges of each sign, rather than just the finished product.

Occasionally, the photographs were accompanied by small arrows indicating the direction of movement (twist/turn/lift/move forwards/backwards/outwards). During class, whenever our teacher demonstrated new signs, I scribbled notes and arrows in my manual, mapping out the movements.

Once at home and reviewing my notes, it felt as if I had a rough set of coordinates but no compass. As I studied each sign, I asked myself: did the hands move in a smooth line? Or did they unfold and change shape via a swooping motion? Alone and confused, I sat in my bed, my hands stilled with uncertainty.

Still (noun)

1. The act of being in a place, not moving away, and not moving at all. Idiomatic English = freezing.

Make a fist with both hands. Hook your index fingers forward then pull downwards, as if stopping and dragging someone in towards you.

Learning is never linear. New information collides with old, sometimes in ways that is helpful; at other times only a slow process of unlearning allows space for new ways of thinking. Some signs folded into my body without effort, via association, linking with other muscle movements, other secured memories.

Person: form a pincer grip, as if gripping a button, now pull downwards—from head to toe, a long, straight spinal cord.

People: the downward flick of the index finger off the tip of the nose—flick, flick, people are nosey.

In some instances, I wished I could disassociate from things that I had learned. Perhaps then I would discover new ways of looking. When I began studying physiotherapy, my tutors told us that our sight would sharpen. But first we needed to learn how to look *properly* at people. In a musculoskeletal tutorial we were instructed to study a classmate and describe what we saw. I remembered squinting, as if this would allow my eyes to squeeze more information from my classmate's physique. I made a list: rounded shoulders, flattish feet.

'That's a start,' the tutor said. Then he talked through his own observations: poked chin, overactive scalenes and trapezius muscles, right shoulder hitched, left scapula winging, stiff cervicothoracic junction and so on. His list outlined which muscles and joints were contributing to the student's rounded shoulders and flattish feet.

'It's easy for your eyes to land on something unusual. It's instinctive. But you must learn to be more careful, more deliberate with how you look at someone. Start with the head and work your way down.'

With time, this act of 'scanning' felt less contrived. After years of practice, my eyes now automatically swept over the length of a body. I had learned to *see* stiffness and muscle spasm. My eyes had sharpened, supported by my hands, which always followed the contours of muscles and bone to confirm what I had seen. Analysing posture and movement patterns had become an essential part of my diagnostic process.

In the Auslan classes, I had to learn how to soften my eyes. As I watched my teacher signing, I found myself focusing so closely on the mechanics of her movements that I couldn't see the words she was creating. It was as if I could only see in piecemeal—muscle, sinew and bone. I wanted to go back to seeing people like I had before becoming a physiotherapist, with delight and abstraction. Bodies as holding stories instead of a list of potential symptoms.

As I had no sense of how my body was moving when I signed, I decided to record myself. Propping my phone up against a stack of books in my room, I introduced myself to the camera and ran through a dull but brief monologue: age (twenty-nine), occupation (office worker) and current living situation (two flatmates in North Melbourne). Then I stared at the phone for a few moments, before attempting to describe the layout of the flat. It was a modest space (three bedrooms, kitchen, laundry, one bathroom, balcony), but I lacked the range of signs to describe even my small corner of the city. I began to fingerspell the words I didn't know the signs for, relieved by my inventive and clever solution.

Afterwards, when I watched the recording, I could see my arms seesawing from sign to sign, radiating tension. On a second viewing, I noticed that my face was flat and unblinking. It matched the blank expressions of the models in the manual.

In sign language, your face is of equal importance to your hands. Each movement—from fingertips to the edges of nostrils and lips—converges to create meaning. In the mirror attached to the back of the toilet door, I tried to parse my features grammatically. Unable to ignore the hitch in my right shoulder, I became distracted, thinking about stretching out my pectoral muscles and then mobilising my spine with a cat stretch. Focus. Eyes shut, I attempted to quieten my inner monologue. Eyes open again, I studied my facial expression. Small, tight mouth. Tension in my temples. Shallow cheeks, the insides sucked in, pinched between my teeth. I cajoled myself to loosen up. I imagined myself reflecting a little more confidence, a little more feeling than before.

By the end of the level one course, the hollow at the base of my thumb, where the muscles had atrophied, begun to fill in again. A shapeliness had returned. My thumb could roll in its socket. My hands were starting to feel like a pair again. Perhaps I'd be able to return to physiotherapy in the next year or so.

After a short break, level two commenced. About half of my class-mates had continued. We learned the signs for animals: a closed fist rubbing the tip of your nose (*pig*); keeping a closed fist, touch the tip of your nose, then bring your fist forwards and down, a long trunk (*elephant*); the pointer finger and thumb opening and closing like a beak (*chicken*); a swishing motion of an open hand (*fish*). Laughter rang around the room as we tried to guess more joyful signs for other animals.

Over the weekend I recorded another video of myself. Watching it, I realised that my features continued to be as flat and stiff as a sheet of paper. I stood in front of the bathroom mirror contorting my mouth, cheeks and brows, trying to stay animated as I moved my hands. The more I focused on my face, the more fragmentary my signing became.

I recalled watching a YouTube video of an acting masterclass run by Helen Mirren. She told her students: 'Never act in front of the mirror. You are doing the exact opposite of what acting is all about. Acting is all about what is happening within you.' She was right: talking to myself in front of the mirror was not helping me loosen up and express all the feelings that were churning inside me.

Talk (noun)

1. The act of saying things to someone (in speech or sign). English = talk.
2. The things that someone says to someone (in speech or sign). English = comments, remarks.

Hold up the second and third fingers of your right hand (the peace sign). Point your left index finger. Now, keeping these handshapes, cross your right wrist over your left wrist, then tap your wrists together twice.

Level two was challenging: we began to practise our conversational skills. The teacher kept swapping our partners so we could look at different sets of hands. Although we attempted to replicate the same movements, we each had slight variations in speed and style—our own particular accent. Unlike my English-speaking persona, my Auslan persona was emerging as slower, shyer. I missed being flexible in conversations, choosing how and when to reveal or conceal my feelings.

During the conversational exercises, we often paused to fossick through the manual, or we simply slid into English. The room filled with chatter until our teacher reprimanded us with a rap on a table.

'No speaking,' she said. 'Otherwise you'll never *really* learn sign language.'

There were other habits I needed to break. I'd always used writing to consolidate new information. During university, I diligently copied out lecture notes and vast passages from textbooks. The process was slow but felt anchoring.

Every so often, during conversation practice, I turned to my manual, stopping the flow of a role-play in order to jot down notes. My teacher immediately signed *no writing*. Her palms faced one another, separated by a few centimetres. She simultaneously rotated each hand in a clockwise direction three times: *signing*.

Socrates predicted that writing would stop people from using their memory properly. I don't think that's necessarily true, because my mind feels porous without a pen in hand.

One night during level two, I dreamt in Auslan. When I woke, I pressed what I could into my conscious memory. The conversations were halting, but, instead of feeling embarrassed by my lack of fluency, I felt sociable and at ease. There were hundreds of us, standing in a field speaking until we were too tired to stand, so we lay in the grass, our hands still moving, moving, moving.

Sign language is intimate; it necessitates looking at others closely, continually. While this came readily to me, I was not used to being watched with the same unbroken gaze. Although I wanted it, receiving the full brunt of someone's attention felt terribly exposing.

During spoken conversations people generally shift their focus, establishing eye contact then breaking it, again and again. Direct eye contact typically occurs for zero to forty-five per cent of a conversation, depending on the circumstances—increasing in instances of intimacy or intimidation, decreasing in instances of fear or disinterest—and yet participants perceive eye contact to have occurred for seventy per cent of a conversation. The wide discrepancy between reality and individual perception doesn't surprise me. I am used to people multitasking mid-conversation: rifling through their bag; unpacking groceries; scrolling on their phone. I have learned to mimic this, to conceal the fact that I am looking closely. But now, to be watched so intently during each interaction using Auslan felt as though I had lost some small power I had.

And yet each Auslan class felt like a revelation. Sign language exalted everything I craved in a conversation: people automatically positioned themselves in view of one another, and it was essential that everyone paid attention. There was always an emphasis placed on clarity and inclusion. Even when the bells of the nearby cathedral tolled—long, echoing clangs—they didn't disrupt a single conversation.

With each class the content became more difficult, the slog of learning a language more evident. The role-plays we performed became less scripted. Our teacher wrote open-ended questions on the board: *How was your day? What did you do at work?* Now I began to dread going to class.

My hands were clammy during the role-play exercises. I experienced frequent flights of panic, when my mind went blank. I felt as though I spent most of the class standing still, unsure. Typically, in my life outside class, if I was confused, I would prattle about the weather or make self-deprecating jokes. In the classroom, with such a limited vocabulary, I had no way of distracting others from my miscomprehension. When I did respond to questions, the phrases that came most readily were: *sorry, I forget*; *can you repeat that*; and *what?*

After class, I wrote myself reminders in my diary, hoping my urgent handwriting would hector me to 'PRACTISE AUSLAN'. Instead, as the weeks passed, I mostly ignored my reminders.

Apparently, people with perfectionist tendencies tend to procrastinate. But I began to suspect that my shyness in class centred on pride: I didn't want to make mistakes in front of anyone. Before each class I told myself—don't take yourself so seriously. I forced myself to move, to speak with my hands.

Practise (verb)

1. To obtain knowledge of the facts or gain the skill to do something as a result of studying and especially training (i.e. through practical experience). English = learn.
2. To keep on doing something regularly in order to be able to do it better. English = practise.

Raise hands to mid-chest. Point index fingers forwards as you rub them side by side.

When level two finished, the teacher explained that, to continue learning Auslan, we could either enrol in a TAFE course or attend community meet-ups. I felt compelled to continue. At some point during the past five months, my motivation had shifted from wanting to rehabilitate my hand to wanting to become fluent. But it wasn't as if I needed the language; I didn't even know anyone who signed or identified as Deaf.

There was no way I could afford to give up full-time work to study at TAFE. But the idea of conversing with a group of strangers at a meet-up prompted a series of unsettling questions. What if they asked me about my deafness? Would they accuse me of cultural appropriation? I kept thinking about the audiologist who, in the early 1990s, told Mum and me that Auslan was something that only *real* deaf people needed.

Since the Auslan course had finished, I'd googled questions like: What is Deaf culture? How many people speak Auslan? What is the easiest way to become fluent in sign? Are half-deaf people allowed to learn sign language? Are half-deaf people allowed to call themselves Deaf? How deaf do you have to be before you are allowed to learn sign? Most of the search engine results directed me towards medical websites or hearing-technology companies. I rephrased each question, again and again, hoping for clear-cut answers.

Confusion (noun)

1. The act of making a mistake about a person or thing and thinking that they are another person or thing. English = confusion. Idiomatic English = mix-up.
2. A situation where it is not clear what is happening. English = confusion.

Right index finger taps the right temple, while the left-hand hovers above the abdomen with the index finger pointing forward. Then both hands fan open and cross at the wrists.

Over the summer, I did what shy people tend to do when learning a language: I turned to reading and writing as a way of hedging against the hot awkward flushes that accompanied every mistake I made when talking to others.

I tried my hand at translation, taking poems—short, simple passages—and transferring them from the page to my hands. I didn't anticipate how difficult and exasperating this process would be. Translating revealed how many gaps there were in my knowledge. I knew only a negligible number of signs, and didn't know how to construct a grammatically correct sentence, as the order of signs is completely different from English.

As the days slouched by, hot and bright, I turned away from poems about birds and towards textbooks about grammar.

Orientation

The beginning of my relationship with reading and writing was so fraught with anxiety that the memories continued to resonate: the grinding repetition; the dullness of constantly circling back to the basics; the flush of embarrassment whenever I made a mistake. I had hoped that, as an adult, I would find learning a language a simpler, faster, more refined process. That I would be better equipped to problem-solve and be on more of an even keel with my emotions. With planning and diligence, surely I could overcome any difficulties.

I became obsessed with considering the body as a system of grammar, in the same way I had begun studying anatomy: I had a voracious need to learn more. And while the canvas was the same—all flesh and bone—it felt like discovering the body anew. The human body is capable of producing an endless variety of postures and movements, but, like spoken language, sign language has its own constraints and conventions to create meaning.

As Melbourne sweated through a heatwave, the textbook

Australian Sign Language: An introduction to sign language linguistics, by Trevor Johnston and Adam Schembri, became my compulsive reading. I learned that, until 1960, there had been no formal research into sign language. This seemed shockingly recent. No wonder my parents knew so little about sign language: they had grown up in an era when signing was considered to be primitive gestures and pantomime.

I began to tell more people that I was learning sign language. Mostly out of excitement—I wanted to talk about how intricate Auslan was—but also to excuse my new behaviour. I had regained a sense of urgency about moving my hands. It was the same feeling I had when I first started to study physiotherapy and discovered that my hands had the potential to be precise and powerful. Back then I practised on my family, now I couldn't help moving my hands all day long. At my desk or waiting for my lunch to heat up in the microwave, my hands floated up, fingers hooking and pointing. When my colleagues asked, I told them I was practising the Auslan alphabet. It turned out that one colleague had worked for years as a teaching assistant in a small deaf school. Another had done an Auslan short course years ago and had been meaning to return to classes. One of my managers simply laughed. I was too shy, too uncertain, to ask why she considered it funny.

The only time I told people at work that I was deaf was when someone asked why I was bothering to learn sign language. I assumed these conversations would be easier than the ones I'd attempted to have with friends. I anticipated that my colleagues' responses would be contained by our workplace's professional standards. Unfortunately, my disclosure was seldom treated in an easy way. Most of my colleagues were surprised, which was understandable, as I hadn't mentioned my hearing loss when I applied for the job eighteen months earlier. Their sense of surprise shifted to confusion. Some pressed me for further explanations and physical details. Others explained how they had a grandparent/uncle/niece who was *actually* deaf. Whenever the latter happened, I pinched myself hard to stop feeling angry. Their words hung in the air without a rebuke from me.

I have yet to figure out which of their questions were reasonable and which ones were just plain rude.

Linguist William Stokoe first identified that American Sign Language (ASL) has an internal structure and logic. His framework consists of Handshape, Orientation, Location and Movement (HOLM). Johnston and Schembri use HOLM to explain the structure of Auslan: while there are just sixty-two handshapes listed in the Auslan dictionary *Signs of Australia*, there are hundreds of distinct signs, each with its own orientation, location and movement pattern.

Orientation, in a broad sense, means whether the sign is directed towards the signer or away from them. A simple example would be the difference between signing *me* or *you*. If you're referring to a separate person—*them*—you would point away from the shared space in the conversation. Johnston and Schembri also detail the bodily locations most frequently used in Auslan. The face alone has an exhaustive list of landmarks used in signs, from the tip of the nose to earlobe.

It was a relief to read that movement was considered the most complex aspect of the grammar framework. I felt validated in my lack of confidence and rhythm. Sometimes referred to as 'the path movement', the hand may journey 'away from the body, towards it, upwards, downwards, to and fro, in an arc, a circle, or spiral'.

There is nothing random or haphazard about sign language; the slightest error, the misshaping or misplacement of hands, can result in significant miscommunication. Some signs look remarkably similar: 'minimal pairs' are signs that have only one key difference. *Beautiful* and *well*, for instance, only differ in location (the chin vs the right side of the chest). The signs *brother* and *paper* merely have a different movement pattern (the knuckles rub vs the knuckles bang together). Whereas *work* and *talk* differ only in handshape (flat open hand vs pointer finger).

The minimal pairing that caused me continuing confusion was *how-old*, *how-much* and *how-many*. For each of these questions, the handshape and orientation are the same—a flat hand, facing towards the signer, the fingers wiggling rhythmically—but the location shifts from the tip of the nose, the chin or the side of the body. During class, I had asked people either *how-much* or *how-many*, when I wanted to know their age. Upon discovering my error, the same sensation I'd had at school returned: tensing to withhold tears and frustration, tensing to make myself smaller and unseen.

I knew that a summer spent reading about sign language alone in my bedroom wouldn't make me a more competent conversationalist. At some point I would need to talk to people. The more I read about sign language, the more I realised that, to become fluent, I had to learn how to become comfortable in my body. My fear of ridicule raced through me, clarifying my fears into a single question: would the Deaf community accept me?

'A study group in a pub?' Alison asked as she chopped up a capsicum.

'Yeah! I found out about it on Facebook. A bunch of people meet up and chat in Auslan.'

'Chat? As in talk? Is that the right thing to call it?' She raised an eyebrow as she pulled the skin off an onion.

'Yeah, of course it is.' I didn't tell her that I had only recently googled the same question.

'So, what will you talk about?'

'Dunno? Maybe about work? The weather? Sport?'

On the tram I tried to picture signs related to work. I could only think of *meeting, happy, angry, slow*, words that didn't come close to describing the details of my life. As the tram swung onto Swanston Street, I was struck by the enormity of the task—how would I talk to strangers in a different language?

Alison's question came back to me as I strode up Collins Street. What would we talk about? I'd spent the past week randomly thumbing through my Auslan manuals and now regretted spending so much time reviewing the signs for cat, kangaroo, horse and dog.

It took me a few moments to push through the crush inside the pub. I didn't know what anyone attending the meet-up looked like, but I figured it would be easy to see a group of people signing. Of course, everyone was using their hands as they spoke, mostly in a volley of yells, competing to be heard over the loudspeakers' barrage of guitar riffs and the bank of blaring televisions on the wall.

I felt a hand on my shoulder.

'Excuse me!' a woman shouted into my face, as she pushed me out of her way. Perhaps I hadn't heard her when she was standing behind me, or perhaps she always barged through crowded spaces.

'Sorry,' I said, as I stepped back to let several people past. Once I had tucked myself into a corner, I wiped my hands on my pants, before rehearsing—*Hello, my name*. My hands low and my movements tight, I spelled my name with my fingers. Then I glanced around the pub, before raising my hands higher. I hoped it looked as if I was casually adjusting my shirt. After a moment, I flicked up my thumbs—*how are you?*

What should I say next? I thought back to class. I pictured the room, the arrangement of desks, the whiteboard covered in conversational gambits, but none of the signs. Why couldn't I remember any of them? The noise was setting my teeth on edge. At any other time, I would have left by now, but I decided to go to the bathroom for a moment of respite. If it was quiet, I could practise for a few minutes. I followed the arrow to the toilets. As I walked around the corner, I spotted a small group of people with a reserved sign on their table. One woman had her hands raised, but I couldn't work out what she was signing. As I got closer, I heard them talking. Wrong table.

Maybe it wasn't meant to be? I decided to do one more lap of the pub before going home. On my way back to the front of the bar I spotted a group of people lounging around a table, blocking the thoroughfare. None of them had bothered to push themselves into the table. People are so rude, I thought. As I turned to leave, I noticed their hands rising and falling, fingers forming hooks and fists, palms slapping and cupping. Of course, they had to sit further back from the table to have enough room to sign.

Before I could escape, I waved—*hello*. I dashed off my introduction. As the group waved back, I plonked myself down in the closest chair, weakened from the effort of not fleeing.

Eight people swiftly signed their names. I caught one or two letters per person. Their fingerspelling was so fast it ran together like continuous cursive script. I pointed to myself, then made a circular motion with my palms facing each other, before sliding my right index finger down the length of my left arm. I shrugged, hoping I'd said—*I signing slow.*

A woman with blonde curly hair sitting across from me smiled, maintaining eye contact as she signed. Then she pointed at me and shrugged. I realised she had asked me a question. I mimicked her shrug, hoping it conveyed my meaning—*I'm confused.*

Then a woman with long black hair waved for my attention. She spelled *S-L-O-W* before running her finger *up* her forearm.

I'd already stuffed up. I nodded—*yes,* then raised my right hand to my chin and brought it forward—*thanks.*

The woman with the mop of curls waved at me again, signing the correct spelling of *Y-E-S* then knocking her right hand twice—*yes.*

After fumbling through a few signs—*yes, hello, sorry*—I sank into my chair, tucking my hands under my thighs. Then I stood up. I gestured *drink?*, using the same charade mime—tipping my hand to my mouth, as if holding a glass—I'd used for years, but I had no idea if it was correct signing. I added it to the list of signs I needed to look up.

At the bar, buying time, I stood in the longest queue, even allowing others to push in. Relieved to have a drink in my hand, I headed back to the table, where I clasped my cider, keeping my hands occupied in order to avoid any possibility of conversation.

As the evening progressed, new arrivals commandeered spare chairs from neighbouring tables. Conversations ran like criss-crossing currents. I shifted my gaze back and forth, trying to figure who was talking to who. I had imagined the meet-up would be a small, studious affair. This was more akin to a party. An older woman told a joke about a Deaf person and an interpreter going skydiving. Even I got the punchline—the interpreter misunderstood when they needed to pull their safely chord—as she signed their plummet to earth with vigour.

More stories were recounted with joyous abandonment. I thought I grasped that one member of the group had got married recently. I recognised a few signs, but failed to follow any single conversation. The syntax of Auslan is completely different from English: for example, small linking words don't exist in Auslan (or most sign languages). I told myself that I really had to focus more on studying the grammatical structures. For now, I settled into my seat, happy to play the role of spectator. Just as I considered getting another drink, the woman with curly hair waved at me from across the table—*your name? I forget.*

My right index finger ticked off the vowels in my name. I felt pleased that I didn't have to look too closely at my hands as I signed.

Your name?

She spelled with smooth precision, responding to my confusion by repeating herself. I mouthed each letter as I recognised it: M-E-L-A-N-I-E. It took me a moment to press the letters together into a familiar shape.

'Melanie!' I cried out in delight. Then I clapped my hand over my mouth.

She rapped the air in front of her twice—*yes!*

I signed back—*Yes, yes! Hello, hello!*

Melanie asked me a few questions. I responded as best I could. Even concentrating keenly, I was floundering. After she had rephrased one question in several ways, I grasped that she was asking me where I lived. I tried to compensate for my limited vocabulary by gesturing behind me, hoping to communicate that I lived in the north of the city.

What? Where?

I apologised again and tried spelling out North Melbourne, but got lost among the letters. She must have registered the desperation on my face: she waved at me. Checking that I comprehended each letter, she began to spell. I tried to keep up, but couldn't hold many letters in my head. Seeing my confusion, she traced the words on the palm of her hand, before showing me the signs for *Melbourne* and *north*. Then she asked me to put them together. North Melbourne. She signed—*quick, quick! Fingerspelling slow.*

Yes, yes. Slow. I exaggerated the slowness of my index finger trailing up the length of my left arm.

She smiled, then followed the same process to show me other words: *south, east, west, work, Sydney, physiotherapist.* The space between us felt inconsequential. It was the first time I hadn't had to do battle with the acoustics of a crowded room. Usually, by now, I would have left the pub with a pounding headache. Tonight, the music and the bank of televisions didn't interfere. Tonight, I didn't need to sidle up to someone, twisting my body to catch each word they said. Tonight, I didn't know who was deaf and who was hearing—it didn't matter when everyone was communicating in the same language.

After chatting with Melanie, my fear of making mistakes faded just enough for me to attempt conversations with other people around the table. Finally, I stood up and waved *goodbye*. Then mimed a yawn.

Melanie signed—*no*. She pointed her hands to her chest before letting them flop down, like a body folding with fatigue—*tired*.

I copied her.

She gave me a thumbs-up—*good*.

I smiled as I walked down Collins Street. When I reached the tram stop, I realised that I hadn't spoken English for over three hours. I felt expansive, energised.

•

'It is all too easy to take language, one's own language, for granted—one may need to encounter another language, or rather another *mode* of language, in order to be astonished, to be pushed into wonder again,' said Oliver Sacks in *Seeing Voices: A journey into the world of the deaf*, which he wrote after spending time with deaf communities during the late 1980s.

It would be entirely inaccurate to suggest that I experienced an unfurling state of wonder as I sat in the pub. Instead, I swung from feelings of inadequacy and confusion. But as I lay in bed that night, I realised how useful sign language was—not just in general, but for me.

Since finishing the course, I had daydreamed about becoming an interpreter, especially after reading that there was a shortage of interpreters. It would mean quitting my job and returning to full-time study, but I thought it would be an exciting career change, one that would allow me to be useful to *real* deaf people.

I could actually have benefited from the help of an interpreter. I imagined not having to strain to hear people talking in large or crowded venues, not having to guess or simply miss information. Not to mention how much energy I would have if I didn't need to recover each day after feeling harrowed by sound.

Why weren't people with hearing loss encouraged to learn sign language? Should I have been learning Auslan all along? Could all those years of exhaustion and uncertainty have been circumnavigated? I had been relieved at not being placed in a class with the deaf children, but perhaps that was exactly where I belonged?

Mother tongue

A few weeks after that first meet-up, I spoke bracingly to myself on the number 59 tram: tonight, you will talk. At the pub, drink in hand, I approached the table. Everyone said hello; some replied when I asked *how are you?* Throughout the evening I repeated a handful of well-practised signs, wedging them into conversations, all the while willing myself to be more carefree in my delivery.

After attending a couple more meet-ups, I began to tick 'maybe' whenever I received Facebook invitations to the upcoming events. I told myself that I was being polite, that perhaps my availability would change. The organisers thoughtfully varied the meet-up times, acknowledging that everyone had different work and care responsibilities, and selected meet-up locations across the range of Melbourne suburbs, ensuring that every venue was close to train and tram lines.

Yet whenever an event rolled around, I stayed home. Eventually, I stopped receiving notifications. The Facebook algorithm was more decisive, more honest than I was. It knew I would ignore the invitations.

•

Why my sudden disinterest in learning Auslan? Was it laziness? Shyness? Boredom? Perfectionism? I implemented 'productivity hacks' to reverse my inertia: schedules; SMART goals (Specific, Measurable, Achievable, Repeatable, Timely); accountability apps. Nothing stuck.

Auslan briefly allowed me to consider my body as something other than abject. It allowed me to recognise that the vast silent spaces within me had been waiting to be filled with language. This idea, although so warm, so full of new self-esteem, didn't last long.

With each ignored Facebook notification, I distanced myself from Auslan. It seemed easier to stay absent from the Deaf community. That way I could continue to dissociate from the deafness in my body.

Even though I wasn't practising sign language, I found myself buying books about Deaf history. Google hadn't provided me with any clear answers. I still didn't know the correct way to describe my body: was I medically or culturally deaf? Or both?

I began to wonder if my craving for accurate terminology was a result of working within the medical model, where everything in the body carries a label. Conditions with unknown origins— including my deafness—are called idiopathic, from the ancient Greek *idios* (one's own) and *pathos* (suffering).

By reading Deaf history I hoped to discover whether my questions about identity were just my own, or whether they were typical among people with hearing loss. I told no one about my research. Mostly because I worried about what I would find. Was my uncertainty over the past twenty-odd years symptomatic of self-obsession and self-suffering, rather than any real form of stigma?

While everything else in the body has been mapped by name and function, the brain remains a mystery. We cannot see it in full flight, twitching with thinking-ness. Unlike the defined architecture of bone, or the ropy strength of muscles, its appearance is merely lumpy. The outer layer, the neocortex, where our intellect prowls, looks like nothing more than a poorly folded fitted sheet. Scientists suggest that it's this neocortex that separates us from animals: we think therefore we are.

In 1637, when René Descartes coined the phrase *I think therefore I am*, he set the body free of God. Until then, it was widely believed that our thoughts were whispers from the Divine and not our own creation. It's sickening to know that this philosophical argument has been used to supress countless deaf lives.

Cogito ergo sum. In three words Descartes' Cartesian Dualism made a swift and bloodless incision, dissecting the body in two, mind over matter. A bodily hierarchy was established: the tongue—anatomically described as 'the blade' as it twists, rolls and flicks air through the lips—became the brain's weapon. 'Language', *lingua* (tongue), or more specifically speech, was considered an indicator of intelligence and sanity. Whatever words arose from flesh (gestures, facial expressions, handshapes) were considered wild, animalistic. For hundreds of years, deaf people who used their bodies to speak were deemed subhuman.

I needed to find the point in history when this brutal thinking dissolved and was replaced by the heft of reason. Over the next few months I asked several local university and public libraries whether they had a Deaf history archive or access to one via a database. One library had a handful of books, most of them printed in the late nineteen-eighties and early nineties. Their pages were yellowed and gritty with dust. As I read through them, my desire to find a hinge point in Deaf history began to feel untenable.

In *Seeing Voices*, Oliver Sacks writes that 'the congenitally deaf, or "deaf and dumb", were considered "dumb" (stupid) for thousands of years and were regarded by an unenlightened law as "incompetent"—to inherit property, to marry, to receive education, to have adequately challenging work—and were denied fundamental human rights'.

The word 'incompetent' struck me with the full force of recognition. All those years of enduring my internal monologue exhorting me to the point of exhaustion to prove my competency: work harder, prove you deserve to be here, prove your worth, prove you're capable. The unease I carried—of being deaf in a hearing world—felt ancient and inescapable.

In 1880, the majority of delegates at the Second International Congress on Education of the Deaf in Milan agreed that all deaf students must be taught using the Pure Oral method. Signing was considered so primitive that it was thought to stunt brain growth. Henceforth known as the Milan Agreement, this decision essentially banned the use of sign language. Worldwide, teachers and students would communicate using speech. The delegates believed they were helping the deaf *become* people.

I read accounts of deaf people being punished for using their hands to speak in classrooms, of having their wrists tied and their bodies beaten. It was hard to stomach these accounts, but I forced myself not to look away—and I learned that history was not confined to the distant past.

Following changes in educational philosophies in the 1960s,

the emphasis shifted to 'normalising' the education of deaf children as much as possible, and residential schools began to close down. By the 1980s, deaf children were increasingly integrated into classes with hearing children or attended classes in small units attached to regular schools...The use of signed language came to be seen only as a last resort for those who failed to acquire spoken English.

I read this passage from *Australian Sign Language* a dozen times. With self-recognition came relief. But the feeling quickly curdled into anger. I hadn't invented my life-long craving to be normal—I had been dutifully following public policy.

Until 1997, ASL was classified by the Modern Language Association as an 'invented' language, a category that included Klingon. Auslan was only recognised as a community language in 1984. But even now, Auslan lacks legal status—it is not an official language of Australia. Without this designation, Auslan hasn't received the same recognition or resources as English.

Some one hundred and thirty years since the Milan Agreement, the preference for oral education continues to dominate education systems globally. The justification has not changed: sign language is inferior to spoken languages. Educators and medical professionals still argue that hearing is essential for brain growth and development.

I touched the left side of my skull, wondering if there was nothing but darkness in the shadowlands. It seemed doubtful, given everything I'd been taught about neural plasticity. The geography of the brain is not static; it reflects how we accumulate as well as use knowledge from our lives, our bodies, our experiences.

In deaf people, the areas of the brain responsible for processing sound have not shrivelled up, nor has the overall size of the brain shrunk; instead, neuronal connections creep in from visual and tactile centres. Deaf people feel and see sound: the entire body becomes a receptor, a giant ear if you like, readied to collect information from the bounce, vibration and texture of sound waves.

Every brain needs to be soaked in language in order to thrive. Yet despite robust evidence proving that signed languages have the same positive impacts on brain development as spoken languages, they are still widely considered an inferior mode of communication and treated as such.

The first National Auslan Curriculum was only implemented in 2017; up until then, Auslan was taught according to frameworks for languages such as French and Japanese.

According to the World Federation for the Deaf, only one to two per cent of deaf people access education through sign language. In many developed countries, where there is a push towards technology (hearing aids and implants), educational success is often measured by the level of speech acquisition. For many years, although illiterate, I was classified—from the medical and educational perspectives—as a 'successful' or 'high-achieving' deaf person, simply because I could speak. In less developed countries, however, deaf children often have no access to any language, either spoken or signed—approximately eighty per cent of the seventy million deaf people in the world receive no education at all.

Oliver Sacks describes the state of language deprivation: 'And to be defective in language, for a human being, is one of the most desperate of calamities, for it is only through language that we enter fully into our human estate and culture, communicate freely with our fellows, acquire and share information.'

Language deprivation can occur to children with any degree of hearing loss—mild, moderate or profound. Even children equipped with hearing technology (including cochlear implants) can still experience difficulties in language acquisition if they are not adequately exposed to the three main ways of learning: formal, informal and incidental. While formal learning might involve structured lessons, equally important is the informal learning acquired during conversations in school hallways, on the bus, around the dinner table, on the sports field. During these moments we learn about self-expression and social cues. Incidental learning, when the brain synthesises information about how the world works, is a lifelong process and can occur in any setting.

Without exposure to all facets of language acquisition, there is a greater likelihood that children with hearing loss will experience delays in cognitive development, which will also adversely affect their ability to navigate social interactions.

As I read about how language deprivation can result in a cascade of unexpected outcomes—disruptions in mood, thinking and behaviour—a memory surfaced.

I had always had a strong sense of pride about being a quick, easy talker, able to follow any thread of thought and interject with jokes or observations. And yet, for years, my siblings were irritated with me during conversations. I would retaliate with ragged exasperation: just *listen* to me!

Finally, when I was fifteen, one of my brothers snapped: 'Fiona, what are you talking about? I can't read your mind.'

'I know you can't!'

He and my siblings pointed out that I had a habit of starting sentences, then abruptly stopping and waiting for the other person to respond.

I began to catch myself doing it. While I didn't imagine anyone could read my mind, I would become frustrated that they couldn't 'keep up' with what I was saying. Eventually, I realised that I was speaking in a rhythm that reflected my experiences of conversation. I was used to hearing in fragments and assumed that everyone had to exert a similar degree of effort and guesswork to fill in the blanks when conversing.

I tried to become more diligent in expressing myself in full sentences. It took time for me to soften my manner from a pedantic, hectoring mode—hammering out every single thought—to a looser, convivial one. Even now, whenever I am excited, I speak in rapid non sequiturs. Or if I am tired, I revert to the habit of swallowing the tail end of sentences.

Do I think I experienced language deprivation? Yes. Even with enormous privilege and a supportive family, there were gaps and spaces in my understanding of words and communication.

The first five years of a child's life are essential for language acquisition and cognitive development. Part of the withholding of sign language from children has been the mistaken belief that lip-reading is an accurate means of communicating.

Since 2006, the WHO has recommended that all children with any degree of hearing loss must have early exposure to sign language. By shifting away from predicting learning abilities against a decibel range, the WHO acknowledges that language acquisition is complex. A mild degree of hearing loss doesn't predict mild learning difficulties, nor does profound hearing loss equate to profound learning difficulties. A bilingual approach to education removes the risk of any child with hearing loss being labelled as failure for not 'keeping up' or not 'trying hard enough'. While some may argue it is costly or unnecessary, a bilingual approach should not be seen as a luxury; on the contrary, it provides the same opportunities and human rights that hearing children have had for hundreds of years—easy access to information.

In 2019, the WHO released another bulletin in an attempt to dispel stubborn misconceptions about educating deaf children: 'There is frequently ideological resistance to the use, and lack of understanding, of signed languages among medical and education professionals who promote spoken language-only approaches, and the use of cochlear implants.' As a consequence, '[t]he global community's failure to support the acquisition of signed languages by deaf and hard-of-hearing children has adverse, lifelong effects on education, socioemotional, and cognitive development'.

Language has a clear lineage, rolling from one generation to the next. What happens when this line is untethered by 'ideological resistance'? When deaf children become adults, we have to find language and community for ourselves. This is not a straightforward experience, especially when we have been taught to blend in.

Nearly ninety-six per cent of deaf children are born into hearing families; often it is the first time the parents have met a deaf person. It is a time of heightened emotion, when parents should be given clear, unbiased information.

My parents followed the prevailing advice: I didn't learn sign language. But they also didn't place their faith in the 'whole language' approach to reading that was widely endorsed during the 1980s and 1990s. Instead, they did whatever they could to make sounds visible.

Mum qualified as a teacher of reading using phonics. When I was seven years old, she enrolled in one of the Spalding Method's first courses offered in Australia. Aimed at university graduates, the content was academic and rigorous. Having trained as an enrolled nurse while working in a hospital, Mum hadn't been in a classroom since finishing high school.

Neither of my parents had ever spoken fondly of school. Their classrooms in Ireland heaved with students and were governed by teachers who preferred corporal punishment to correcting spelling mistakes. Dad left early to get a trade in bricklaying. Mum grew up in a Gaeltacht, a region officially recognised as Irish-speaking. She only ever spoke obliquely and infrequently about school, so it wasn't until I was in my mid-twenties that I asked her about it.

I'd just learned that the valley where she lived had been designated an International Dark Sky Reserve in recognition of its lack of light pollution. A gushing press release read: 'This is the ONLY Gold Tiered Reserve in the whole of the Northern Hemisphere. It is the only Reserve that has a playground, a church, a little pub, a hostel, a graveyard, several beaches…and…a chocolate factory.'

I know that graveyard, set high on the sundrenched side of a mountain, angled so the dead can overlook the sea. That same light turns red and blue and holy as it falls through the church's stained-glass windows. The cottage where Mum grew up now houses a dozen hens and peat for the fire. On the dark side of the mountain is the village bog, where orange nylon string hooked between spikes demarcates each family's plot. The press release doesn't mention the sporting field, which has been blessed with blood and holy water. Or how the heft of waves, whomping against the sea wall, can be felt in the middle of your chest. I wanted to know more about the sky and the sea, so I asked Mum about the valley's geography.

'I've forgotten it all.'

'All of it?'

'I was taught the names of the mountains and rivers and battles in Irish. Those memories are now long gone.'

She told me that a government inspector would visit once a year to assess whether she and her brothers were fluent. If they passed, they would be given a grant, ten pounds each family.

'We were so poor, we had no choice but to pass,' she explained.

Finishing primary school meant catching a bus to a state high school beyond the valley. It also meant a swift transition from Irish to English.

'Suddenly we were having to learn how to do everything in English—maths, science, history, everything. God, it was awful. We were as lost as anything.'

Only then did I realise that her lingua, her tongue, had been completely soaked in Irish. Mum had passed on to me all her careful and diligent habits of feeling out the shapes of English words.

My transition from illiterate to literate was not fuelled by my own desire and motivation. Without those hundreds of hours spent sitting with her, I would never have felt comfortable reading and writing. Even now, I still need to break up words into small units of sound and clap and click my hands, feeling out each letter.

I read a Facebook post in an Auslan group about a teacher with a hard-of-hearing student. Although the boy communicated in English, the teacher discovered he had begun to learn Auslan at home. During a routine spelling test she had read a list of words aloud. The boy scored four out of ten. Having watched the boy squirm and hook his arm around his worksheet, and knowing the crushing weight of shame that can descend after a student receives a low score, the teacher encouraged the boy to play for ten minutes—to jump and stretch, allowing the frozen block of fear to melt and his small body to shake off any discomfort. Then she sat him down and repeated the test, only this time she signed each word in Auslan.

He sat up straight and watched her hands, before taking his pencil to the page with clear strokes. When he passed the sheet back, every word was correct. Although obviously chuffed by the boy's result, the teacher didn't gloat at her cleverness. Instead, she just wished she'd realised sooner how hearing-centric her teaching methods had been. I felt a sense of hope that attitudes towards deafness were changing, mine included. Although born into a body that was both hearing and deaf, since becoming literate, I took immense pride in believing that I had *beaten* deafness. This belief in my own victory lived unchallenged within me, even as my research into Deaf history continued into the autumn of 2018.

More of my writing was being accepted for publication. Here was external validation—proof!—that I could string words together. But when I began to receive the mark-ups from editors, most of my sentences were full of tiny holes. I consistently omitted single-syllable words—a, of, an, the, it, and, so, on. Mortified by these simple errors, my confidence unravelled. To salt my wounds, I analysed old emails, drafts, text messages—everything was pinpricked with small omissions.

A few weeks later, when I learned that omitting single-syllable words is common in deaf children, I immediately thought of the boy in the Facebook post—I would never want him to feel ashamed of making these 'mistakes'. So, instead of continuing to admonish myself, I'm now somewhat delighted how my deafness continuously asserts itself—it cannot be pummelled into submission.

I kept returning to *Seeing Voices*. For me, the most important aspect of the book is Sacks' honest account of his changing perspective: 'Whilst I never forgot the "medical" status of the deaf, I had now to see them in a new, "ethnic" light, as a people, with a distinct language, sensibility, and culture of their own.'

Changes in perspective like this are not inconsequential. They often come incrementally, rather than as a thunderclap. Having documented my questions, my confusion, my misunderstandings, even when I am not proud of them—I remind myself that, until very recently, I hadn't realised Auslan was a language with its own syntax and grammar. There is so much about sign language, and even deafness, that I still need to learn. It is ironic that, although Descartes' philosophy continues to influence how deaf children are educated, he in fact thought highly of signing, considering it to be the representation of true human language. When I read this, I realised with a start just how much hatred I had been funnelling towards him. Mean, spiteful thoughts. I had taken comfort in blaming Descartes as the source of Deaf oppression. In reality, Deaf history has been less linear and much more complex, with modern policies and healthcare advice continuing to be insidiously informed by ancient myth and rhetoric.

At times, out of habit, my spite was directed towards myself. At other times, my anger spun outwards, taking aim at healthcare and education practices that cordon off Auslan. Eventually, however, I conceded that there were any number of people complicit in maintaining the status quo of hearing culture. Including myself. I had to acknowledge all the years I had quashed my shadow: stay quiet, don't say a word.

As I tried to become more open about my hearing loss, I was met with endless questions or incredulous remarks. In response, I strove to provide an explanation that was both clear and plain: I described myself as half-deaf. In return, people would ask: which one is your good ear? Am I on your bad side? And I would point to my right ear and say—this one, this is my good ear.

These situations always left me unsettled. It was as though, in order for my body to be valid, for it to be accepted, it needed to be both examined and explained. For an individual ('that which cannot be divided'), words like 'half-deaf' are violent in so many ways; the self, once whole, is obliterated. Split in two again and again: the good and the bad.

I realised that the division—half-deaf and half-hearing—was purely a distinction driven by philosophy, policy and societal opinion. Living in a body with two opposing sides meant never feeling whole and well. It meant living in disagreement with and at a distance from myself.

But, having read widely, I now finally understood that my feelings were not singular or self-generated.

I stopped thinking in halves.

My body has always been deaf.

A couple of months after my binge-reading of Deaf history, while heading to work on the tram, my eye was caught by two women in grey-haired bobs and heavy winter coats. Sitting across from one another, they were signing, chatting with ease in the crowded space. I stared at them from the back of the tram and felt a low, tugging ebb of shame. I still hadn't gone back to an Auslan meet-up.

Pain points

A letter addressed to me arrived in the mail. A question was printed on the outside of the envelope: Which Sound Would You Miss Most? The bold font felt like a punch. Inside, the letter read: 'Whether it's the sounds of waves gently lapping on the shore, the delicate rat-tat-tat of rain against a window pane or the sounds of children playing, we'd like to help you rediscover the beauty of sound with the new smart hearing device from Phonak.'

Those joyous moments—the rolling sea, cooling rain, chatty laughter—had been stripped of dimension, texture and taste. Their aural quality had become their single defining feature. I felt ropeable; I was spoiling for a fight with the hearing technology company. Given that this was impossible, I laced up my joggers and ran through the streets of North Melbourne towards Royal Park.

I hadn't felt this riled up since the hearing-aid trial. As I reached the native-grass circle, I paused to catch my breath. It had been three years since the trial. Until reading the letter, I'd thought that with time I would feel less emotional about hearing technology.

I looped around the park's grasslands, trying to extinguish

my flare of anger before Alison and Megan got home. After living with some volatile housemates—the sort who would storm around, lashing out at others when upset about their work or relation-ships—I never wanted to infect the mood of a share house with my own foul temper or sadness.

A few weeks later, I flew to Sydney for the October long weekend to celebrate my dad's birthday. While unpacking my bag, I had a sudden urge to find my hearing glasses. I wanted to put them on and compare the experience with the memories I had of wearing them as a child. I also wondered if the glasses would now suit my older, fuller face.

That evening, after eating birthday cake and fobbing off dozens of questions about whether I planned on moving back to Sydney, I returned to my childhood room. I pulled everything out of the wardrobe that I had shared with my sister until I was twenty-one—clothes that no longer fitted; boxes of university notes; my accordion and my sister's fiddle; bottles of cheap perfume that I instantly regretted spraying; swimming costumes ruined by summers of salt. Unable to find the large black case, I gave up and went to bed.

After I flew back to Melbourne, Mum continued looking. A few days later, she rang to tell me that she had no luck.

'You wouldn't have thrown them out. I wonder where they could be?' She paused. 'God, you hated them.'

I was surprised. My memories of that time must have mellowed. More worryingly, it occurred to me that I had been hoping the glasses would be a back-up plan. It would take years for me to acquire any degree of fluency in Auslan, and I was becoming increasingly worried that my body's perfect symmetry of sound and silence would, at some point, deteriorate.

•

Hearing loss has been solved, or so I always read in advertisements selling hearing devices—The cure was so *simple, elegant, and cost-effective!* The cure was essential to live a *full life!* The cure came *in a range of discreet flesh tones!* The cure allowed you to live *just as nature intended!* The copy was so smug, my teeth ached as I read it. And yet, craving certainty, I stayed subscribed to mailing lists for hearing-technology companies and audiology clinics. This was how I learnt that I was selfish and vain.

Most people absorb stories about deafness long before they acquire hearing loss. There hasn't been a government-led national awareness campaign focusing on hearing health since at least the early 1990s. Most of the health promotion has been left to organisations with commercial interests.

Narratives of deafness are dressed up like journalism, with emphatic headlines, supposedly reputable quotes, typeset columns— all the cues of unbiased authority. These carefully parcelled sales pitches, 'native advertising', appear in print publications, website banner ads, posters on public transport, places where people with hearing loss will find them. They don't appear on the television or radio. In most of the advertisements, the potential consequences of hearing loss are listed: dementia, social withdrawal, anger, lack of focus, depression, muscular tension, headaches, constipation, mental and physical exhaustion, dizziness, sexual problems, increased risk of falls, suspiciousness, sleeping problems, low self-worth, increased blood pressure, loss of income, dependence, early mortality, and on and on it goes. The inference is that hearing loss means a life of misery. Unless, of course, you invest in solutions, which are promised to be 'high-tech' and 'miraculous'.

By figuring out the emotional drivers, the specific details that carry emotional valence, hearing-aid marketers can address the fears of potential customers and motivate them to purchase their solution.

In medicine, pain is measured on a ten-point scale that allows healthcare professionals to track something that is invisible, to give shape to sensations, no matter how diffuse. Some marketing companies are adopting this scale to evaluate consumer pain points. A score of two is 'very mild' and ten is 'excruciating and unbearable'. It is easy money to aim for the high end of the pain scale. As one marketing blog explains: 'you effectively have to help your prospects realise they have a problem *and* convince them that your product or service will help solve it.'

Advertisements for hearing aids push hard into pain points. Vanity is often cited by audiologists and researchers as the key reason why people don't wear hearing aids. And this is why, regardless of complaints, Victorian Hearing considered their 2015 advertising campaign as something akin to public health promotion. The ad featured a photograph of a young woman with bold cat-licked eyeliner and a prawn slung over her ear. The accompanying text in capitals was blatant: 'HEARING AIDS can be UGLY.' They offered customers an 'invisible' product.

The response to the advertisement was swift and scathing. People from the Australian Deaf community argued that it perpetuated the stigma of hearing aids. In a Facebook post explaining their actions, the group of audiologists stated: 'Victorian Hearing sincerely apologises if our current invisible hearing solution add [sic] was hurtful, it was certainly not our intention. However, we are fighting a war with a large population of Australians (1 in 5) who refuse to seek hearing amplification because they are embarrassed.'

War. The word has an undeniable heft. It centres deaf people as the enemy.

Hearing-aid advertisements don't just focus on the pain points of deaf people, they also target the concerns and frustrations of family members. There is a body of research about how deafness affects family dynamics. Multiple studies have found that 'hearing impairments [are] a source of annoyance within a family, requiring efforts for mutual adjustment'.

It doesn't take much for annoyance to escalate to resentment. As one study notes: 'The male's inadequate behaviour, for example not answering the telephone or door bell, or too high volume when listening to the radio or the television, often invoked irritation and aggressiveness from the other family members.'

Many studies have been based on interviewing the entire family as a group. It wasn't until researchers Lillemor Hallberg and Marie-Louise Barrenäs interviewed only the spouses of men who had noise-induced hearing loss that a more complicated picture of family dynamics started to emerge. None of the men wore hearing aids; their partners reacted to this in a range of ways. Hallberg and Barrenäs classified the strategies used by the spouses into four categories: co-acting, minimising, mediating and distancing.

The first category of spouses become 'co-actors in their husbands' game of rejecting or denying hearing difficulties'. In striving to preserve their pre-existing dynamic, the co-acting spouse views her husband as 'perfectly normal', denying that anything significant has changed: 'You just have to adjust to each other. As a spouse you have to be patient.'

The second category, 'the minimising spouse', adopts a conflict-avoidance strategy. One such interviewee said: 'During the last years I have become more and more silent…there is no use in discussing the problem with him…it doesn't work, it always ends up in a conflict and you want to avoid that…especially me.'

The next category is the 'mediating spouse'. In order to maintain the social status of their partnership, she uses strategies that include controlling, navigating and advising. One interview participant explained her new role in her marriage:

All the time I have to work extremely hard and I have to be very attentive…I have to listen to what others say and at the same time make sure my husband is able to hear and if he is involved in the discussion or not. He is the same charming person as ever with all his positive attributes. However, when we are at a party with my friends, and if my husband is unable to hear what they say…that's really very embarrassing. My friends are not aware of his hearing loss…and I am frightened that they might view him as a stupid person if they knew. Otherwise the hearing loss has no impact on our close relationship. I have the feeling of being his mother and therefore I must take care of him.

The final category includes those spouses who fully acknowledge that hearing loss has impacted their relationship. These women spoke candidly about the loss of intimacy and the distance that had emerged: 'It is hard to get in touch with one another…we are on different levels, so to speak…sometimes it is almost impossible to reach each other. You may say that there is a mutual irritability between us.'

What struck me most was that each woman interviewed resented the lack of initiative her husband showed to buying hearing aids. After all, they fully expected that hearing aids would work. I wanted to scream: it's not that simple!

'The challenge of getting used to hearing aids is widely recognised in both research and clinical practice,' write Piers Dawes, Michael Maslin and Kevin J. Munro in their 2014 research paper, 'Getting Used to Hearing Aids'. Yet individual stories have seldom been documented. The trio worked to fill this gap by interviewing adults who had less than twenty-four months' experience with hearing aids.

One participant described walking out of the hospital wearing hearing aids 'and hearing very, very strange noises that I realised were my feet. And my car, which I thought was as good as a Rolls Royce, was making one hell of a racket. Switches going click, indicators going—terrible. It was a bombardment of noise.'

My breath caught in my chest: I remembered my own feet thundering off the pavement as I staggered home from the audiologist's office. Other participants described the sudden influx of noise as 'oppressive', 'weird' and 'overwhelming'.

It's widely assumed that hearing technology effortlessly recreates the hearing experience. While hearing aids suit some people, for others they are unbearable. Unlike the discriminating nature of hearing ears, hearing aids are unable to selectively amplify sounds, so noises swell into a cacophony.

One study consisting of 15,000 adults who had been prescribed hearing aids, found that sixty per cent of the participants aged over seventy-five years did not use their hearing aids regularly. This figure increased to 74.5 per cent when the age range was expanded to include participants aged between forty-nine and eighty years old. This number jumped even higher when participants were followed up five years later, with 93.1 per cent of people not using their hearing aids on a regular basis.

When I learned this, my body went loose with relief. It was a comfort to know about these complicated experiences. I'd spent the past three years feeling like an anomaly. My sense of ill-ease had pushed me into a period of deep, distressing isolation, and created a stark sense of a 'before' and an 'after'. I still don't feel I have completely emerged from this state.

I had assumed that people who wore hearing aids simply had restored to them what they'd had before. I, on the other hand, had been flung into the experience, thrashing through the shock of sound, the shape of sound, the overwhelming fear of sound. I realise now that, no matter how or when someone acquires hearing loss, the experience of trialling hearing technology can be confronting, exhausting and disappointing.

Back in 2003, Louise Hickson and Linda Worrall wrote in the *International Journal of Audiology*: 'Hearing aids should not be seen as the treatment panacea for older people with hearing impairment.' They argued that the 'current focus on hearing aids as the predominant form of intervention is inappropriate and/or inadequate for the majority of older people with hearing impairment.'

Hickson and Worrall recommended auditory rehabilitation, the process of teaching people with hearing loss strategies to minimise communication difficulties. While this can be delivered one-on-one, a group setting can provide participants with a sense of belonging. Community-building can reduce stigma and alleviate the loss of social identity associated with hearing loss. Generally, in a group setting, classes run for two hours. The first hour involves instruction about communication skills, followed by an hour of group conversation, and it is this second hour that researchers have found has the biggest impact. Participants collectively and creatively engage in finding solutions to hearing-related difficulties; they might, for example, role-play how to disclose hearing loss or how to ask someone to repeat themselves. The group setting also allows for individuals to adopt a 'normal' identity. There is power and comfort in numbers. The rehabilitation model normalises hearing loss, thus reducing the stigma perpetuated in hearing-aid advertisements.

The four categories of spousal response outlined by Hallberg and Barrenäs—to deny, dismiss, dominate or distance oneself from deafness—validate my casual observations of family dynamics in healthcare settings. I had become nervous asking patients about their hearing; often the question would provoke emotive responses of distress, disgust or disdain from family members. In my own self-centred way, I kept wondering—if this is what they say about one of their own, what on earth would they say about me?

But now my perspective has shifted. Given that it's so clear deafness doesn't just affect people with hearing loss, why do all the responses focus only on them? Some audiologists have been speaking out about this single-sided approach for years.

Group auditory rehabilitation works equally well with partners of people with hearing loss. As well as equipping the pair with robust and flexible communication skills, it has been shown to alleviate feelings of guilt and blame, and even unexpected miscommunication. In one instance, a woman expressed concerns about her relationship after her partner was fitted with hearing aids. She felt hurt that her husband no longer looked at her when she spoke. He was surprised. He explained that he always listened, but now that he had hearing aids, he didn't need to see her face in order to hear.

•

I looked for more stories about hearing aids written by deaf people. Reading Donna McDonald, I began to understand my own experiences with hearing technology.

> My hearing aids are personal. Intimate even. I hate people asking me questions about them and only answer such questions out of the long-ingrained sense of duty drummed into me as a child by my mother. 'Answer their questions. They are not being unkind. They are just interested, that's all.' But questions about my hearing aids by hearing people feel intrusive. I am fiercely protective of them and rarely entrust them into the care of others, not even my closest friends. I certainly don't like other people touching my hearing aids. It is a shocking breach of intimacy, as if they are exploring my ears, using the tips of their fingers to trace the outline of the vacuum where sound should echo. I don't even like people looking at them for any longer than passing curiosity warrants.

My hearing glasses and the CROS device made me feel shy, strained, protective. While neither device was stylish, in both instances I was less worried about my appearance and far more concerned that they made my deafness visible. I too feel a 'sense of duty' to answer strangers' questions, even though I would rather just blend in.

My issue isn't with hearing technology. It is with the language used to sell devices.

'Hearing aid advertisements have a powerful effect on purchasing decisions. The ads must be accurate and truthful,

171

especially given that many of the people buying hearing aids may be vulnerable due to their age,' said Australian Competition and Consumer Commissioner Sarah Court, after putting 'hearing clinics on notice' in 2017 following concerns that some clinics were creating 'a false sense of urgency' in consumers.

Despite their well-documented limitations, hearing aids continue to be marketed as a definitive fix. The words *cure* and *solution* are often used by doctors and hearing-technology companies. Robust, reassuring words that don't even sound like promises; rather, they assume the status of fact.

Cochlear implants, for example, are simply described as a 'miracle', a narrative that overlooks the amount of rehabilitation and ongoing effort required for the implant to work. In quiet environments, some people with implants have ninety per cent sentence recognition. This drops to fifty-five to sixty per cent accuracy when words are spoken without context. The immense cognitive effort required of individuals to decode sounds doesn't appear in a typical sales pitch. It's no wonder the general public believes that deafness can be 'fixed'.

And even though McDonald clearly expresses a great fondness for her hearing aids, she goes on say: 'When I choose to turn my hearing aids off and switch off the world of sounds, I experience delicious relief. It is as if a sigh is breathing into my ears…everything in me relaxes.'

For some people, hearing aids may be a useful even key part of their life, but that doesn't mean they are easy. There is no technology that can 'unmake' a deaf person. Hearing aids and cochlear implants work best when the environment is set up for success via a range of means that improve the comfort and efficacy of hearing technology—noise-dampening building materials, such as soft furnishings and carpet; efforts to reduce background noise; good lighting to minimise glare and shadows; closed captioning on televisions and cinemas, as well as for announcements at airports and train stations.

Unfortunately, however, instead of promoting flexible communication skills, resources and awareness, the current message to the community is that people with hearing loss *just* need to buy hearing aids.

The global hearing-aid market is expected to be worth US$13.54 billion by 2026. The simplification of the deaf experience to a sales pitch is widespread. In Australia, this has been encouraged by government policy, which permits audiologists to make commissions from selling hearing aids.

In 2017, the Australian Competition and Consumer Commission (ACCC) released a report expressing concerns about the industry: 'commissions can be as much as fifteen per cent' and 'more expensive hearing aids generally attract higher commissions'. Some clinicians surveyed by the ACCC reported that 'devices may be recommended on the basis of commissions rather than consumers' needs'. This sales-focused culture has been deliberately fostered by the industry, with indicators used to assess the performance of clinicians, including 'the number of hearing aids sold, their average price, and the number of high-end and "top-up" devices sold'.

Most worrying are the reports of vulnerable individuals being targeted: 'In another instance, an older consumer with dementia attended a free seminar run by a hearing-clinic operator at a local community organisation. The consumer, who receives a government pension, subsequently purchased a pair of $13,000 hearing aids through a two-year finance plan from the hearing-clinic operator.

The hearing aids are unsuitable for the consumer's needs and abilities, and are not used. Despite the efforts of the consumer's family member, the finance plan could not be cancelled.'

The singular, unflinching focus on sales has shifted the relationship between the clinician and the client. In Victorian Hearing's defence against the complaints about their prawn advertisement campaign, they claimed to 'have been able to help many who would have never stepped foot inside an audiology clinic as they were not aware of all options available'.

Their advertisement was, in my opinion, more galling than educative. It failed to highlight other options, including hearing-assistance technology (such as visual alerts on phones, doorbells and smoke alarms), auditory rehabilitation and hearing-assistance service dogs, all of which have been shown to improve the quality of life and social participation of people with hearing loss.

Sociologist Graham Scambler coined the phrase 'weaponising stigma'. Scambler suggests that 'heaping blame on shame' is a by-product of neoliberalism, which 'allows for the state's abandonment of people with disabilities'. This is a distinct shift in how stigma was perceived by Erving Goffman, whose book *Stigma* became the cornerstone of research into the marginalisation of people. Goffman defined stigma as being situational, as a reaction to social interactions. His theory, however, negates systematic and perpetrated stigma, whereas Scambler analyses the impact of power structures, both interpersonal and societal. He considers stigma a means of asserting the norm as the dominant dynamic.

Scambler categorises the differing power relationships that can exist between blame and shame: 'the normals' (who are neither shamed nor blamed), 'the losers' (who aren't shamed but get blamed for being different), 'the rejects' (who experience shame for being different but are not blamed for their difference), 'the abjects' (who experience both shame and blame). He explains that the 'abjects are both beyond the pale and deserving of their lot and misery'.

Before hearing aids were considered to be a definite cure, deaf people were considered 'rejects'—hapless but blameless individuals. In my opinion, we have now become 'abjects'. There is an assumption that anyone with hearing loss has been wilfully reckless with their hearing health. If they are older, the assumption is that they didn't follow work health and safety rules; if they are younger they are labelled as part of the 'earbud generation'. This pattern of 'blame and shame' is not only present in media and advertising; when working in hospitals and aged care, I have seen it play out in couples and families—if individuals do not 'fix' their hearing, they are considered selfish, vain even, and are shamed for choosing not to integrate themselves into society.

Maybe it should come back to pain points? To frank emotion and feeling? After all, hearing loss must not be treated as a technological problem. Communication is a human concern and should be considered humanely.

When I work as a physiotherapist, I ask people about the specifics of their pain. How would you describe it? Does it keep you awake? Has it ever woken you up? When did it start? Is it getting better, staying the same or getting worse? And finally: on a scale of one to ten how would you rate your pain?

In talking to others, asking them about their bodies, I have learnt that most people carry secrets of some kind, or have an internal knot of resistance or shame that they may have spent years trying to untangle. There is nothing simple or even textbook about any of the patients I interact with. Their pain points are a messy constellation of previous ailments, worries, responsibilities. Pain is rarely predictable; it is always entirely personal. And once healed, we continue to carry the memories of pain in our bodies. These memories are not inconsequential; they inform how our bodies react to future ailments.

I think back to the early days of my clinical practice, when I first began to use the pain scale. The goal was always to get patients as close to 'normal' function as possible. I cringe when I think about how I would chastise patients—*don't cheat!*—if they performed their exercises in a manner I thought was sloppy. I remember the impatience I felt whenever they 'took too long' to recount their stories, the relief when an assessment shifted from subjective to objective.

After a few years in the workforce, I began to hear phrases such as patient empowerment and patient-centred care. By then, I had fumbled my way to an understanding that stories mattered. Without empowering the patient, including them in the decision-making of their treatment plans, the process of care would be a passive and ultimately ineffective exchange.

Even given my deep, unrelenting pain, I didn't think my own story was significant. For years, I believed that I had 'beaten' my deafness; I had bent to the logic that asking for help would be akin to 'giving up' on myself, conceding defeat. I now understand that I have always been at war with my deafness.

Learning about the experiences of other deaf people has challenged my deep-seated beliefs. I now see that society has been sold a simple story about hearing loss when it's really not simple at all. Deafness is only measured in decibels. Yet these numbers don't take into consideration the complexity that is involved in conversations.

Until there is an understanding that communication is a collective responsibility, it seems unlikely, even impossible, that the stigma-tisation of deaf people will dissipate. Conversations don't fall on deaf ears; on the contrary, deaf people pay attention, engage, think deeply.

On topics of conversation

I was amazed to learn that, as an artilleryman, Eric Fallon, an American military audiologist, had *wanted* a hearing loss, because everyone in his unit had a hearing loss. 'If you didn't have a hearing loss, that meant you hadn't done anything.'

Fallon now develops hearing-protection equipment for military use. Tinnitus and hearing loss are the two most prevalent injuries sustained by US service members. Currently a billion dollars a year is spent on treating these injuries. Communication challenges and hearing loss are very much part of the culture of combat, says Fallon:

> We're just so accustomed to finding work-arounds with hearing loss that you'll sometimes find soldiers that have a significant degree of hearing loss, but their unit leadership may be so dependent on that person that they also want that person to remain where they are.

A marine who sustained hearing loss during active service describes how prevalent hearing loss is: 'When we get together, everyone knows who has the worse amount of hearing loss. Typically, if it's a good set of friends we tend to know which ear they have hearing loss in.'

When I enthusiastically relayed these facts to a friend, she snorted before roundly dismissing any soldier's desire for deafness as vapid and irresponsible.

I wanted to tell her that the military could be proof that deaf people can work anywhere, that we shouldn't be classified as a risk or liability. Instead, embarrassed by my naive optimism, I shyly confessed that it was the first time I'd read anything positive about deafness, before quickly switching the topic of conversation.

Months later, when I stumbled across the story filed on my desktop, I was struck by the marine's description of returning home with hearing loss. '[My family] actually end up getting frustrated at me. You just have to play it off sometimes, pretend that you've heard what they have had to say. Then pick it up later on the conversation or ask them as though you forgot.'

No matter how whole I might feel, the facts remain the same: the hearing world rarely welcomes deaf bodies.

Reasonable adjustments

I wasn't shocked the first time I touched a dead body. It looked exactly like the photographs I'd studied in my sister's anatomy books when I was supposed to be preparing for my final high-school exams. I'd been fascinated by those deconstructed bodies: limbs skinned and deboned; ribbons of muscles untethered and fanned out across tabletops; the kidneys, liver and gall bladder scooped out of the thorax, each given its own portrait in the textbook.

It was during my first anatomy lesson that I learned to refer to them as 'cadavers', not 'dead bodies'. The word placed the body parts at an even further remove from what felt familiar, and, truthfully, what seemed human. The cadavers reeked of the tang of formaldehyde, the preservation chemical that turns flesh stiff and leathery. I leaned in close and with a gloved hand touched a dissected leg. After leaving the anatomy lab, I began to view people as a series of moving parts, distinct layers of muscle, sinew and fat arranged like strata beneath their skin.

The French have a phrase for how our occupations uncon- sciously and continuously inform our worldview: *déformation professionnelle.* Chefs might use the seasons of fruit and vegetables as a way to earmark the passage of time. Engineers might automatically assess the structural integrity of each bridge they cross or staircase they ascend. After my four years of physiotherapy training—in which I learned the *correct* ways a body should function, as well as all the ways it can fail or falter—my professional bias meant I viewed the world through the prism of perfect body parts.

I also learned to keep my disability well hidden.

In her essay 'A Writing Life', Annie Dillard ruminates on how our bodies are shaped by work. She notes: 'In working-class France, when an apprentice got hurt, or when he got tired, the experienced workers said, "It is the trade entering his body."'

When did my trade enter my body? Was it when I first lifted up a leg to examine someone's bones? I can remember the sudden pain in my shoulder when I underestimated the weight and sheer awkwardness of moving someone else's knee. Or did my trade begin to shape me when I slipped my T-shirt over my head and stood in front of my fellow physiotherapy classmates? My posture mimicked an anatomical drawing, chin level, expression neutral, arms stretched long and palms facing forward—I ignored my instinct to cross them over my chest as my joints were examined. Or did my trade settle in my body while I was studying at my desk? My textbook open in front of me, I would palpate my muscles in order to understand their shape, leaving bruises, deep blue and green, scattered along the length of every limb.

During my new-graduate year, I raced through hospital corridors, assessed bodies swiftly and decisively, laid my hands on hundreds of patients, wrote clinical notes about dysfunction and maladaptive movement pattern. By the end of the year, my trade had definitely entered my body: my palms had collected calluses and the webbing alongside my thumb had thickened into dense muscle; my eyes were now quick to detect abnormalities in people's movements. And when I returned to Sydney and looked for my next job, I didn't mention my deafness on my CV or in any interviews, as I knew it would be considered a risk, a liability.

In Australia, deafness is a strike against your name. Despite improved access to education, the overall employment rate of Australians with hearing loss is fifty-eight per cent. Those who are employed are in part-time, low-paying roles with limited career progression. In economic terms, they are a deadweight loss, 'a loss of economic efficiency'. A recent report found 'the total deadweight losses due to hearing loss were $1.9 billion in 2019-20.'

I think about my working life, which, for the past sixteen years, has consisted of periods of part-time work, short spurts of full-time work, stretches of burnout, and overall limited career progression. I am a deadweight. It's likely I will always be one.

As my work history has wavered, so too has my health. It's been a boom-and-bust cycle that I failed to understand until my early thirties. Not from a lack of dissonance, as my body was so obviously weighed down with fatigue and frustration, but because I kept trying to find solutions. This, I realise now, was my own professional bias. The medical model I was trained in proposes that 'any economic or social deprivation encountered by people with disability is located within the individual and their impairment'. I believed that I was the problem. Or rather, I was *taught* that I was the problem.

Many university courses medicalise disability—labelling the body as working or malfunctioning, normal or abnormal—without considering a person's autonomy and human rights. According to a paper published in the medical journal *The Lancet*, 'Professional training can lead to an erosion of empathy and growth in cynicism. Some studies have found that medical students have more negative attitudes to disability than the general norm...'

I had been diligently trained to view the world, and my own body, through an ableist gaze—seeing disability as a series of deficits that *must* be overcome in order to live a meaningful life. In my twenties, as I shifted from one job to the next, I desperately focused on trying to make my body fit into each work environment.

Every so often, I thought about retraining, changing careers entirely. In my early twenties I enrolled in an MBA, but dropped out before the classes began. In my late twenties, I started learning how to code. The following year, I considered specialising in Occupational Health and Safety. I became so fixated on finding a job that involved little personal interaction that one of my brothers sent me a job advertisement for a lighthouse keeper. It was a joke. But one I did consider briefly. Instead of moving to an empty stretch of coastline, I began a degree in writing and editing, hoping to work only with words.

I did online career quizzes. The Myer–Briggs assessment told me I had the same personality traits as Steve Martin, Margaret Thatcher and Stalin: planning, consistency, rationality, analysing and 'likes criticism'. The website didn't clarify whether the enjoyment came from giving or receiving criticism. In an effort to distance myself from those 'celebrities', I resolved that the assessment was simply a result of my momentary self-critical mood. Years later, after what felt like a period of self-growth, I redid the quiz and got the same result.

•

In 2019–20, the loss of wellbeing in individuals with hearing loss totalled $21.2 billion. In part, this is thought to be due to the physical and psychic stress experienced by deaf and hard-of-hearing people trying to live in a hearing world. The compound effect is devasting. Hearing loss is associated with a higher risk of premature death due to cardiovascular disease. My own heart is so used to thrumming through the tight grip of anxiety that I only notice my hyper-vigilance, my rapid pulse, my jittery temperament, when I see family and flatmates unwind with a level of ease that feels unattainable.

Single people with hearing loss have an even greater risk of premature death. Having been single more often than not, I can now see how my deafness has influenced my approach to dating. After a slew of disappointing dates in crowded bars, music venues, sporting events and cinemas, I learned what locations work best for first dates—places with bright lights and low ambient noise, such as art galleries, picnics in parks, afternoon drinks on rooftops. Even with this kind of planning and awareness, it has only recently become clear to me why some relationships didn't work out. In each instance, I would initiate the break-up. A physiotherapist who was a kind and attentive listener, but whose voice was a few octaves too low. A barista who shared my taste in music, but who constantly preened his moustache, making lip reading impossible. A primary-school teacher who had a wonderful sense of humour, but, at six foot five, was too tall for me to see his face. We dated for a while, before, in a cruel way, I ghosted him. A few years later, I dated another man of a similar height to the previous guy. The conversation was easy and interesting. It lasted for a few months, before I suggested we should be friends. Another obvious pattern emerges—I had told none of them about my hearing loss.

I'm alarmed to read that deaf and hard-of-hearing people live longer if they have a partner who is hearing. Not because love keeps hearts healthy and strong, but 'being in a relationship may also serve as a buffer against the detrimental economic consequences of hearing loss'.

I think about how I've developed a habit of deleting dating apps within days of downloading them. I'm neither shy nor without desire, but the thing I love most, or really *need* the most, after each workday is to sit in quiet, unpeopled spaces. Time to rest and recover. Instead of scrolling through apps, exposing and exerting my heart, I've focused on saving my strength for things that matter—namely, staying employable.

As proving one's employability is an ongoing worry, disabled people conduct an informal risk assessment before making any workplace requests. Will the answer most likely be yes? Has anyone else at the organisation got a disability? If so, has that person received any accommodations? How will my colleagues react? These sorts of questions have become so innate in me, so reflexive, that I can't imagine what it would be like not to have to calculate risk. My fear feels corporeal, so full of consequence. Too often, even if accommodations are needed, the risk of reprimand, ridicule and rejection is considered much too high—requests are never made.

I've only requested workplace accommodations once. I was twenty-nine and working in an entry-level admin job. A small part of my role involved typing up meeting minutes using audio recordings. After several attempts to complete the task, I realised that I couldn't understand the conversations without reading lips. Having recently learned about disability rights while participating in the comedy workshops, I felt brave enough to disclose my deafness to my supervisor and tell her how it was impacting my ability to complete tasks.

When I asked if I could attend the meetings, she said: You just need to practise. And that's what I did. I showed up early and left late. I jammed my headphones into my ears. I turned up the volume so loud that my colleagues could hear the babble of voices, which to me, still sounded meaningless. The next time I spoke to my manager, she said: You just need to try harder. Not long afterwards I resigned.

Although the *Disability Discrimination Act* (DAA) was passed in 1993, the disability unemployment gap has been increasing in recent years. The DAA hinges on the phrase 'reasonable adjustments', a strikingly ill-defined set of words. Of course, the DAA needs to be flexible, but it is left to the discretion of employers to act in a reasonable manner. When employers are asked to assess adjustments, their judgement of reasonableness is influenced by how *they* themselves work. It's not surprising then that the 2017 Disability Confidence survey found fifty-nine per cent of small-to-medium-sized Australian enterprises didn't even consider hiring disabled job applicants. Thirty-six per cent of the businesses claimed that 'our type of work doesn't suit people with disability'. Frustratingly, these employers assert that they are being reasonable—they cannot see the world, or their work, from any other perspective. They are judging potential applicants via their own professional bias. Research also shows that employers are unlikely to treat disabled people equally unless they have had personal experience of disability. Equality only seems reasonable when you've experienced inequality.

Of all the complaint cases received by the Australian Human Rights Commission (AHRC), the vast majority relate to disability discrimination in matters of employment. The DDA assumes that employers wish to deal proactively with disability, whereas the statistics reveal that many discriminate against this group. Legislation that promises to defend human rights is often used only as part of a cost-benefit analysis.

How do employers get away with this behaviour? Most don't realise that they are failing to comply with their legal duties. In 2016, researchers from the University of Technology Sydney examined all available complaint cases received by the AHRC in relation to disability discrimination, and found a clear trend that 'employers misunderstood key legal concepts that underpin the DDA including: unjustifiable hardship; inherent requirements; reasonable adjustment; direct; and indirect discrimination'.

Even if an employer understands their responsibilities, the DAA is couched in abstract language and linguistic malleability that safeguard the status quo. On the OECD scale that rates employment of disabled people, Australia is ranked twenty-ninth out of that many countries. The DAA is being used as a brutally effective tool to exclude disabled bodies from employment opportunities.

The Law Institute of Victoria has been critical of the complaints-driven function of the DAA: '[P]eople are required to pursue legal action to achieve their entitlement to freedom from discrimination. In this context, it seems crucial that some form of guidelines or standards covering all the areas in which discrimination is prohibited under the Act be developed.' Until there is clarification of how the DAA should be used, employers are essentially encouraged to apply their own professional bias to determine what is fair and reasonable.

In *Far from the Tree: Parents, Children, and the Search for Identity*, Andrew Solomon writes:

Difference and disability seem to invite people to step back and judge. Parents judge what lives are worth living, and worth their living with; activists judge them for doing so; legal scholars judge who should make judgements; doctors judge which lives to save; politicians judge how much accommodation people with special needs deserve; insurance companies judge how much lives are worth.

He fails to note how much judgement a disabled person may direct towards themselves. It's something I find myself doing: the chronic calculating of costs and risks. The tedious, ongoing reckoning: will my body be welcome here or not?

After resigning from my office job, I was apprehensive about the physical cost of returning to clinical work. I was equally apprehensive about applying for other office roles, worried I would be asked to perform transcription or similar tasks that involved intense listening. After much deliberation, I decided to apply for physiotherapy roles in aged-care facilities. In that setting, I hoped, my deafness wouldn't be as striking or even unusual.

'Do you have any questions? Or anything further you'd like to add?'

I wrapped the telephone cord around my index finger. It was less of a question and more of an opportunity. Perhaps this time I'd take it. Would life be easier if I were honest?

'Well?' the woman on the other end of the line asked.

My confidence flickered. Did I really need to say anything? What would happen if I told them? Would things be different this time? For so long my secret had informed every sentence I uttered: even at the age of thirty, I couldn't imagine what plain, easy honesty felt like. It was harder still to judge this situation without seeing her face. I covered my pause with a rough cough and tightened the cord.

'Sorry about that,' I said quickly, clearing my throat. 'No, I don't have anything else to add.'

'Well, your CV is great. I'll need to call your references, but I'll get back to you soon.'

Only after I'd hung up did I release my finger from the cord. It was cold and white. I watched the blood return and wondered when, if ever, I'd stop lying about my body in order to get a job.

A few months later, now employed in steady part-time work as an aged-care physiotherapist, I found myself idly filling out 'The Common Secrets Questionnaire'. Just two pages long, it seemed as harmless and appealing as a quiz from a glossy magazine. I had discovered the questionnaire when googling: What is the difference between a secret and a lie? Lying is deliberating telling things other than the truth, whereas keeping a secret means avoiding the truth. I oscillated rapidly between the two during any given interaction, consciously tacking away from the truth whenever possible.

Sitting in my bedroom, I circled yes/no with faint pencil marks, checking to see how I measured up to the average on questions about drug use, relationships, fantasies, illegal behaviour, emotions and so on. By now I had actively hidden my deafness for well over two decades. It was hard to imagine living and moving in a body free of its burden. If each cell in a body renews itself every seven to ten years, then my secret had threaded and rethreaded itself through me into a tight knot.

I left the finished quiz on my desk and headed to work. All day I helped elderly people in and out of bed; encouraged permed and cardigan-wearing residents to walk another lap of the nursing home corridors; documented my treatment sessions, detailing each resident's mood, motivation and level of physical exertion. Within days of starting at the aged-care facility, I felt I'd returned to work that suited my tempo and temperament. During my shift, however, the task of exposing my secrets in the questionnaire played on my mind.

When I stopped for a tea break, I fretted that a gust of wind would snatch up the loose sheets of paper and carry all my secrets to the living room for my housemates to find. The anticipation of embarrassment was excruciating.

At home that evening, I erased my secrets: with frantic strokes of the rubber I got rid of all the careful tracings of truth. While checking the questionnaire for any lingering mention of deafness, I realised that most of the other so-called secrets—my catalogue of unrequited loves, fantasies, misdemeanours and experimentation—had already been dissected in the pages of my diary and with a group of close friends. But my deafness continued to be the oldest and most safe-guarded secret of all. One that I didn't know how to dissect.

There was certainty in the silence of a secret. A predictable sort of pain. I was not alone in my silence. The WHO estimates that about fifteen per cent of the world's population have some form of disability. With ninety per cent of disabilities not visible, studies consistently show that the vast majority of people choose not to disclose that they are disabled in workplace environments. Hundreds of millions of people are concealing parts of themselves for fear of social stigma and economic disadvantage. When I first read those statistics my sense of relief was immense and dizzying. The past twenty years of hiding seemed worthwhile, sensible even. It soothed me: my lies hadn't been a by-product of a furiously active imagination. My fears of stigma were not unfounded; it was a common concern. Millions and millions of people, like me, were concealing their disabilities. This invisible community felt reassuringly close. After a few moments of consolation, however, my loneliness rushed back. The statistics were cold comfort; they did nothing to dull the pain.

As my career progresses, my professional bias has shifted to accommodate the fact that bodies are more than just moving parts; they are unpredictable; they have histories and muscle memories. As it has turned out, I chose a career that demands careful and close listening, and I realise that, rather than limiting me, my deafness allows me to be good at my job.

When talking with patients, I try never to be casual or distracted. I do my best to listen keenly. I avoid making assumptions. And I always try to check that every patient feels heard and understood.

But even while working in the aged-care facility, I still felt it was too much of a risk to explain to my employer that my deafness made me a careful and attentive listener. Afterall, it defied expectations. And while I was confident that my deafness made me an empathic healthcare professional, especially given that the majority of my patients had hearing loss, I was also hesitant to disclose it to my colleagues. Even though they were often kind, ordinary, *reasonable* people, I still feared they would say: *Our type of work doesn't suit people with a disability*.

Currently, forty-five per cent of Australians with a disability are living either near or below the poverty line. To put that into perspective, the OECD average is twenty-two per cent. The level of disadvantage among disabled Australians is not accidental; it is a symptom of our attitude to the body in social policy—we consistently perceive someone's worth as based on their economic contribution. Conversations about access and reform are halted because disabled bodies fail the cost-benefit analysis. This analysis is fundamentally skewed: there is language to articulate the costs—deadweight losses—but there isn't a similar economic language for securing basic human rights and safeguarding wellbeing.

Only measuring contribution in dollars and cents means that no one has any inherent value—you must prove it. As long as this narrow definition of productivity is stitched into policy, it reinforces the myth that this country has been built from two hundred and thirty-two years of hard labour, rather than from invasion, genocide, unpaid labour and unceasing systemic human-rights injustices.

The overlooking of disabled bodies is so consistent, so rampant worldwide, that the United Nations has created a checklist for parliamentarians: 'Why I should be interested in the rights of persons with disabilities.' Each of the six dot points is a rallying cry of common sense, unfortunately not yet common enough to go unstated. The list begins: 'The human rights of persons with disabilities should be promoted for the same reason that human rights are promoted for all other people: because of the inherent and equal dignity and worth of each human being.'

I laugh bitterly about the checklist with another disabled friend, whom I had met in a creative-writing workshop. We trade stories about how we cope, the ways in which we find ourselves backed into corners or avoiding, avoiding, avoiding the places that cause us to ache. Others, with able bodies, experience the world in seamless ways, entering and exiting buildings without friction or calculation, because parks and schools and workplaces and homes, and even our Parliament House, have been designed for their bodies only. We know just how necessary that checklist is.

Care work

John Wayne was strutting across the television screen. I knocked on the doorframe. Tony looked up as Wayne aimed his pistol at me.

'Tony! Tony!' I waved, my voice straining to compete with the volume of the television.

Tony smiled at me as the cowboy walked away from the blood-soaked body.

The body thins and thickens with age. Skin, no longer cushioned by deep layers of fat and muscle, becomes a light cover over bone. It tears with shocking ease. You need soft, steady hands when transferring an elderly person in and out of bed—even friction from sheets can slice skin, causing blood to gush. Just as skin thins, joints thicken. The spine no longer twists like a pivot or folds like a hinge; it becomes stiffer, shorter. And while some aspects of ageing are predictable, most aren't—each body accrues the weight of time differently. Care work requires a deep interest in individuals, and I was glad to be back in such an environment.

•

I did all the right things. Muted the television, faced front on, made sure I had his attention, enunciated my words, kept my face and hands animated.

'Can we go for a walk, Tony? Do some exercise?'

Tony sank deeper into his recliner. His face became impassive, only his eyes flittered back and forth, assessing the situation. It was the same expression I used whenever I couldn't hear anything. I tried again, gesturing to his frame. 'The walk will do your legs some good.'

'What talk?'

'Walk!' I started marching on the spot. 'Exercise, Tony!' My voice took on an edge of impatience.

After several more attempts to communicate, we were both left strung out.

On my way home, as the train rattled past the sewage-treatment plant that has become an internationally recognised bird habitat, I stared at the rush of blue sky, hoping to ease the slosh of shame in my gut.

Once home, I searched for an alarming story I'd read a few years earlier and that had been nagging me since I left Tony's room. Sadly, the facts aligned with my memory. In 2013, as a result of a UK hospital's failure to keep accurate records, the staff were not aware that a patient was deaf, and so treated him as if he had dementia. Although not incontinent, he was fitted with a catheter. He was not informed that he might have cancer. He died a month later. Apparently this was not an isolated incident; other deaf people have been incorrectly diagnosed with dementia. A wave of horror rolled through me. The medical and legal implications of such a diagnosis were unbearable to contemplate—complete loss of autonomy; everything a deaf individual did could be disregarded. Images of my own workplace's locked dementia wing—residents pacing the corridors or staring dully out the windows—stayed with me all night long.

While there is evidence of an increased risk of dementia in deaf people, it is not a simple cause-and-effect relationship. Anyone with hearing loss experiences increased social isolation—just as a young deaf brain needs language to flourish, so too does an older deaf brain. Along with a lack of conversation and companionship, people with hearing loss are also prone to 'brain overload'—trying to decipher sounds requires immense cognitive energy, which leaves fewer reserves for thinking, reasoning and remembering. Although these complex factors impact on cognitive function, hearing-technology companies advertise that hearing aids prevent dementia, without also providing the appropriate education to individuals or families about how they must adjust their communication styles, and be aware that, after a certain degree of hearing loss, technology may no longer be effective.

So much of the loneliness and confusion in my aged-care facility would disappear, I thought, if we focused on language, rather than treating technology as a panacea. None of the residents knew Auslan, nor did the staff. Many residents had stopped wearing their hearing aids, preferring the softness of silence to the screech of sonic feed-back. Staff and family, however, insisted they wear them anyway. Everyone was frustrated, including a number of residents who were annoyed with other, deafer residents, some even refusing to sit next to them. Many of the deafest residents sat alone day after day. The nursing staff compared the petty and resolute behaviour to high-school cliques. My heart ached.

•

'Tony!' I waved from the doorway.

He lifted his head and smiled. A newspaper was spread across his lap. I had learned that Tony was a morning person; he only turned his television on after lunch, often falling asleep before a film ended. Now I planned my schedule around his, trying to get to his room around the same time each morning.

I made a walking motion with my hand. 'Keen to go for a stroll?'

After several sessions of trial and error, I had discovered that Tony understood me when I said 'stroll' instead of 'walk'. It made sense: 'stroll' came from lower in my chest, whereas 'walk' clacked off my tongue.

'Thought you'd never ask.'

I looked for ways of rephrasing and repeating, without resorting to loud hectoring. I started to incorporate signs into my treatment sessions, not sophisticated, standardised signs, just small gestures to amplify meaning. Whenever possible, I wrote notes and questions, passing pieces of paper to residents: fancy a walk?

Slowly, over months, I found ways of communicating with most residents. And as I was learning their individual ways of expressing themselves, they were getting used to me. We shared jokes, stories. We did gentle exercise and rehabilitation. As immensely satisfying as I found my work, after each shift I boarded the train home feeling knackered. The very reason I had been so keen to work in aged care was quickly becoming a reason to leave. The facility was louder than I anticipated. Televisions or radios blared from every room; announcements crackled through the loudspeakers; the dining room was chaotic with conversation and cutlery. My body felt full of noise. Without intending to, I began to curtail conversations, close off questions, so that residents only needed to give me short responses, thumbs up or down. I worked my way through packets of pain relief. Nothing could loosen my headaches. It was all too much. And yet the thought of the deaf residents sitting alone, without conversation, made me reluctant to leave.

In circles

Recently a friend asked: what would your perfect day be like? I answered readily, as if I had been waiting for someone to ask: wake up without an alarm clock; sip home-brewed coffee on my balcony; read and write, first for leisure and then for work; a ramble through the native grasslands, stopping to watch the man flying kites in the shapes of animals, their limbs loose and sunlit; snack on a crisp apple and a wedge of aged cheese while standing in my kitchen, hips pressed against the sink, feet bare; read some more; watch the curra-wongs fly in large, lazy circles around the communal courtyard; a heart-belting run; suck on a gin-soaked cucumber as I make a second drink; fall into clean bedsheets, accompanied by a new book whose spine I would crack…On I went, detailing small and large moments, each perfectly formed in my mind.

'So, you wouldn't want to see anyone at all? You'd prefer to be all alone?'

Her response startled me. I hadn't realised that I'd crafted an entirely solitary day. My chest tightened. I'd tried to become more mindful of the allures of self-isolation. My most enduring hobbies, however, have always been solitary in nature—distance-running, reading, writing—activities that do not easily lend themselves to companionship. But they didn't feel solitary to me. Whenever I can, I retreat from noise. I feel the most embodied, most enlivened, when I am in the thick fold of silence. But now, in my early thirties, I know that this is a dangerous desire.

'Friendship is the single most important factor influencing our health, well-being and happiness. Creating and maintaining friendships is, however, extremely costly, in terms of both the time that has to be invested and the cognitive mechanisms that underpin them,' declares R.I.M. Dunbar in his article 'The Anatomy of Friendship'. The word 'anatomy' presents friendship as a physical entity—with its own pulse, rhythm and breath, in need of nurturing to thrive. For several months after first reading Dunbar's work, I referred to the paper as 'The Architecture of Friendship'. When I returned to reread it, after a particularly lonely weekend in Melbourne, I was stunned by how readily my mind had swapped a more mechanical metaphor into the title, something solid, constructed, almost scientific. While I don't think I considered friendship in mathematical terms, as Dunbar does—estimating how 'costly' each friendship may be—I did calculate the cost of each conversation, with friends or otherwise.

For people with hearing loss, deciphering what somebody is saying requires conscious effort—every interaction consists of thousands of micro-decisions. A brain can only handle so much before it brims over.

Listening fatigue. Whenever I use the phrase, it's interpreted by friends and family as being 'sick of people'. They say that they too experience it: *yes, yes, we all get tired of listening to people go on.*

It is hard to explain that it's more than just a feeling of weariness or disinterest in others, but rather an inability to process auditory information. When I'm fatigued it's as if I am submerged in murky liquid: suspended in silence, eyes straining.

Until recently, listening fatigue, also known as concentration fatigue, had not been considered worthy of scientific attention. No audiologist had ever asked me: how do you cope with fatigue? It wasn't until I was thirty that I learnt about listening fatigue from the Deaf community on Twitter. People shared their stories, tweeting their frustrations, often saying that friends and family, colleagues and managers 'just don't get it'. I got it.

It explained why I'd feel dimwitted and washed-out after even a brief conversation on a busy street corner or crowded tram; why watching TV never felt relaxing; why I had never managed to binge-watch anything—I took months to work through a single season, pressing pause halfway through each episode, no matter how much I enjoyed it. And why school felt like a grind, and why I would lose the ability to follow instructions, grasp simple concepts or even pronounce words by the end of each day—I had always assumed I was innately lazy, feckless.

Now aware that my concentration had a finite supply, I recognised whenever I was losing my ability to focus—words ran together, morphing into an indistinct drone. Even moving, coordinating my limbs, become an effort—I'd veer while walking, trip over my own feet or collide into furniture.

I began to consciously calculate the costs of each social interaction and compare it with the demands of my working week. A simple question—should I catch up with friends for coffee?—would be accompanied by dozens of other questions. How many work phone calls did I have to make? How long would each call be?

Did I have any meetings scheduled? More often than not, I played it safe and reserved my energy for work.

This method of calculating costs is common among people with hearing loss. A study by Lillemor Hallberg and Sven Carlsson proposed that people with hearing loss tend to use two different coping strategies in demanding auditory situations: 'control the social scene' or 'avoid the social scene'. I recognised my life as eddying between controlling and cowering.

I usually concealed my grasp for control with an enthusiasm for obscure facts, reeling off detailed histories of hot-air ballooning or submarines. Or by simply rolling from one anecdote to the next—that time I almost walked backward into an active volcano while taking a photo; my family's folk band, which dominated the Western Sydney supermarket talent-quest circuit during the late nineties; my first job, in a fabric store, and how, at fifteen, I assumed I had to answer every consumer query—I spent my weekends doling out sewing advice without ever having threaded a needle.

But I didn't always do all the talking. In large groups, when the flow of conversations changed quickly, I would cower. With each tangent, the currents shifted. I hung back, didn't dive in, preferring to bob quietly along the edges. Even this would require a degree of control. I would remain in a constant state of adjustment—checking and changing myself to suit the particular social dynamics.

As exhausting as it was trying to be in control during conversations, it didn't stop when I was alone. People with hearing loss often review conversations, testing their comprehension. One participant in Hallberg and Carlsson's study explained: 'I call a couple of people and tr[y] to reconstruct the meeting afterwards.'

I thought about how often I would lie awake, re-examining sentences for all the ways I could have misconstrued, misheard, misunderstood their substance. Turning and weighing each word, checking for double meanings. It never felt like an anxious habit, just a necessary act of housekeeping.

Hallberg and Carlsson's second category of coping, the desire to be alone, is described as 'avoiding confrontation'. It's easy for me to amass a list of situations that I have left—share houses, workplaces, relationships—fearing the potential and complexity of conflict. I always want to avoid the impossible task of accurately reading a face bristled in rage or masked in resentment.

Hallberg and Carlsson touch on how even the most innocuous settings can be unsettling for people with hearing loss:

> The hearing-impaired prefers to be alone and takes his coffee break alone in his/her room or in another quiet place instead of being exposed to hearing-demanding and threatening situations: 'I know that people communicate, they go to the cafeteria...I can't go there, I can't relax in there. Do you understand...I become an isolated person in a big group in that way.'

I do understand. So, wherever I go, I carry a book. When I worked for the not-for-profit, I used to prop it open and shovel food into my mouth from behind the small paper wall. Then, while working at the aged-care facility, I carefully timed my breaks so that I would be the only one in the tea room, my book open on the table, ready for me to hide behind. The body doesn't listen to logic when adrenaline is released, it merely reacts. So even though I *knew* I wasn't in a threatening situation while eating reheated pasta, my heart hammered and startled at the slightest noise. The layout of the not-for-profit's tea room—the table in the centre, two entry points, heavy foot traffic from all directions—held too much potential, too many possibilities. It was easier to sit at my desk, alone.

It was comforting to read tweets and scientific studies about others who had fallen into the same patterns as I had. And to recognise that devising coping strategies wasn't conniving or contrived, but essential. Had I known this earlier, it might have made me more forgiving of my fluctuating moods, given me a way of explaining to friends why I seemed to switch dramatically from being an extrovert to an introvert, never settling as one or the other. All through my twenties I swerved between vivacious partying to months of being a recluse. I've learned that it is only when I am alone that my body expands with boundless energy, and I can sit among my own thoughts. Without this time to listen to myself, I feel turned inside out. Emotions unspool—flashes of anger, tears.

Recognising how intertwined my deafness is with my physical and psychological wellbeing has allowed me to manage my fatigue. Often deaf people to find the transition from school to working life rough going: balancing demands and desires, social interactions and work, the costs of fatigue. It takes sensory overload to understand the limits of your body, to understand the signs of impending and explosive fatigue. Looking back, I acknowledge with some regret the instances when I should have taken myself off into corners of quiet solitude.

'The problems of deafness are deeper and more complex, if not more important, than those of blindness. Deafness is a much worse misfortune. For it means the loss of the most vital stimulus—the sound of the voice that brings language, sets thoughts astir and keeps us in the intellectual company of man,' wrote Helen Keller.

This comparison has been condensed and widely paraphrased as: blindness separates people from things; deafness separates people from people. Both descriptions of deafness strike a chord within me. I don't have complete control, of course not.

Separation can be causal: the turn of a shoulder or a hand hovering in front of a mouth. Or it can be more intentional: 'don't worry about it' or 'never mind' if I've asked for some missed phrase to be repeated.

So I separate myself, quickly and cleanly, from conversations, house parties, meals, drinks—acting before someone gets a chance to cut me out. This act of self-isolation, frequent among people with hearing loss, is known as self-stigmatisation. When I spend evenings and weekends alone, I call it self-care. Where does the line between self-care and self-isolation lie? I suspect there must be a line, for at times I have found myself too far removed and unable to find the enthusiasm or courage to socialise.

The graph of Dunbar's 'circles of friendship' looks like a bullseye, each circle annotated with ascending numerical values moving out from the centre: 5, 15, 50, 150, 500 and finally 1500 people. The average personal social network hovers at around 150 friends. Sitting in the North Melbourne library on a Saturday afternoon in mid-2017, my eyes lingered on the innermost circle, the 'ego' or 'circle of oneness', quantified as 1.5. I shifted uncomfortably when I read that this innermost circle of the social network indicates emotional closeness, the sort often shared with a significant other.

I glanced away, but not quickly enough. In my mind, the circle had split into two: what my hearing-half wanted and what my deaf-half wanted were distinct, divided things.

•

For as long as I can remember Dad has always told us: your siblings will be your first friends and they will be your last. If we were bickering, he'd say it as a way of corralling us back to gentler behaviour. Often he would say it without any clear trigger or context, turning away from the television or steering wheel, reminding us that we were all friends. It was something his father used to tell him and his eight siblings. It was something we had all readily agreed with. Even after moving out of home, we continued to talk almost daily. We hung out so often, friends referred to us as a collective: The Murphys. They joked that once you were friends with one Murphy, you were friends with them all.

Dunbar suggests that the inner circle of friends, the group who supply your emotional and social needs, typically consists of five people. Perhaps it is no coincidence that I failed to recognise how few friendships I actively nurtured until I moved out of home: as one of four siblings, I had been fortified against loneliness.

Growing up, I always looked forward to dinner. We would all sat down together, the television switched off. Then the talking began. We didn't simply recap our days; we re-enacted them, one by one bounding into stories as though striding on stage. We each strove for the biggest laugh. As we got older and all my siblings were working in healthcare, the stories shifted. The dinner table became a place for us to talk about death and dying.

After moving out of home, I found it challenging to converse over meals. Eating out often meant having to contend with background noise. I would sit in any available seat, even if I knew that it would place me at a disadvantage during the conversation. Round tables were easier, as I could scan each face. Long tables were next to impossible. More and more, I realised how smoothly my family had always accommodated my deafness—facing me and speaking clearly without food in their mouths.

The experience of this specific kind of isolation is so prevalent in the deaf community that it has been called 'Dinner Table Syndrome'. Winston Churchill's personal physician, Dr Charles Wilson, describes it in his diary of June 1955:

> It does not seem a long time since Winston did all the talking at every meal; now he sits all huddled up in silence; he can no longer hear what is being said, he is outside the round of conversation and not a part of it, though at times, it is true, when there is a burst of laughter, someone will explain to him what it is all about.

Not yet understanding that I was experiencing loneliness even when surrounded by others, I tried to remedy the sadness by putting myself out in the world more and more. I accepted every social invitation going, until my mid-twenties, by which point I was unable to deny how physically and emotionally draining it was trying to keep up.

Loneliness kills. I know the statistics well. Six months after moving to Melbourne, and as I waited for the surgery on my thumb, I began to volunteer as a copywriter for a fledging not-for-profit whose mission was to reduce the stigma of loneliness. After work and on weekends, I attended meetings; got pulled into long email threads; drafted blog posts and tweets; wrote fundraising reports. One of my research documents claimed that loneliness 'heightens health risks as much as smoking fifteen cigarettes a day or having an alcohol-use disorder'.

I learned that we can carry loneliness, taking it with us into even the most crowded of places—work, public transport, the pub, the dinner table. So personal, so distinct, it adjusts to our individual outline, to the very curve of each cell. These cellular changes, or 'accumulation of deficiencies', as scientists call it, have been shown to increase vascular resistance. Loneliness troubles the blood, forcing the heart to work harder. No wonder we lose any sense of orientation when living in loneliness—we are soaked in it. Our thoughts spiral in on themselves. Not from selfishness, but from just the opposite: a loss of self.

I delved deep into the data, but it still took me until that summer, some eight months after beginning my volunteering, to recognise how miserably lonely I was. One afternoon, the founders of the not-for-profit asked me to join the board, explaining the opportunities that would come once I took on more responsibility. I sat in the meeting, smiling, nodding, thrilled to have my work recognised. Once home, I lay on the couch and sobbed. A messy outpouring of pent-up feeling. And it was only because Cassie was out for the night that I allowed myself to fall so fully into my feelings of loneliness.

It wasn't the first time I had isolated myself, though it was the longest. I am still shocked, however, by how easily, how quickly, I withdrew into myself that first year in Melbourne. Not long afterwards, I moved to North Melbourne, knowing that it would be healthier for me to return to a bustling share house.

I still regularly ask myself: how do I choose between feeling alone and enlivened in an empty room, or alone and exhausted in a crowded one? I try to monitor my moods, as well as commit to a reliable schedule of rest and socialising. But sometimes, even when in a steady routine, I lose track of myself, unsure how to judge whether I am relaxed or lonesome, bored or yearning. By all respects, everything might seem to tick along—I go to work, exercise, pay my bills, cook basic but nourishing meals, sleep well most nights. But even within a scaffold of routine, I can suddenly become aware of not being present either in my body or in my life. I'm on 'autopilot' and only ever intervene, change course—hustle myself out of the house, call friends and make plans—when the edges of solitude sharpen and alarms flash, forcing me back into the pilot's seat.

Then again, that's not quite true. This habit of withdrawal, this slippage into solitude, doesn't always happen without conscious intent. I have endless proof of my deliberate acts of self-isolation— the closely guarded gaps in my weekly planner, which ensure that I have stretches of quietness during each week; the ready excuses I use to pull out of invitations to dinners or drinks; the ignored messages and unanswered phone calls; the missed gym classes; the often replenished stack of books beside my bed, ready to be picked up during yet another long night spent alone.

Will introversion and self-isolation always be the tides of my body? I picture a set of waves. Every few months I tumble forward full of vigour, then spectacularly crash, before pulling back from everyone, quietly regaining momentum once more.

It was a hot afternoon when I wrote the previous paragraphs. My fingers raced over the keyboard: a rare moment of feeling my mind coursing through my fingertips. Later, when I reviewed the sentences with an unsentimental editorial gaze, a *conscious* gaze, I saw that I'd typed: 'deliberate acts of self-sabotage'. I quickly changed it to 'self-isolation'. A small narrative erasure, a constant desire for control.

During my time at the not-for-profit, before I was required to do transcription, I often left work feeling bright, sure-footed. It was a new and unusual sensation. With energy to burn, I started volunteering at a community radio station as a weekend 'reader': I read out the newspaper for listeners Australia-wide who were blind or had low vision. Three readers rotated on each four-hour shift. I hadn't anticipated how technical and precise the broadcasting would be. As a new volunteer, I was enrolled in a short course, Voice Training for Performance. Some of the twenty attendees in my group were there for an annual 'tune-up'. Our instructor was a stage actress. Over the two days, the only time she slouched was when she demonstrated how such posture 'traps your breath in your stomach'. In response, we sat like primary-school children looking for praise.

After receiving instructions about pacing (go two beats slower than you think), breathing (don't gasp) and popping (watch your p's), we each had a chance to read aloud and receive critiques from our fellow readers, some of whom relished the task—too fast! too much popping! where was the colour? the emotion? maybe keep your shoulders back a little more?

By the time I read, even the new volunteers had lost their shyness. Everyone was ready to criticise, or at least that was how it felt to me.

I had been assigned the weather forecast. During the prep time I had made faint pencil marks, trying to find the 'natural' cadence in the numbers, but that didn't help. I focused entirely on maintaining a measured pace, aiming at a muscular pronunciation of each set of temperatures for the upcoming week

'That was fine. But could you try and put a little more personality into the article?' said the actress. She scrunched up her nose. 'It was a little…dull.'

The group nodded in agreement.

I took a sip of hot tea (no milk, the actress warned, you don't want your vocals to go claggy). This time I tried to feel the daily lows and highs, the sun on my skin, the taste of sea spray as I worked my way around the coastline, savouring each mouthful of numbers.

The room remained quiet. A few participants raised their eyebrows.

'Well, that was a remarkable difference!' The actress leapt up. 'You've got the ability to pull people in or push them away with your voice. That's a real talent.'

Later, as we washed our mugs in the tea room, some of the seasoned volunteers patted me on the shoulder, reiterating what the actress had said. Not sure how to respond, I peeled off and headed home. I felt mortified that the actress described my voice as a weapon—pushing and pulling my voice betrayed more of my feelings than I had been aware of. How often did it tear out of me wildly, clawing and striking?

Almost every year since graduating high school I'd lost my voice, usually only for three or four days. Occasionally, it vanished for almost a fortnight. During one of these long, frustratingly quiet spells, my sister fixed me a hot whisky. As she poured the hot amber liquid into a tumbler, she told me that she'd read about people losing their voice whenever they felt as if they hadn't been listened to. Unable to reply, I sipped on my whisky and burnt my tongue.

As loneliness seeps through your veins, it distorts your perspective. I learned from a behavioural psychologist that mapping out your circles of friends is a useful way of reorientating yourself to reality. The behavioural psychologist is a friend.

She had rung me towards the end of 2017 and told me that I was 'an essential part' of her life. She explained that during a period of acute anxiety, she wrote out a list of 'the people who mean the most to me'. As she thanked me for years of conversation and kindness, I felt a swell of pride. The unexpected compliment knocked me sideways and continued to give me gentle shocks of delight for weeks afterwards. Each time it came into my head, I considered myself anew, as someone useful and solid, a perspective that was in contrast to how I felt in 2016. Throughout 2017, since emerging from that year of recovery and reclusiveness, I had been keenly monitoring myself. Making sure that I wasn't pulling away from friends again. I formed habits of calling and texting.

Inspired by my friend, I mapped out my social network following Dunbar's bull's eye graphic—I filled in the first ring (five people who offer 'emotional support'), the second ring (fifteen people who are 'regular social partners'), and then the third ring (fifty people who I'd invite to a 'social party'). Each circle came quickly, but I stopped at the fourth ring (150 people in my 'broad reciprocal support and information-exchange network')—the task had served its purpose; I could see things more clearly. Most of the people in my circles had been there for the past decade, a few from the years before that, and a substantial proportion from the last twelve months. Despite the slow start since moving to Melbourne, I had been pursuing friendships.

The only consistent factor between the people I had befriended seemed to be that they all prioritised deep, engaging conversation. This made me think of an aspect of control that Hallberg and Carlsson didn't mention in their framework of coping: deaf people control their focus when socialising by being wholly present and attentive to others. What a rare gift we give.

I pictured Churchill huddled at his dinner table, surrounded by conversation, yet without any support. Initially I had considered everyone at the table as cruel and senseless. But now I wondered whether Churchill had attempted to renegotiate the terms of his friendships. Dunbar suggests that 'friendships are cognitively demanding because they are implicit social contracts—in effect, promises of future support'.

I've started to understand that deafness doesn't have to diminish a relationship, but it *should* change it. As I begin to ask my friends if I can sit in a certain chair at a dinner table or even suggest quieter venues, I am continually surprised. Not because they are so instantly accommodating, but because they remember each request. New rituals have folded into friendships—the tables selected are bathed in light; there's a pause prior to everyone sitting, *Fi, which seat would you like?*

And yet, even when warmly ensconced with company, loneliness lingers. The *physical* memory of it remains fresh, easily accessible, a cauterised edge on a deep cellular level. Even when I am not actively feeling lonely, I know that loneliness is still in my blood. This is what frightens me most of all.

On learning

I can remember precisely the moment when I peered into my own brain and saw my deeply rutted tracks of thought. It was the winter of 2018, I was sitting at the kitchen table in North Melbourne, my back to the weak afternoon sun. As I read *The New York Times* on my laptop, a single sentence triggered an insight about *how* I had been living for almost thirty years:

> Becoming disabled demands learning how to live effectively as a person with disabilities, not just living as a disabled person trying to become nondisabled.

At the time, I felt as if I was still failing to cope with every sphere of my life. This plain but pointed sentence—written by Rosemarie Garland-Thomson in the essay 'Becoming Disabled'—articulated the source of my anguish. It allowed me to clearly see the vast and shocking amount of mental space I devoted to trying to be nondisabled.

•

The word 'learning' unmoored me. People born with disabilities may need to undergo a process of 'becoming disabled'—that is, learning to live in your body as it is, rather than how it is measured by society.

I thought about how I had always divided my body in two distinct, non-symbiotic sections—hearing and deaf. My deafness was a vacant space that had to be circumnavigated or, at the very least, something I could willingly disassociate and distance myself from. In the last few years I had learned to first live alongside and then with my deafness. I had not yet learned to live inside it.

Disability is widely considered to be incompatible with living a complete and worthwhile life. Although I had worked in health-care for over a decade, I knew very little about disability beyond how to assess someone's loss of function or independence. I felt good helping people to become as normal as possible.

'This impulse to rescue people with disabilities from a discred-ited identity, while usually well meaning, is decidedly at odds with the various pride movements we've come to know in recent decades,' writes Garland-Thomson.

Even though healthcare has been shifting towards empowering patients, the underlying ethos remained unchanged: disabilities are deficits. Through rehabilitation exercises, manual therapy and patient education, I had been steering patients away from thoughts of 'giving up' and 'giving in'. I had learnt about disability discrim-ination and equality, but my internal ableism was still undeniable.

The idea that I could consider my deafness with pride felt too strange, too at odds with everything I had been taught about bodies. As I sat in front of the computer re-reading the article, Garland-Thomson's words coursed through me, connecting everything I had read and learnt over the past three years. It was like meeting myself for the first time.

Even after the sudden insight that afternoon, my body is still unlearning the habit of secrecy. Whenever somebody discovers that I am deaf, I react with churning terror. How do you build up a sense of robust pride when your body has taught itself to be fearful?

RELEASE

The smallest bone to pick

During December 2018 and into the new year, I was annoyed with my neighbours. Every night I lay awake for hours thinking hideous thoughts about them. Their air-conditioning unit, which sat just outside my bedroom window, droned loudly. The machine sounded vexed, overworked. How did they put up with it? Couldn't they just call somebody to repair it?

Then my fridge started to whir and groan. I hoped it would trundle on, and once I had a bit more money, I would buy a new one. Whenever I did the dishes, or unpacked groceries, I said a quick prayer to extend its life.

It was only when I stayed in Sydney with my parents for a week—sleeping in my childhood room and raiding their well-stocked fridge—that I realised the noises had followed me. The droning, humming and rattling was all in my head.

When I woke, the ringing was at its most insistent, rising from inside my skull and travelling out through my right ear. I read that tinnitus is the brain singing, stirring up noise. As the weather turned cold and the days shortened, the sad recital continued unabated.

The ringing rankled me. It made me gripe, loudly and at length. During my melodrama, I discovered that others also heard humming or buzzing sounds in their heads. My new housemate's boyfriend, a part-time DJ, said, 'That ringing? Yup, I hear it all the time. I have to turn up the beats to drown it out.' My sister told me on the phone from Tamworth that she heard a hum when her house was finally dark and she was settling into bed. Moving from inner-city Sydney to the country had made her tinnitus more noticeable. 'I try not to think about it,' she said. 'Unless there's a clock ticking, then that drives me mad.'

I took my sister's advice and tried to ignore it.

In January, she sent me an advertisement for a physiotherapy job at her local hospital. 'You should apply. You've been complaining about share-housing for months. Come live with me for a bit.'

Since moving to regional New South Wales two years earlier, my sister had sent me job advertisements about once a month. She texted me photographs of wide-open spaces, blazing sunsets. Videos of her dogs, all slobbery and joyful.

The role was a senior position; the remuneration would be life-changing, allowing me to experience the security of accumulated savings. I kept the advertisement open on my computer, looking at it throughout the day. I'd always dismissed her suggestion of moving to the country, and listed off all the reasons why I *had* to stay in Melbourne: work, study, friends, the theatre, galleries, coffee and so on. But it was true, I had been complaining: I'd had enough of the noise and chaos of share houses. Moving away for a while seemed like an appealing solution. It would be nice to live with family again. It might even allow my body to loosen up a little.

For weeks, my neck muscles had felt like ropes, thick and

knotted. Unable to turn my head, I swivelled my torso whenever I needed to look from left to right. My neck had not been this sore in years. The last time it had stiffened up, so completely that it felt fused, was when I had first moved to Melbourne. Within days of moving into that first flat near the Yarra, my neck had begun to ache. Night after night, I woke up with my head lifted off the pillow, hovering high and still. My right ear would be exposed to the night air, alert and listening—a habit I had developed from child-hood, occurring whenever I slept somewhere new. It had taken a week or so in each new share house before I lowered my guard. My head only settled once I feel settled in my new surrounds.

But now, despite living in North Melbourne for almost two years, my neck spasms lingered week after week, even after my routine of stretching, bending, twisting and deep muscle releases with a hard, spiky ball. No matter how much I tried to treat myself, every morning my neck was stiff again—because my body was always nervous come nightfall.

From my kitchen window, I watched as the insides of every other flat in the complex was carried up or down the stairs. It was a transient sort of place; nobody seemed to live there for more than six months at a time. But to me it seemed secure, even cosy. The building had thick walls, free of black mould, and the laundry only flooded every so often. Most of the rooms had glimpses of warm sunlight.

While I stayed, Alison and Megan moved on. It wasn't hard finding replacements. The rent was cheap, the location was central. On the edge of the CBD, it was where roads from each quadrant of the city intersected, ribboning out into expressways. Traffic was steady all day long, especially on weekends, when carloads of footy fans drove through. There was constant motion. And yet, to my ear, the thousands of cars sounded like the melodic curl of the sea. Soft, even soothing.

Nevertheless, I found myself becoming uneasy, even frightened of living there. My newest housemates liked to rave, play techno music, deep bass drone. As did their friends. Glitter matted the dining table. Feathers drifted, lost from the edges of costumes. Pre-drinks usually began hours after I'd gone to bed. My flatmates and their friends smoked on the balcony, littering the concrete with butts and matches. I lay in bed, reading John Cage's theories about silence—a state he suggested doesn't exist. I'd press my ear to the pillow, proving him wrong.

In the morning, when I walked into the living room, I had to step over sleeping bodies—on the couch, in the beanbags or in a large sunken air mattress. I'd slept through everything. For years I was proud of this gift I had. But now I was unsure. My housemates were casual with their keys. I'd come home to find strangers in the living room, eating our food and watching TV. Even more unnervingly, sometimes I'd arrive home to discover that the doors and windows had been left wide open. I never really knew if I was alone or not.

I tried to talk to my housemates, but the rhythm of the house was already well established. I began to lock myself into my room at night. As I fell asleep, I'd roll towards the safety of the walls, cocooning myself in a fort of pillows and plaster. When I woke, I needed to rub liniment into my neck muscles. By the time my sister sent me the hospital job advertisement, I was ready to move on.

Audiologists have a shorthand way of describing a run-of-the-mill hearing test result: 'on banana'. On a graph, the decibel range required to hear speech sits in a curved, banana shape. After the audiologist described my latest audiogram as 'off banana', I learned that I had acquired moderate hearing loss in my right ear. The clean symmetry between my good side and bad side had eroded.

The hearing test was a 'routine HR requirement'. Filling out the form for the job in Tamworth was the first time I had declared my deafness on an application. While ticking the box for sensory disability and writing down 'hearing loss' felt like a small act of bravery, it seemed to diminish the likelihood of an interview. But then I got one, followed swiftly by a job offer, and then a request for a health check. I had been flagged in the system.

Now, as I sat in the audiologist's office in North Fitzroy, I sobbed.

'I'm guessing you weren't expecting bad news.'

'No, not at all.'

She patted my knee and passed me a box of tissues.

'Sorry, I think I'm just premenstrual,' I blurted. Her expression softened as she readily accepted my lie. Not wanting to burden her with my messy emotions, it felt easier to explain them away with hormones. I wanted to give her an excuse not to ask me how I felt about the diagnosis. As always, I wanted to be a good patient.

'Ah well. The good news is that your hearing loss is a little unusual. You've lost some of the lower frequencies—they are ones we don't tend to use for speech—which is the opposite to what we would normally see in age-related hearing loss.'

'So it's not age-related? Does this mean that it's due to loud noise? I've tried to be careful.' I felt my throat tightening. 'I avoid loud noises as much as I can. Really I do.'

'I'm sure you try your best,' she said.

I focused on her small, pearl-coloured earrings in the shape of hearts. I was too embarrassed to look at her face, as my own felt flushed from crying.

'Besides,' she said, 'it doesn't fit that typical pattern.'

'So, what could it be?'

'Look, I'm not a specialist. It could be due to a number of different things.'

'I've got an appointment booked with an ENT, about my sinuses. Should I raise it with him?'

'Sure, why not. Why don't you get a cup of water from the cooler in the waiting room while I finish writing your report.'

The reception area had been a set for *Offspring*, the television series I had watched obsessively after breaking my arm. Photographs of the actors hung on every wall. Each scene prompted visceral recollections: my body wedged into the corner of my bed, my face lit by the laptop propped on my thighs, my stale, unrelenting loneliness. I slumped in the waiting-room chair, pulled down by muscle memory.

After the hearing test, I needed to have a doctor verify that I was physically capable of performing the role.

I went to a GP I had only seen once before. After reviewing my audiogram and the report noting my pre-existing and new hearing loss, he turned to me and said, 'I guess this means you wouldn't be able to do the job?'

'But I've already been offered the job. Besides, I've been a physiotherapist for almost a decade.'

'So, what's this for?'

'HR wanted it.'

He raised an eyebrow. My heart skipped a beat. I stayed quiet and still, hoping HR wouldn't revoke the job offer upon receiving the audiogram report.

Finally, the doctor picked up a pen and signed the form.

•

'So, what brings you in today?'

'I've been getting sinus pain.' I gave the ear, nose and throat specialist a potted history of my headaches. By way of wrapping up, I mentioned my recent hearing loss, pulling the audiogram out of my bag, then apologising for tacking it onto the appointment. 'It's just that the audiologist said it was a little unusual.'

'Let's have a quick look.' He spread the piece of paper out on the table. After a moment, he turned back towards me.

'How old are you?'

'Thirty-one.'

He nodded, then stood up. Methodically, he peered into each ear, tested the response of my ear drums to pressure, and passed a small camera up my nose. Then he sat down.

'I think you have otosclerosis.'

I recognised the name—I'd recently read a book about Beethoven, who most likely had the same condition.

Shit.

The specialist described how the smallest bone inside my ear, the stapes, was ossifying—growing bone. As it thickened, it was becoming less limber, less able to beat on the ear drum.

'It is an issue with conduction, how sounds travel through the ear's apparatus,' he explained, with the aid of a plastic model, the same one I had seen in countless audiological appointments, without ever looking at it closely. I kept my eyes on it now, willing them to stay dry.

He said it was possible the bones might eventually fuse together, becoming immobile, and sound would cease to ring through my ear. I thought of Beethoven, his wretched moods, his terrible sadness. Was that why I'd been feeling so frazzled the last few years? My greatest fear had been of losing the use of my 'good' ear. Ironically, just as I had come to terms with that eventuality, it has been occurring all along.

In an effort to reassure me, the specialist said it was difficult to estimate the progression of otosclerosis, given how rare the condition is. There is scant research, but it is known that it often starts in women in their late twenties.

'So, what now?'

'Most people elect to have their stapes surgically replaced. It's a terrifically effective procedure.'

I sat forward in my chair, admonishing my internal dialogue of despair. Of course there are treatments; this isn't the nineteenth century.

'But this option carries about a one per cent risk of completely deafening the ear. In your case, I'm afraid, there is simply no surgeon in Australia who would be willing to take that risk, as this is your only working ear.'

Straight after the appointment, back home, slumped in among boxes of books and a rucksack packed for my move to Tamworth, I began to research the condition. I told myself there was comfort in putting things in context. 'About ten per cent of adults have otosclerosis but in only about one per cent of the general population does it affect the stapes, or stirrup bone, where it can be detected by its interference with hearing.' This information was really not comforting at all.

No one is quite sure why the stapes starts to form a kind of exoskeleton. It shouldn't. Typically, the ear's apparatus finishes growing in the womb. And yet at some stage, perhaps in my late twenties, my stapes started to grow again. As if it suddenly no longer wanted to be the smallest bone in my body.

I visited the GP again for the final booster shot of vaccinations required to work in a public hospital. He told me that the condition was hereditary. 'Does anyone else in your family have it?'

'Not that I know of. My father has noise-induced hearing loss, but I don't know if anyone else has lost their hearing.'

I knew little about my family's medical history beyond that of my parents and siblings. I wasn't about to explain to him that the more distant family histories hadn't been passed on to my parents, that rural people had lived and died for hundreds of years without the stories of their bodies being catalogued in medical language— it all felt too far removed from the clinical confines of the doctor's office.

The first Irish poem I can recall reading was about the bog people, whose bodies were preserved in the wet ground, flesh still anchored to bone.

Thinking of deafness as ancestral was calming. If my stapes wasn't the smallest bone in my body, maybe it was the oldest.

I was referred to a surgeon, who told me I would be an ideal candidate for a Bone Anchored Hearing Aid (BAHA), essentially a bolt drilled into my skull, through which sounds would be conducted, bypassing my inner ear.

'And if we implanted it behind your left ear, we could eliminate your head shadow.'

She went on to explain how the hearing processor connected to the screw, which would allow me to 'keep up with technology'. As she talked, I thought about my shadow: I still hadn't forgotten how exposed I felt being surrounded by sound.

'Are you planning to have children?'

'Maybe? One day? Perhaps? I don't know.' I stumbled over my words.

'Pregnancy has been shown to accelerate the rate of hearing loss, but that shouldn't matter if you get the BAHA—the sound will travel past the stapes.'

I was still thinking about my shadow, so thick and comforting.

'Sorry, you're probably wondering about the cost?' said the surgeon, registering my silence.

She reassured me that the procedure would be covered by Medicare, as it is an implant. I was struck by how unfair the system is, with standard hearing aids classified as an out-of-pocket expense. Finally, she asked if I had any questions.

'What if I don't like the BAHA? Will I be stuck with it?'

She paused, and leaned back in her office chair. 'You don't have to connect the hearing processor, but you would be left with the bolt in your temporal bone.'

There are competing theories about the origins of the name 'temporal bone'. Some suggest it has been called the 'time bone' because the first signs of grey hair often appear there. Others argue that because you can feel blood pulsing through the superficial temporal artery en route to the brain, it is a ready reminder that time is marching on. Or perhaps it is a gesture towards the bone's thinness and connected to the Greek verb *temnion*—to wound in battle—as it is so vulnerable to a deathly blow.

The surgeon suggested that I think about the procedure and contact her when I felt ready. Later that afternoon, as I washed my hair, I lightly touched my skull until the water ran cold.

•

Between medical appointments I organised a storage unit, chased up the real estate agent, sourced cardboard boxes, donated books, cancelled my gym membership, updated my contact details for endless utility or subscription services, and showed up to work at the aged-care facility with bloodshot eyes and a ready smile. While I kept myself busy and on task, my feelings spiralled. My body shook whenever I thought about my ever-expanding shadow. My housemate found me weeping as I scrubbed the empty fridge. She stepped around me, filled a glass of water for herself and went back to watching television. I was grateful that I didn't have to explain my tears. By now, I wanted nothing more than to leave Melbourne and see my sister.

Every night I lay awake, listening to my brain drone. Despite unknowingly losing my hearing, the world had felt like it was becoming unbearably loud. But it was all in my head. The tinnitus tugged at my attention, an unassailable presence. I learned that as my hearing range shrank, my body was 'helpfully' filling in the gaps. Losing my ability to hear while gaining a deep unrelenting drone felt brutally ironic. How I missed the quietness in my body.

Approximately one in ten Australians have tinnitus, due to a range of factors, including prolonged noise exposure; head or neck injury; infections; increasing age; or being male. Or, as was almost certainly the cause of my tinnitus, hearing loss. The sounds of tinnitus differ from person to person, and shift from day to day. Some liken their tinnitus to *blowing like the wind* or *a swarm of bees*. In one case study, a woman describes her tinnitus as being like 'high ringing sonic cicadas on a hot summer's night...I have a physical sensation like a vibrating piercing needle.' Overwhelmingly, sufferers talk about their desire, and need, for silence.

Tinnitus has been labelled a 'medical enigma'. Part of the

controversy concerns the source of the sound. According to the current theory, the body's central nervous system generates the noises; quite literally, they arise from within. When brain scans of people with tinnitus are performed in silence, activity is still detected in the auditory cortex, proof that these sounds are not just delusions. The brain appears to be actively listening to itself ringing, humming, buzzing and whistling.

Tinnitus can cause distress, depression and fatigue, a corrosive trifecta. As the summer months dragged on, my mood dipped low. I tried to follow my sister's advice, but failed to ignore the sounds. Next, I tried to adjust my expectations, to think positively, or at least realistically. Up until now, I had only ever experienced absolute silence when I slept. Sleeping in a share-house had been straightforward; even when a collective of amateur DJs practised in the living room until daybreak, my sleep had been deep and undisturbed.

After snatching a few hours, I woke up feeling worn out by the incessant ringing. The sound felt like a constant reminder of otosclerosis. It took time to muster the energy to pull myself out of bed. I still had so much to organise before my flight.

Looking out the window of the small plane, I was staggered by the vast expanse of dry earth. I had read about the drought, but I hadn't fathomed its endless reach. I arrived in Tamworth, in north-west New South Wales, on a Sunday afternoon at the end of March 2019. The heat was shocking. My sister greeted me with a hug at the airport arrivals lounge.

After she'd driven us back to her house, she showed me my room. The linen was bright blue, the pillows plumped. She poured me a glass of wine and cooked me an enormous dinner, and as we ate, she told me about living in the country—the pace was less intense. She couldn't imagine returning to Sydney.

That night my tinnitus rang high and clear.

The following morning, I started my new job. My manager took me on a tour of the building, set into a hill on the edge of the hospital campus. When she opened the back door, she scanned the ground before stepping out. Once we were outside, she moved swiftly, glancing around the patio.

'There was a snake sleeping out here during the summer,' she said. 'Good spot, eh?'

She introduced me to the team. With firm, friendly handshakes they asked where I'd come from. When I said Melbourne, each asked: 'But originally?' Ireland, I said reflexively, still unable to break the habit of concealing the truth. They nodded, before responding with the quiet, tense refrain: 'I hope you've brought the rain with you.'

My manager showed me to a large sunlit room, my private office, fitted out with a set of stairs for rehabilitation exercises; hooks where I could tie elastic resistance bands for strengthening exercises; and a long countertop for patients to steady themselves as they practised balance exercises. The walls were covered in anatomical drawings of the cardiovascular system—the heart, lungs, arteries and veins. I remembered that the Auslan sign for *blood* is the combination of the signs *red* and *flow*. I flexed and extended my fingers, comforted by the warmth and quietness of my new space.

I wondered whether my manager would ask me about my deafness.

It took several weeks for me to settle into town. Unlike my life in Melbourne—where I went out a few nights a week to meet up with friends, attend book clubs, author talks or art installations—now I did little outside of work. My sister invited me to dinners and drinks with her friends, but I shrugged off most of the invites. She understood how taxing I found pubs and restaurants.

Although my days were slow, I still didn't sleep well. Or rather I fell asleep, but then woke after midnight and lay there for hours listening to my brain, waiting to lose consciousness again.

My job in falls-prevention involved conducting strength and balance assessments, and listening to patients' stories about falling over, the injuries they sustained, and sometimes how they lay for hours on the ground before being found. During these very personal conversations, they described their new-found fear of stairs, uneven ground, car parks, shopping centres, their own bathrooms, and admitted to feeling embarrassed by their anxieties. They reassured me, again and again, that they hadn't always been like this, that they used to be so carefree, so unaware of their bodies.

After work, as I hung out washing, I thought about how hazardous a task it would be for some of my patients. A flock of cockatoos flew low over the backyard. Wings stretched wide and brilliant against the darkening sky. They returned the next evening, and the next. I began to wait for them, my body unwinding whenever I watched them wheel through the air.

Once I'd found a narrow track along the Peel river, I realised how much I needed to move my body each day—to walk off my own anxieties, my attentiveness to sound and voices.

The hospital car park was full of utes, four-wheel drives, campervans and the occasional tractor. Patients travelled hours from around the region for specialist appointments, surgery and comprehensive care. The helipad was in constant use, transporting more complex cases to Newcastle or Sydney.

My job involved driving to towns scattered across a region the size of England. I would assess elderly people's risk of falling and prescribe balance exercises. Most days, there were delays, whenever cattle were grazing on Crown land. Temporary road signs announced safe speed limits, which dropped from 100 kilometres to 40 kilometres for long stretches of the road to Gunnedah or Barraba. The cattle trundled slowly, their heads lowered, searching for grass, unbothered by the slow procession of cars.

I got used to the rough roads, but my eyes were in a permanent squint, still adjusting to the light in New England. The sheer expanse of sky, so broad and blue that even a cavalcade of clouds failed to shield the sun. The fields were bald, weather-beaten.

By mid-May, I felt as if I had settled into my sister's house. She automatically switched on closed captions when we watched TV or ensured she had my attention before asking me a question. It felt effortless to live with someone who naturally accommodated my hearing loss. I tried not to think about the future. I stayed within the weave of routine: wake, eat, work, walk, sleep. The mindless sameness of each day slid over me like a balm. At night, my tinnitus rang without reprieve; there was nothing to mask my brain's warble.

My sister would leave for work before me, starting her nursing shift at 7.30 a.m. I got up early and ate breakfast with her. We took turns cooking. Every Monday morning, I bought eggs from the secretary at work. I loved opening the carton, thrilling at the dozen different shades of beige, so unlike the orangey uniformity of store-bought eggs. At home, I gently washed the stray feathers and grit from the shells, patted them dry, and rehomed them in the carton. Each morning, as I cracked the eggs open, the yolks slid out in a burst of joyous yellow.

After breakfast, my sister would rush out the door, I'd wash our dishes, turn off the gas heater and wave the pups goodbye, before walking to work. One afternoon a few weeks later, my sister sent me a text: *Can you please make sure you switch off the heater before you leave the house?*

I texted back, apologising. But I was confused: I was usually so diligent about turning it off. I resolved to be more careful with my morning routine. A few days later, my sister raised it again over dinner.

'Can you please start switching the heater off? It's getting kind of annoying.'

'But I have been. I even double-check that the bars aren't glowing red before I leave.'

'But you haven't been switching off the fan.'

'There's a fan?'

'Can't you hear it?'

'No.'

As she pointed to the small switch, I wondered what other sounds were slipping away from me.

For the June long weekend, my sister and I drove out of Tamworth along the Waterfall Way and stopped at Wollomombi Falls, in a valley of deep silence. Once out of the car, we stopped our loud chatter and walked quietly along the bush track, not wanting to disturb the stillness. At one of the lookouts, we stood with our hands curled over the railing, staring at the monumental bare cliff face. Breathtaking also by its absence of water. We read the information boards diligently, and stood in reverence in front of the faded photographs of water flowing over the lip of the gorge.

•

A friend, a poet, told me that Judith Wright grew up in the New England region. And that she, too, had otosclerosis. Years earlier, I'd read a poem by Wright describing birds flying on the wing. While my memory of the words had faded, in Tamworth I began to feel a sense of awe whenever I saw birds, feathered and full, moving through the air. In the evenings, I read all of Wright's work, selfishly hoping it would recount the process of her body building new, unnecessary bone. I picked each line of her poems clean, looking for any mention of deafness.

Her eye roved over the region, which she described as 'clean, lean, hungry country'. Her poems also talked about water. The rivers she used to sit next to, the waters she watched slide over rock and funnel through fields, have all gone now.

In 'Northern River', Wright captured the enormity of the sea, both in complex emotion and geographical scale: 'the sea that encompasses/all sorrow and delight/and holds the memories/of every stream and river.' I repeated the words as though reciting an incantation; each word held softly in my mouth felt true. Everything comes back to the sea. We too are tidal, pulled by the moon, rising and flattening, immersed in our own feeling.

'God, it's got so dry, there isn't even roadkill anymore,' a colleague said as we ate lunch in the staff tea room.

That afternoon, as I walked to the shops, I saw the cockatoos gathered on the side of the road. They scattered as I approached, flying up to the telegraph wire. They had been feasting on stale bread. Of course, I thought, no wonder they flew so low over town—they were hungry. The bare earth was breaking into dust; there was nothing of sustenance for hundreds of kilometres.

In company

At work, I listened to classical music. At least for brief periods of the day, the bold, sweeping scores coming through my right earbud masked the drone in my head. Next I tried listening to rain. In the Rain Library on Spotify, each soundtrack had a description of its particular rain: rain under a steel bridge, monsoon rain, rain on a tin roof, thunderstorm in an open field, dripping rain. I was drawn to rain recorded in rainforests, where the earth reacts to the downpour and water gathers in pools and rolls over rocks. The sound made me feel as if I was lying on a forest floor, cool and energised.

From the number of downloads, I could imagine the thousands of people listening to the recordings in houses and offices across Australia and beyond, rain-soaked and serene.

But I soon stopped. Some of my colleagues and patients were suffering from drought stress—their family farms were under immense financial hardship and they were forced to buy feed for their livestock. It felt extravagant, cruel even, to listen to rain.

According to the internet forums I wandered through, many tinnitus sufferers try to mask their tinnitus. There are whole communities online who trade tips and soundtracks. The trick, apparently, is to find something that matches the sounds in your head, which can help externalise the experience, and perhaps reduce the physical and mental drain.

I spent long evenings clicking through clips on YouTube, trying to find a sound that matched the one in my head. The sounds have been conveniently categorised by colour according to their frequency. Pink noise, one of the most popular frequencies, is considered smoother, more mellow than white noise and has been compared to TV static or the sound of the shower running. After playing several pink noise soundtracks, I decided the pitch was too high. Next, I tried brown noise, a deep-bellied rumble, which I discovered sat outside my hearing range. Blue noise sounded closer to the drone in my head. Under each video there were comments of appreciation and thanks—they are the most wholesome threads I have ever seen online. The relief among the community members was palatable. After hours of searching, I landed on a series of sound combinations: a sandwich, as they are sometimes called, of pink and brown and blue noise matched my tinnitus. I turned up the volume and sank into the sound.

And then, after a few days, the sandwich stopped working. Instead of masking my tinnitus, it made me feel vexed each time I pressed play. Whenever I yearned for silence, my brain responded, amplifying the drone. I continued searching for a solution.

Tinnitus has been recorded as far back as the seventh century BC. Yet even after more than a millennium's worth of medical advances, it is difficult to treat. A raft of pharmaceuticals from antihistamines, diuretics and antidepressants to anticonvulsants have been trialled without any particular effectiveness. There is little scientific evidence that acupuncture, herbal remedies containing ginko biloba, low-power lasers or ear candles work any better. Accounts of surgical interventions are alarming: case studies of cutting both auditory nerves was proof enough that the brain, and not the outside world, is the source of these incessant sounds.

The focus has shifted from finding a cure to improving the quality of life for individuals. Currently, the most popular form of treatment is cognitive behavioural therapy—equipping tinnitus sufferers with a series of strategies to dampen the swell of feelings that accompanies the sound—to help them to reach a place of acceptance. This was the exact opposite of the approach I had been taking to manage the noises in my head. I had been too nervous to write about tinnitus, or specifically my tinnitus: I was worried that if I thought about the droning noise openly and deliberately, it would somehow become hardwired into my brain. Or, more worryingly, that my attention would amplify the noise. Instead, whenever I became conscious of the humming, I swung my gaze around the room; played music loudly; started conversations; walked quickly and with purpose; began meal prep for the week, clanging pots off the stove, boiling the kettle; anything to stop myself from focusing on the hum. This, I learned, is classified as a panic response.

The success of acceptance-based treatments can be measured using the 'Tinnitus Acceptance Questionnaire' (TAQ), which gauges an individual's relationship with the sounds they hear. Even before I was halfway through the questionnaire, I knew I had not accepted my tinnitus. That would mean having to accept my otosclerosis, which felt impossible.

As the weeks passed, my dreamscape took on strange qualities. I was strumming a ukulele, playing feather-soft scales for what felt like hours. In another dream, I was attempting to play in an Aussie Rules game. During the dream, as my uncoordinated body ran and tumbled and bumped into more skilful players, I could hear the sirens wailing, the crowd whistling and yelling, feet stomping, hands slapping. When I woke up, I felt rested.

Later, when talking with friends, I discovered that my dreams weren't strange; rather, they were quite normal. Having always slept with my hearing ear pressed into my pillow, I'd never experienced noises like pouring rain, rushing wind or heavy footsteps permeating my dreams. In fact, prior to having tinnitus, sound had seldom featured in my dreamscapes. Now, as I lost my hearing, my brain was playing with sound. I couldn't decide if it meant my subconscious was wildly ironic or deeply sentimental.

Exhausted from the sounds in my head, I tried to think of the buzzing as something belonging to my body, as obvious and unthreatening as a shadow. That felt forced. I tried to make the droning familiar, as though it were a friend or a form of company. That too required an impossible degree of cognitive dissonance. Then, instead of trying to impose a narrative, I tried to listen, both to the sound and to my reaction. It took practice. At first, I shied away from my anger, not wanting to acknowledge it at all. In the mornings, I lay still in bed, simply noting my reactions, instead of trying to wrestle or suppress them. It took effort. I tried to treat it as a priority. As I pegged out my washing, I thought: yes, there you are, my body. As I walked my sister's two pups, their bodies waggling with joy, I copied their loose-legged stride and tried to think of my body as equally full of verve. At night, as I lay still and my brain buzzed the loudest it had all day, I breathed deeply, rubbing my belly in slow circles, as though trying to still a restless child.

On some days, for up to several hours at a stretch, the dull droning folded itself into my other bodily sounds—sniffing, gurgling, rumbling—and became just another ambient feature of my internal soundscape. On other days, however, especially on days when I was high-strung from the effort of listening, my tinnitus became unbearably shrill.

Anxiety has been identified as a trigger for tinnitus. Now, I think of my tinnitus as a siren. It has made me consciously aware of whenever I am experiencing deaf anxiety.

Mostly my anxiety is triggered by particular circumstances: rooms with poor acoustics and dim lighting; soft or muffled voices; background noise; large groups scattered across the expanse of a room. In these instances, when I am struggling to hear, my brain begins to screech with unease. Annoyance descends on me, hot and mean. Sometimes, when I don't try to shepherd or suppress my annoyance, my tinnitus dissolves quickly. But, more often than I'd like to admit, my body becomes tense and resistant and I'm reminded that my stapes is thickening, that these difficulties of navigating the hearing world will only intensify.

But now, instead of suppressing my worries, I try to address them, reminding myself that being deaf is not a terrible thing, not at all. While this process of confronting my anxieties does not immediately dampen my tinnitus, with time, my shock and anger about the diagnosis of otosclerosis has softened.

It obvious to me now that I can't trick myself into a false sense of acceptance of the noise in my head, in my whole being. Achieving a sense of acceptance is not an act of stasis or submission. My body only settles back into a softer, steadier rhythm when I engage in an ongoing negotiation with the world around me, when I listen to what my body is saying.

Location

On my work desktop, I kept a shortcut to the Sign Bank dictionary, a series of videos, each only a few seconds long. Whenever I got a chance, I randomly clicked through the index and practised signs. Even though I was alone in my physiotherapy office, I kept my hands low, hovering over the keyboard, hooking and curling my fingers into the shapes on the screen. My vocabulary grew in a slow, eclectic way, as I learned signs such as *egg beater*, *gardener*, *canapes*, *jigsaw*, which, of course, without regular use and no one to sign with, quickly fell from my hands forgotten.

I got to know the faces and bodies of the people in the online dictionary: the woman with cascading curls that I always looked at before taking notice of her hands, the man with cropped hair and exceedingly upright posture, the other man, with round, impish features, who always seemed to be on the verge of smiling. But, much like in the manual, there was little motion in their faces.

I began to use my hands more freely as I spoke, hoping to maintain my loose grasp of Auslan grammar. Using different tenses was especially confusing, so I made an effort to remind myself of how time is represented spatially.

In Auslan, time sits around the body like a compass: the past sits behind us, the present is within us and the future lies ahead. Yet, in practical terms, time can't exist on a linear plane. The majority of signs occur in front of the body; when signing about the past you don't simply hook your hands behind your back. Instead, temporal shifts are organised around 'timelines': the deictic timeline (extends from the signer's dominant shoulder and runs perpendicular to their body, representing specific units of time such as *yesterday*, *tomorrow*, *next year*), the anaphoric timeline (runs diagonally and indicates anything that is not happening in that moment, but whose temporality is established by the context of the conversation) and the sequence timeline (sits parallel to the body and represents an ordering of events).

On paper, the timelines were easy to map and contain. But in conversation, I became disorientated as time spun along each axis. It was only when I started to think of my face as a clock around which my hands rotated that deictic time started to make more sense.

Yesterday: Place your right index finger on your right cheek with the nail facing backwards. Now slide your finger forwards along your cheek.

Tomorrow: Place your right finger on your cheek with the nail facing upwards, run your finger forwards tracing the curve of your right cheekbone.

It took constant repetition for me to remember how my fingernails related to time, especially when they spun several times when signing *next week*, *last month* or *next year*.

When I conversed with my colleagues in the tea room, I moved my hands vigorously to indicate the passage of time. Eventually, after several of them pointed out how 'theatrical' and 'dynamic' I was, I made my gestures smaller.

Although I had intended to be more open and honest about my hearing loss, I still avoided telling my new colleagues that I was deaf. I wasn't sure how to talk about otosclerosis, particularly as my condition was progressing along a timeline that I couldn't predict. I was discovering that the process of losing my hearing wasn't a slow fading out of sound. It was a much more muddling process. Sounds became garbled. Some days were worse than others. I tried to preserve my energy and focus by resting, meditating and being more deliberate with my attention, which only amplified my tinnitus, making voices more difficult to decipher.

One colleague mentioned that she was enrolled in an Auslan course at a local neighbourhood centre.

'It's only six weeks. It's been fun. I thought it might help when I chat with older patients.'

'That sounds brilliant!' I explained that I had been learning Auslan in Melbourne but hadn't found anything when googling classes in Tamworth.

'I don't think they advertise the course online.'

'Do you have her contact details?'

'I'll pass you her email address. You wouldn't be able to call her. She's *completely* deaf,' my colleague said almost reverently.

After a few emails, Kathy agreed to give me lessons. She arrived at my sister's house on a Wednesday afternoon in June. The weather, unlike in Melbourne, was still sunny and warm. We sat across from one another.

It had been over a year since I'd conversed with anyone in Auslan. I felt exposed and shy. I couldn't fade into the background like I could at a meet-up at the pub.

Realising that I had oversold my abilities via email, Kathy pointed around the room, *so who lives here?*

I told her about my sister, then my family in Sydney. Then she told me about hers. I sweated through the hour trying to remember basic phrases.

When she left, I marked our next lesson in my diary, my handwriting trembly with relief and satisfaction.

During our conversations my hand regularly touched my temple. The signs—*understand*, *forget*, *think*—all originate there. Often, mid-sentence, my mind went blank and I signed *I can't remember*. Fed up with myself, and desperate not to break the flow of our conversations, I began fingerspelling the word for each sign that I had forgotten.

It wasn't the best solution. I would get lost in a word and seize up; each error felt cataclysmic. I shrank in my chair, a shy schoolchild once more.

Kathy didn't allow for sloppiness and patiently pointed out my spelling errors. I kept going, for sometimes five or six attempts, until I spelled the word correctly. After a few weeks of marginal improvement in my fingerspelling, Kathy told me I needed to practise more.

This, she tapped her fingers, ticking off each vowel, *is not real signing*. Then, to make sure I understood, she said aloud, 'You need to stop thinking about English and start thinking in pictures.'

•

I later learned that Kathy was just being polite—fingerspelling is like shoehorning English into an Auslan conversation. It doesn't fit. It is the equivalent of having a half-written and half-spoken conversation. In Auslan, fingerspelling is only reserved for nouns—the names of people, places and everyday objects. Even so, many common nouns have become signs. I used to think it was only to speed up the process of communication, but each sign has a story. For instance, *Sydney* is the first three fingers of each hand coming together to form a triangular shape, indicating the Sydney Harbour Bridge. The sign for *Melbourne* is the right-hand swooping under the chin, representing the curve of the southern coastline. Signs can also mark a moment in time: the sign for *Darwin* is the right index finger spinning downwards, Cyclone Tracey.

Over the weeks, Kathy taught me the sign for *Tamworth*: tap the right temple, first with a closed hand and then with an open hand, like doffing a large Akubra. The sign for the neighbouring town of *Armidale*: tap the left forearm twice, which is a play on the word 'arm' and the town's pride in its two large roundabouts. My favourite was the sign for the town *Singleton*: the straps of a singlet.

People also have sign names, which have been given to them by the Deaf community. Most names articulate a distinctive characteristic such as the individual's curly hair or a visible tattoo. Some older people have names that designate the number of their locker at Deaf school. Each time I spelled my name out, I wondered if I'd ever have a sign all of my own.

Sign language is passed from hand to hand, and signs are often imbued with Deaf history. The sign for *Perth* is the letter P in American Sign Language—the second finger points straight ahead and the third finger points down. Now, keep your fingers still as you swing your wrist up then back down—a movement to indicate that the city is far away. The handshape is a throwback to the schooling system in Perth, which used the single-hand ASL alphabet from 1868 until 1927.

The histories of signs are not always clear-cut, or have been lost when passed through thousands of hands. It has been suggested, for instance, that the sign for *rich* represents stroking fine garments worn by the elite. Other signs are incredibly specific to a time, place or even person. One sign for *library* originally meant *hairclip*, the sign name of the librarian at a school for the deaf in Victoria.

The earliest known written record of sign language was created by John Bulwer in 1648. He described signs that were used by two deaf brothers. Some of the descriptions closely resemble signs used in contemporary British Sign Language (BSL), Auslan and New Zealand Sign Language (NZSL), including *good*, *bad*, *wonderful*, *shame*, *congratulate* and *jealous*. It strikes me that these emotive words—raw, distinct feelings—have remained unchanged for hundreds of years.

The ongoing legacy of colonisation can't be separated from the origins of Auslan. There are dozens of Indigenous sign languages throughout Australia. These are the world's oldest sign languages and are completely different from Auslan.

Auslan developed from BSL, introduced to Australia by settlers. Given Australia's huge expanse, two main dialects quickly emerged: Northern (New South Wales and Queensland) and Southern (the other states and territories). The deaf school established in Melbourne in 1860 used a dialect of BSL from London, and the deaf school in Sydney, which had opened only a few weeks earlier, used a dialect from Edinburgh.

Moving from Victoria to New South Wales meant that I

switched dialects. Was that why I felt lost when signing with Kathy? After consulting the Sign Bank and a series of textbooks, I learned that, in some instances, the same sign is used in both dialects for different words. The sign for *beach* in Victoria means *yesterday* in New South Wales.

As I researched both dialects, I sometimes had an instant preference for a new sign, and wanted to use it immediately. This was the case with *blue*, which in the Northern dialect is the right hand arching over the left hand like a wave, whereas in the Southern dialect it is the right hand rubbing the back of the left hand. I made wave after wave: *blue, blue, blue.*

I became greedy, wanting to use both dialects rather than choosing one. The sign for *dog* is a thigh-slap in Sydney, as if saying: come here, pup! In Victoria you form a loose fist, as though holding onto a leash. Both perfect signs. An equally perfect pair include the signs for *cat*—I'd been taught a soft, stroking movement, whereas Kathy taught me a whisker-like shape. I became determined to learn as much as possible, clicking through video after video on Sign Bank.

But despite all my revision between lessons, my conversational skills didn't improve. If anything, I got worse. I tripped myself up now that I had multiples of each sign. Kathy stared at me in confusion as I started and stopped sentences. After one particularly jumbled monologue, she signed *stop*.

You're doing. She took her hands and twisted them together several times. *Mess.*

Sorry, I think out signs. I hoped that she understood I meant that I was thinking out loud.

Just sign, okay.

Yes.

She looked at me for a moment, then pulled out her phone, scrolled through her camera roll, and passed it to me. Pictures of fields. Kathy rapped the table. I looked up.

See, snow. Her hands ran diagonally, snow lightly falling from each fingertip. *My home.*

P-r-e-t-t-y

Kathy stroked her chin. *Pretty.*

I raised my hands, fingers fluttering. Then I stroked my chin. *Snow pretty.*

She told me about her weekend, the sudden, unseasonal dump of snow over the Great Diving Range, the snowman her daughter made. She fingerspelled signs that I didn't understand.

After that lesson I felt relaxed. Usually, I was drenched in sweat—I assumed it was from nervous energy, but it struck me that for the past few months I had been signing *at* Kathy, flinging out streams of signs, rather than signing *with* her. It was my habitual compulsion to retain a sense of control whenever I felt uncertain. I was still treating sign language as if it were a location I would arrive at one day, if I could just study hard enough. The truth is, conversing in Auslan requires continual focus and flexibility. The only way I would ever gain a degree of fluency would be if I learned to direct my attention beyond my own body, with all its fear and vanity.

After a flight to Sydney, my right ear started to ache. At first the pain was dull, but within hours of landing it had intensified. After a day of me rubbing my jaw and temple, complaining about the pain, Mum sent me to the doctor.

'You obviously have an ear infection,' she said to me in a brisk tone.

The doctor confirmed her diagnosis and prescribed me ear drops. The drops sealed my ear canal. My world was now without sound. During dinner that night, I pushed food around my plate, occasionally I looked up and saw that my parents and brothers were talking. I looked down.

The next morning, Mum rushed into my room, a look of panic on her face. She must have been startled to find me still asleep. She grabbed my phone off the floor.

I watched her lips moving, eventually realising that she was asking me how to turn off the alarm. My phone's alarm—a rapid, high-pitched beeping I can usually hear from several metres away, and impossible to sleep through—had been going for over twenty minutes. The incident left us both unsettled.

A fortnight later, when I was back in Tamworth and my hearing had returned, Mum called to ask how my Auslan lessons were going.

'Good, I think. I'm slow.'

'Don't worry, keep practising. You'll be quick soon enough.'

After hanging up, I cried. I was relieved that she was beginning to understand why I felt it was so pressing, so urgent for me to learn the language.

Eventually, Kathy and I fell into a conversational rhythm. At the beginning of each lesson we talked about the weather. As the months went on, I learned the signs for drought, rules, restrictions, wind, fire and hail. We talked anxiously about the smoke that hung over the town, stinging our eyes, sticking to our skin. On the Fires Near Me app, we studied the red alerts multiplying as we approached summer, and we lamented the areas that had already been razed. The conversation about pretty snow seemed so long ago.

In parallel

When I thought back to the summer when I learned that my ear bones were hardening, my memories alternated between faint outlines and firmer, almost brutally cemented recollections. I had been creating two parallel streams of memory. There were moments I was keen to fix in my mind—the expanse of sky, the yellow of eggs, the elegance of birds in flight. Then there were the memories that lacked shape, obscured by a gauze of terror, that returned in awful flashes: the memory of sitting on the plane from Melbourne to Sydney, trying to figure out how to tell my parents about the otosclerosis diagnosis; the sobs that rankled in my chest when I stood alone in a boxed-up kitchen, my hands submerged in the warm sudsy water; emailing and texting close friends, letting them know the news, drafting each message to sound casual and untroubled.

I only recognised that this wilful process of memory-making and erasing was occurring when a surgeon suggested that there had been a misdiagnosis. I had flown down to Melbourne in June 2019 for a surgical review. Although I had yet to decide whether I wanted to have a BAHA inserted into my skull, it felt good to be back in the city. My trip coincided with a writers' festival, and I planned to meet up with friends for dinner and drinks.

The surgeon was apologetic. The CT and MRI scans taken at Footscray Hospital six months earlier had been misfiled.

'I wish I had the scans in front of me. The condition is so rare, it's highly unlikely that it's actually otosclerosis.'

For a brief week, my heart swelled and for the first time in months I felt lighter, less agitated. Feeling free and untethered, I let my mind roam. I could read and *think* again.

And then the surgeon emailed with another apology. The scans of my skull had confirmed that my bones were indeed hardening. As the feeling of agitation returned, I realised it was panic—panic I had been trying to suppress. The week without worry had clarified that my apprehension was not so much a fear of silence and miscommunication as a sense of heavy, unrelenting responsibility. For now, I would need to work harder, save money, for the day when my body would go beyond 'reasonable adjustments'. For when I would need to find another use for my hands.

In marginalia

The casual references to eugenics laced throughout research about deafness didn't stop me from trawling through scientific databases. Every so often, there was a direct quote from a research subject. As they described their deaf body, their Deaf life, I couldn't help writing in the margins—Yes! Yes! I feel this too!

'I don't want to be labelled…' said one subject. 'I don't want people to be like, that's the deaf girl. I don't want to have that label. I want people to see me apart from that.' When asked would she take 'normal' hearing if it were 'magically offered' to her, she replied: 'Deafness is part of who I am…It's made me who I am. And if anything, it makes me a more well-rounded person. So, I think I'd say no.'

I ran my highlighter over the page, illuminating the text in neon yellow. I was reading a transcription of my own thoughts. In these instances of recognition, I also scribbled questions in the margins. Questions I was desperate to ask the research subjects—I wanted more insight, more intimacy.

Deaf writer and academic Donna McDonald describes the

complex loss that comes with a diagnosis of deafness:

> [F]ar from being a death sentence, the diagnosis of deafness
> simply propels a child into a different life, not a lesser life.
> Evidently, a different sort of silence has been created over
> the years; not the silence of hearing loss but the silence of
> lost, unspoken stories.

Researching deafness often left me raw with nervous rage. I found so many instances of deaf bodies being described as damaged. But I risked enduring that sick, electrified feeling for the chance to discover personal accounts. Reading, highlighting and writing questions in the margins was my way of ensuring that these stories weren't just lost in an archive. There was companionship in marginalia, as well as sorrow.

I began to broaden my search, away from scientific and medical data, towards sociological and ethnographic studies of deafness. That's when I noticed uncanny overlaps between my personality traits and those of other deaf people—scheduling each day and sticking rigidly to plans; being overly prepared; striving to feel occupied and busy; a willingness to detach from emotions and take comfort in logic; a reluctance to trust others; conflict avoidance—all aspects of my personality I had always resented.

Through reading, I began to appreciate why I could never change myself: living in a hearing-centric society is exhausting, and it takes endurance and ingenuity to survive. My patterns of behaviour create a constellation of control: monitoring food intake, scheduling sleep, setting incremental and long-term career goals, delaying gratification, tracking relaxation time. My behaviour revolves around the need for certainty. Within myself, within the world.

•

I gasped when I first read the phrase Deaf Gain. A sudden, shocked exhalation.

'Why had all the doctors told me that I was losing my hearing, and not a single one of had told me that I was gaining my deafness?' asked Aaron Williamson, the English performance artist who coined the phrase.

Deaf Gain suggests that there are benefits to being deaf, for both individuals and society. The word 'gain' is round and pert with possibility—profit, growth, yield, boost—dazzling with the promise of community, language and art, shared experiences that mean not having to explain or justify one's body.

Reading a complete inversion of the 'normal' narrative of deafness was both thrilling and disorientating. Without my realising it, my understanding of deafness had always been defined by absence. The phrase 'hearing loss' highlights an obvious absence, but I was also lacking a vocabulary or even the ability to talk about deafness without an undertow of apology.

Although I was exhilarated by the concept, I shrank away from it. It seemed impossible to think of otosclerosis as anything other than a loss. And while I liked to think I had accepted my pre-existing deafness, I still reflexively minimised my deafness. At best, it stayed unseen.

Much of my life has been defined by language and my desire to understand it. First by sight, with spelling and reading. Next by concept, for comprehension and conversational control. Then by touch, connecting concepts of pain and injury to bodies. I spent so many years organising my thoughts—'organise' as in the medical process of divvying up the soft, wet mess in the centre of the body into distinct organs. But Deaf Gain troubled this sense of order. As long as I considered my own body in strictly medical language, the concept would feel incongruous. I spent weeks trying to *think* my way towards feeling a sense of Deaf Gain.

Finally, one Friday night, after a glass of wine, I tried to feel it. I closed my eyes. I imagined the fault line between my 'good' and 'bad' sides closing up, the void filling in: my shadow stretched from left to right, encircling my skull, filling my chest, reaching down the length of each limb, pooling in my toes and fingertips. My body was undivided. It was all deaf.

My breath caught in my throat. I opened my eyes, blinked hard. My thoughts felt forced. While I could map the flow of blood through my cardiovascular system, remapping my deafness felt contrived and entirely unconvincing, more philosophical than physical.

The image of the fault line didn't leave me. Its distinct margins felt as much a part of my body as my lungs, arse and elbows. My body couldn't forget anything it had been told about deafness: you are bad, broken and a burden.

In a staff meeting, one of the podiatrists mentioned that they often had patients confide in them, disclosing instances of abuse, trauma or anecdotes that still filled them with embarrassment.

'It's amazing what people tell you when you're working on their feet. They're sitting in a position of power, no eyes on them, and their most personal stories pour out.'

An occupational therapist agreed. 'People tend to tell us the most personal things during shower assessments. There is something about the intimacy of bathroom spaces. Even though they are unrobed and already so exposed, they reveal their secret histories.

Maybe it *is* to do with the lack of eye contact?' She paused. 'Yes, perhaps that's it. My patients do also tend to unburden themselves when we're in the car—as soon as my eyes are on the road, they start to open up.'

I sat quietly, unable to add anything to the conversation. Having spent so long concealing my own worries and fears, I'd never considered how my need to look so intently at others could be a way of silencing them.

Instead of stewing on this discovery, I sought comfort in reading more deaf stories.

As his deafness progressed, Oliver Sacks wrote about the unpredictability of hearing. He took to recording each instance that he was aware of mishearing words:

> I carefully record these in a little red notebook labeled 'PARACUSES'—aberrations in hearing, especially mishearings. I enter what I *hear* (in red) on one page, what was actually *said* (in green) on the opposite page, and (in purple) people's reactions to my mishearings, and the often far-fetched hypotheses I may entertain in an attempt to make sense of what is often essentially nonsensical… Every mishearing is a novel concoction…The hundredth mishearing is as fresh and as surprising as the first.

Sacks used his expertise as a neurologist to understand his experience: 'While mishearings may seem to be of little special interest, they can cast an unexpected light on the nature of perception.'

In conversation, the brain is poised, ready to fill in gaps in speech so smoothly that we don't register the effort. In trying to determine how this occurs, a group of researchers from the University

of California tested how the human brain performs in noisy environments. They created a list of words that are acoustically identical
expect for a critical phoneme. The list included couplings such as:
faster/factor; voices/choices; novel/nozzle; rigid/ridges; appoint/
anoint; babies/rabies. During the experiment, the key part of the
word was replaced by a broadband noise. The subjects readily
identified one word or the other, never both. They had performed
'phoneme restoration': their brains rebuilt the shape of the sounds
so smoothly that they were unaware there had been a gap or distor-
tion. Are hearing people even aware that they are vulnerable to
misunderstandings? Perhaps it is better to be deaf? It keeps you
alert and curious.

For hundreds of years, stories of deafness have been told by
hearing people: the deaf are fallible and endure grim lives. Yet as
I read Sacks' essay, I felt revitalised by the endless creativity of the
deaf brain:

> And yet there is often a sort of style or wit—a 'dash'—
> in these instantaneous inventions; they reflect, to some
> extent, one's own interests and experiences, and I rather
> enjoy them. Only in the realm of mishearing—at least, my
> mishearings—can a biography of cancer become a biog-
> raphy of Cantor (one of my favorite mathematicians), tarot
> cards turn into pteropods, a grocery bag into a poetry bag,
> all-or-noneness into oral numbness, a porch into a Porsche,
> and a mere mention of Christmas Eve a command to 'Kiss
> my feet!'

I began to note down my own instances of mishearings. Each
time it felt as if I was sharing a joyful in-joke with Sacks, without
the risk of mockery.

•

I continued to think about Deaf Gain. To describe deafness as anything other than a loss is a subversive act. And yet to live in a body defined by loss is to be shrouded in a skein of grief. Even if your sense of self is buoyant and proud, the language of loss is quietly smothering. The very weight of the word *loss* is evident in the synonyms that shadow it, which, incidentally, are the words people use when they talk about deafness: accident, disaster, catastrophe, cost, ruin, bereavement, dispossession, wreckage, deprivation.

Without sufficient Auslan to ask Kathy about Deaf culture, I began spending hours on Twitter finding and following other Deaf people. After some deliberation, in August 2019 I updated my bio, announcing that I was Deaf. This was the most visible I had ever been. Soon other Deaf people found me. They too had grappled with the letters (d/Deaf); learning sign language as an adult; managing the expectations of mangers; finding a sense of belonging and community. Now, we reach out to each other and connect. We share resources. My vocabulary grows:

Audism—discrimination or prejudice against people who are deaf or hard of hearing.

Deaf anxiety—a constant feeling of stress and hypervigilance in situations that require listening.

Craptions—auto captions, which produce inaccurate and confusing text.

With each conversation, my deafness feels larger, more significant than ever before. I laugh at Deaf memes; the jokes are startlingly relevant. My story has shifted since I was trying to write the comedy routine—I find hints of humour in the shadows.

Expression

'You need to fix your face,' Kathy said aloud, which meant that she really wanted me to understand. Even so, she reiterated her point in sign. Her eyebrows and mouth articulated anger, annoyance, joy, concentration, in rapid succession, as her hands moved accordingly. 'See, my hands match my face. When you just signed *pain*, you didn't show pain on your face. That's not right at all.'

She had been teaching me signs that related to my job—*hospital* (two hands moving from your shoulders to your waist, like the long lapels of a doctor's white coat); *nurse* (a tall, crisp cap placed on your head); *physiotherapist* (the right hand rubbing the left forearm, knuckles angled low in a bruising motion). We had progressed to ailments and injuries, when my face fell out of sync with my hands.

Repeat, repeat signs

Okay. As I moved through the signs for injuries, I felt my face stiffen again.

Towards the end of the lesson, Kathy touched her cheeks, rubbed them up and down. *Fix.* I nodded. After she left, I walked to the bathroom and stared at my face. My gut felt fizzy with frustration. Yet my face looked placid.

To pass as hearing has meant over two decades of rigid self-discipline. I have taught myself to control my face, to unlearn my instinct to screw it up whenever I am confused. It's worked. Often when I've felt completely overwhelmed, I've been told that I look calm, even nonchalant.

And now, as my hearing is become increasingly unpredictable, I've doubled down. I work even harder to keep my face free of expressions of worry. My teeth carry the telltale signs of tension: at a recent dental appointment, I was warned about the long-term consequences of clenching and grinding.

'Your right jaw joint looks like it belongs to someone in their seventies. Keep this up and you'll crack a crown.'

The dentist fitted me for a mouthguard for sleeping and recommended a meditation app.

Back home, I looked at myself in the mirror, placed my hands on my cheeks and smooshed them together, then rubbed them up and down, trying to get my face to loosen up and release some of the frustration trapped inside my body.

After Kathy had told me to fix my face, I researched the non-manual features of signing—everything that doesn't involve the hands—which are essential to conveying meaning: the head (shaking, nodding, turning, tilting); the eyebrows (raising, lowering); the eyes (opening, closing, blinking, widening, narrowing, gazing forward and down, gazing forward and up, gazing to the left, gazing to the right); as well as various movements of the nose, cheeks, shoulders and body. The most versatile body part is the mouth: 'opening, closing, poking out the tongue, protruding the lips, vibrating the lips, pressing the lips together, drawing the lips back, stretching the lips, turning up the corners of the mouth or down, pushing the tongue into the cheek, pushing the tongue down below the lower lip, biting the lip, sucking in air, blowing out air.' As I read Johnston and Schembri's list, I noticed that my teeth were gripping the inside of my lower lip. Mentally, I had accepted my deafness, but my body was still striving to be blank-faced and invisible.

Kathy suggested dinner and drinks. We met at the pub, talked about the menu and the weather, and we people-watched. We continued to sign as we ate, taking turns to down cutlery. Was it the food and drinks that allowed me to relax? Or was it the ambient noise of the pub that gave me the confidence to converse with my hands rather than my voice? We traded stories. She told me about her children and her farm. I told her about my hobbies (writing, reading, running) as well as a string of facts about birds, whales and telescopes that I would normally have used to control a conversation, but now thrilled in simply sharing. Kathy raised her right hand. As if forming the letter W, she ran her right hand across her forehead, her fingers wriggling.

What?

You w-e-i-r-d

I burst out laughing.
She signed weird again.

yes

yes

Different sounds of blue

For the longest time, it was thought that the ocean was without sound.

One summer afternoon in Melbourne, in the middle of a heatwave, I watched Louis Malle's film *The Silent World* on YouTube. Released in 1956, it went on to win the Academy Award for Best Documentary Feature and the Palme d'Or at the Cannes Film Festival. As shoals of fish passed the camera, I thought how wonderfully free they looked.

Later, I learned that, during the filming, oceanographer Jacques Cousteau had flung dynamite into a coral reef. Each explosion caused sea life to scatter, producing a performance for the cameras. He argued that his approach allowed him to better understand the silent world.

Of course, we now know that sound travels exceptionally well through water. There's even a theory that whales beach themselves because they can't cope with the cacophony created by industry— their thick, muscular bodies shoulder their way up sandbars as ship engines and sonars shred the sea.

I was reminded of the dynamite during a hearing test in February 2020. My ENT specialist wanted to determine whether I'd acquired any further hearing loss over the past twelve months. I booked an appointment at a local clinic in Tamworth. Distracted by nerves, I took the day off work.

Whenever I have my hearing tested, audiologists always check my left ear. Some apologise. It's a habit, they say sheepishly, to always check both sides. When I was younger, I used to sit poised, listening intently, half-expecting that if I *just* tried hard enough, the result would change.

Today, the audiologist started with my right side, I kept my eyes closed, eliminating any kind of distraction. While she tested my left side, I watched her pressing buttons and turning dials. I couldn't hear anything. But I knew the sounds were getting louder because my skull ached from the rumbling vibrations. The sensation intensified until it made me cry out in pain. Only then did she stop. As a reflex, I had raised my hand to protect my left ear. The audiologist was surprised: 'Wow, I really had to ratchet the dial up as far as it could go.'

'Well, you're definitely completely deaf in your left ear,' she said after the test. 'Your right ear has moderate hearing loss.'

She showed me the graph paper she had been annotating during the test—my hearing hadn't changed in the past year.

On 29 August 1952, several hundred people entered Maverick Concert Hall, New York. The atmosphere was festive; the audience chatty. As the house lights went down, a hush settled over the room. David Tudor walked across the stage and sat down at the piano. The silence intensified, fed by anticipation. And then the performance began.

After thirty seconds of silence, Tudor lowered the piano lid. He shuffled his sheet music, restarted his stopwatch, before lifting the piano lid again. His body was now motionless, the piano keys still untouched. The audience began to murmur. After two minutes and twenty-three seconds, Tudor closed the piano lid. By now the audience's discomfort was turning into an uproar. As Tudor reset his stopwatch, people began to leave. Undaunted, Tudor lifted the piano lid. Then, after one minute and forty seconds of silence, he stood up, took a bow and exited the stage. The premiere of John Cage's latest composition *4'33"* was complete. Critic Clark Lunberry summed up the music world's derision: 'He is either a saintly prophet of new sounds, new silences, or a foolish charlatan leading anarchically astray.' Others described the experience of silence as terrifying.

On 16 January 2004, the BBC Symphony Orchestra was scheduled to perform *4'33"* for the first time in the United Kingdom. As a live radio broadcast, it posed an issue for the BBC engineers, as any silence lasting longer than ten seconds would trigger the emergency backup track. The dead air switch had to be dismantled. Dead air. In my late twenties, a doctor once described my left ear as dead. Even now, it makes me shudder to think that a part of my body was declared deceased.

I first encountered John Cage while visiting New York City in the winter of 2013. The cold air was lacerating, so I spent most days in art galleries, soaking up the luxury of central heating. In the Museum of Modern Art I stumbled across a retrospective of Cage's work. His musical notation was framed and hung on the walls. In primary school I was taught a glib mnemonic to memorise each treble clef line—Every Good Boy Deserves Fruit. Cage's musical scoring looked like the fruit basket had been turned over, the notes scattershot across the expanse of each page. His music notation often failed to follow any standard conventions; it was up to the musician to interpret the score. The resulting music became a process 'like the weather'.

Cage cited the French-American artist Marcel Duchamp's words as his inspiration—'a work of art is not completed by the artist but is completed by the listener or the observer, so that it can change from one person to another'. Yet as I stood in wet socks and a thin jacket, I wasn't bothered to do much work at all.

But then, during my last summer in Melbourne, while avoiding my housemates' drinking sessions and DJ sets, I watched Frank Scheffer's documentary about Cage's work process. The title is an almost necessary pun—*How to Get Out of the Cage*. As I sat at my desk, headphones on to block out the noise in the flat, I didn't simply watch the documentary, I paused it every few minutes to write down my thoughts and responses—sound as movement, as feeling; silence as everything. It felt as though a conversation had begun, one I had been avoiding for years, if not my entire life. In the six years since learning about Cage's work, my body had changed, and so too had my relationship with sound and silence.

After a lifetime of being completely deaf in my left ear, deafness had felt like my natural state. But the process of losing hearing is a completely different experience. Growing up, I was paranoid about my right ear, I would carry ear plugs to concerts or clap my hand over my ear whenever there was the risk of irreversible damage. And so, as my right ear goes deaf, a process I once feared, perhaps the most surprising thing of all is that I now crave thick, cool silence.

For me, silence has always meant safety. Knowing that every-thing is secure and stationary, my eyes can relax from scanning and squinting in an effort to detect and decode sound. As my tinnitus whirrs, however, disrupting the calm within me, I have to accept that hearing loss is not predictable. Now I am having to learn how to live with the discord in my head.

In the documentary, Cage explains that he loves sounds but not the feeling of harmony. Few of the shots in the film are harmonious. The camera is often set up at awkward angles, or the footage is unfocused. There are jump cuts in time and place, an assortment of overlaying images—Cage typing; a plastic bag; an ice-licked fence. When editing the film, Frank Scheffer initially followed the 'chance operations' technique favoured by Cage: 'a faith that each thing that happens is the best thing that could happen.'

Later, I discovered that I had watched the 2012 re-release of the film, a version that has had the chance operations mostly, if not entirely, edited out. Even though Scheffer revered Cage's creative process, he admitted that he 'wanted the documentary to be informative and appealing to a bigger audience'.

In most aspects of life, we demand that stories are presented as neat, chronological narrative. We find ambiguity unappealing. Consequently, silence becomes inescapably symbolic: holy, golden, sinister, terrifying. Even when perceived as an absence, a void, gap, pause, negative space, the implication is that silence is on the margins of sound, never the focal point.

The earliest meaning of the word *sound* is something 'free from special defect or injury'. To be of sound health. That is a sound idea. This house is sound. To have sound reason. Full of life and meaning. No wonder people believe deafness is a kind of death sentence.

An audiogram, or hearing test, is based on the musical scale. Like a musical score, the body is a composition, with rhythms and beats. But this is where the overlap between music and medicine seems to end. Musicians and composers tend to speak of sound with a depth of knowledge and inventiveness that medical professionals have had trained out of them.

In medicine, sound has been stripped back to a single component: noise. Deafness is defined as an inability to detect certain decibel ranges, the results plotted on an audiogram. In music, the musical scale is merely a starting point for conversation. Gaps and spaces and pauses are considered just as important as the hiss of a high hat, or the dull beat of a foot pedal against the belly of a drum. Challenging the musical establishment, Cage pushed this even further. He approached sound and composition from a place of movement, in which sounds travel, settle, collide, meld, infuse and fill spaces—nothing, not even silence, is anchored to treble clef lines. There is no dead air.

And there is no right or wrong way of experiencing his music, or even sound at all. I *know* that sound is more than noise. By its very nature, sound is sensual—it involves more than just one sense but elicits them all. Sound is movement and texture and colour and emotion rolling over our skin. What would it be like if audiograms were treated with the same scope of possibility? If deafness wasn't considered a kind of death?

'We're in an ocean of possibilities,' Cage says, beaming at the camera.

His words take me back to some of my earliest and rawest impressions of the world. Skin wet, goggles tight, tumbling in the community pool, fully immersed in sound and silence.

One of the original meanings of the word 'deaf' in Proto-Germanic indicates a wider, all-encompassing state of being 'empty, barren', which reminds me of the first Irish poems I read about bogs.

Inhospitable tracts of land, they are an accumulation of dead plant material, including fossilised woodlands, packed down in soft, concentrated form.

My high school had selected the poems of Seamus Heaney as the main text for our Year Twelve exams. The module was tedious. Heaney's poems seemed to be about soggy fields; our sports oval was balding and sun-beaten. The people he wrote about were weathered, whereas our faces carried the sheen of youth. He wrote about the ancient rituals and sombre incantations that accompanied death. Our heavy-handed essays in response to his poems were choked with words like synecdoche, intertextuality et cetera, words we hoped would hide our lack of understanding.

It was some months into the school year before I thought about asking my parents if they knew Seamus Heaney's poems. It felt like an act of desperation, as they were always too exhausted from shift work to read for pleasure. But they read the poems and translated the language, most of which wasn't poetic so much as the plain, hard-heeled language of rural practicalities. A language that felt true and familiar to them and represented an Ireland they knew. Thus began a conversation that has spanned almost fifteen years: my parents, having realised how little I knew about their childhoods, now talk at length about the realities of living on the land, the seasonal routines of saving hay, fattening cattle and cutting turf, routines that are still performed by their brothers and sisters, my aunties and uncles.

The Irish writer Ian Maleney was inspired by Heaney's approach: he spent hours at 'the wastes of the bog' around his house, an experience that was informed by his training as a sound engineer. His relationship with sound was slowly and unexpectedly altered by standing in the rain and wind, accumulating 'hours and hours of recorded emptiness'. After fifteen years studying the technical aspects of recording sound, from microphone placement to cable testing, he learned how 'to listen'.

It has taken me years to accept that my way of listening is in no way diminished compared to that of hearing people. While I have to work harder, my attentiveness and synaesthesia has allowed me to see, hear, taste and feel the unexpected or even extraordinary within the seemingly mundane. An exchange in a hospital corridor can take on new dimensions as I watch a swell of pride alter a patient's posture when they receive a compliment, and their voice become bright, almost incandescent. Some music has, for me, the taste and mouthfeel of a banquet. Notes are a heady mix of sweet and tart, chewy and salivating. Even my tinnitus—a condition that has permanently disrupted my ability to dwell within spacious silence—now shifts with the intensities of my mood, each hum, drone and buzz appearing with its own colours and texture.

'If people want to experience what it is like to be deaf, they will very often plug their ears. Well, the absence of sound doesn't give you the experience of being deaf,' said DeafSpace design researcher Robert Sirvage in a lecture about design.

Sirvage explains that walking backwards triggers a true state of alertness, which is for him a more accurate way of limiting your 'sensory reach'. Forced to deeply engage with your surrounding environment, you must continually watch, feel and consider how your body exists in relation to everything else. Information comes from inferences: shifting shadows and wind; the reactions of animals and people; muscle and scent memory.

'This,' he says, 'is an embedded experience throughout deaf lives.'

•

I listened idly to Melvyn Bragg talking about Beethoven as I made breakfast. Fill the kettle, flick the switch, pull the frypan out of the cupboard—my movements quick and clattering. Bragg spoke in a low rush, a smear of sound.

Unable to keep up with what he was saying, I pressed pause on the podcast and finished cooking my eggs. Afterwards, I grabbed my headphones, rewound to the start of the episode, closed my eyes and listened hard.

'In particular, he popularised music without words, transcending language, and it changed the way that audiences valued music. Making it something that could be engaged with and thought about, rather than played in the background and talked over.'

Beethoven, a deaf man, taught audiences how to pay attention.

For the last few years I have turned my attention to the sky, unexpectedly developing a fondness for birds. I envy their ability to take flight together and soar above the sprawl of the city or glide over the countryside.

When not wandering through parks and grasslands looking for birds, I read books about them. In *The Wonder of Birds*, Jim Robbins writes about collective intelligence or metacognition—a pooling together of perspectives to create a 'collective mind' that is both larger and more intelligent than the sum of its parts. There are countless examples of animal species working together.

I can't help thinking about how disabled perspectives have not been included in the 'collective mind'. The thought is galling. The consequences are frightening. Disability activist Eddie Ndopu wrote that '[s]urvival demands imagination from people who exist on the margins. To exist at the centre does not require nearly as much imagination because the centre functions to cocoon its inhabitants. Centring the imagination of the marginalized is key to saving society itself.'

The shock of discovering that the world was not made for you can be devastating. The realisation can come at any point during a lifetime, whether you are born with disability or acquire one, momentarily or permanently. It is almost unavoidable. At least three or four times a week, since I was a new-graduate physiotherapist, patients have said to me: don't get old.

It doesn't have to be this way. But until society starts valuing the intelligence and creativity of disabled people, we will continue to experience the hard edge of being on the margins.

In Melbourne, I had developed an evening ritual of leaving my flat and walking a long, lazy loop around Royal Park. The golden-hour walks were a way of recovering my equilibrium after work, loosening up after intense physical and mental focus. There, in the natural soft edges of the city, among the green spaces and waterways, sound felt light and springy. I caught the fleeting coda of bird chorus. A broad-chested currawong winged its way past me. Moving with, and through, the air. Then more currawongs appeared, black-feathered and flying with undulating elegance.

Even in the country town of Tamworth, my need to be alone after each day persisted. One evening, a week or so after my audiogram, the dusk warm and slow, my body felt off-kilter after hours of watching others closely and angling my ear to catch the flow of conversation. Over the past days, thinking about my audiogram, I had decided to delay my decision about the surgery. I would hold onto my shadow for a little longer. The relief was immense. Even though my audiogram had remained stable over the past twelve months, I had been gaining my Deafness through culture and community.

By the time I reached the bend in the Peel River, my shoulders had loosened. My thoughts started to drift. I watched as birds, one after the other, took to the air in a smooth muscular sweep. My body had recovered—for the moment.

In June 1954, Dr Vern Knudsen, the president of the Acoustical Society of America, marked the society's twenty-fifth anniversary with a speech entitled 'I Hate Noise'. The speech was recorded, with the intention that it would be played in 2029 at the society's hundredth anniversary. Knudsen observed that since the society had begun, maximal noise levels of daily living had increased by about one decibel per year. He worried that by 2029 the world would be an 'inferno' of sound.

A 2011 report from the World Health Organization analysed the health impacts from environmental noise (any noise excluding industrial noise) in Western European cities and calculated the impact in terms of Disability-Adjusted Life Years (DALYs).

> With conservative assumptions applied to the calculation methods, it is estimated that DALYs lost from environmental noise are 61 000 years from ischaemic heart disease, 45 000 years for cognitive impairment of children, 903 000 years for sleep disturbance, 22 000 years for tinnitus and 587 000 years for annoyance...These results indicate that at least one million healthy life years are lost every year from traffic-related noise in the western part of Europe.

For the first time in history, more than half the world's population live in urban settings. According to a 2018 report from the United Nations, this figure is on track to reach sixty-eight per cent by 2050 and noise is predicted to become even more of a public health crisis.

While it might not seem obvious, or even immediately logical, Deaf people can provide valuable insights into how we can manage our ever-noisier soundscapes. Deaf people spend their lives listening with their whole bodies. They know that noise is more than just sound.

'Throughout history, Deaf people have developed an exceedingly practical and elegant means of adapting their surroundings to reflect their unique ways of being, often referred to as DeafSpace,' writes architect Hansel Bauman in *DeafSpace: An architecture toward a more liveable and sustainable world*. 'Inherent within Deaf experiences reside an architectural wisdom and a drive to create, or to dwell, within places that are expressive of Deaf people's ways of being.'

I think about how at each Auslan meeting, we spent time shifting tables and chairs, creating a circular shape so everyone could see one another. Recently, after I complained to Mum that my back faced the office door, she bought me a rear-view mirror to prop on my desk so I wouldn't be startled when someone approached. I later read that Judith Wright also placed a mirror next to her typewriter.

DeafSpace began to be formally codified in 2005 during a two-day workshop at Gallaudet University, Washington DC, the world's first Deaf liberal arts college. Founded in 1864, the college's design was modelled on Harvard University—Victorian Gothic, architecture that focused on aesthetics rather than access. When the university was planning a new building, the Sorenson Language and Communication Center (SLCC), they asked a group of Deaf scholars, students and administrative staff to establish a set of design principles. The group 'described space by telling personal stories of isolation from and connection to place as well as to others... This embodied, very personal awareness of space is a unique and enlightening way to think about architecture more empathetically.'

The two-day workshop evolved into a design-and-research course, the DeafSpace Project, facilitated by Bauman, who identifies as hearing: 'Ten years ago, when I first started working with the Deaf community, it was really a profound time for me because I took on a new identity. I then realised that I was hearing.' Instead of relying on the traditional language of architecture, which revolves around the experiences of hearing people, Bauman cites anthropologist Edward Hall as an inspiration for DeafSpace architecture: 'People from different cultures not only speak different languages but, what is possibly more important, inhabit different sensory worlds.'

Over the next five years, Deaf students attending Gallaudet identified more than 150 Deaf-architectural patterns. Each pattern introduces a specific concept and a new set of design guidelines that articulate the ways that Deaf bodies and buildings interact. This new language of space is striking, and even poetic in its specificity. For instance, the pattern 'Layers of Light' recommends that 'diffuse light, like that of a flat, cloudy sky, is ideal for seeing sign language'. On a practical level, this can be achieved with windows and skylights 'positioned to take in a variety of light intensities... to wash building surfaces with light...resulting in a calm, glowing space'.

The patterns explore concepts of proximity, acoustics, 'visually quiet' backgrounds, the flow of communication (including 'conversation circles'), sensory reach, reflections, static and moving shadows. 'Common to all of these categories are ideas of connection, community building, visual language, the promotion of personal safety, and well-being,' writes Bauman.

I wish the pattern 'Soft Intersections' could be incorporated into every building. Unable to hear if someone is coming around a corner, I often approach hallway intersections cautiously. At Gallaudet, these points of potential collision have been minimised by extending a person's line of sight via curving walls or opaque glass incorporated into corners. I imagine moving freely, quickly, through streets and corridors, without being startled or trampled.

The desire for access and inclusivity also addresses how race intersects with the Deaf experience. The pattern 'Color: Contrasting Surface' is concerned with the design of 'visually quiet' backgrounds, which in turn improve visual clarity when reading sign language: walls should be 'contrasting and complementary to the full ranges of human skin tones. Cool colors within a range of blues and greens are recommended'. This awareness of others has been attributed to Deaf culture's tendency to a be 'collectivist culture', one that pools resources and shares information.

Even though there has been the extensive codifying of Deaf knowledge into formal architectural guidelines, Bauman notes that 'DeafSpace, or Deaf architecture, has not been recognised within popular architectural discourse'.

Yet modern architecture has, in one particular instance, already been shaped by deafness. Regardless of an increasingly scientific approach to acoustics, world-famous architect Frank Lloyd Wright preferred to work intuitively, his design sensibility reflecting his immersion in Beethoven's music:

> When I was a small child I used to lie awake listening to the strains of the *Sonata Pathétique*—Father playing it on the Steinway square downstairs in the Baptist minister's house at Weymouth....When I build I often hear music and, yes, when Beethoven made music I am sure he sometimes saw buildings like mine in character, whatever form they may have taken then...So when you listen to Beethoven you are

listening to a builder. You are seeing him take a theme, a motif, and building with it…You cannot help, when you finish listening to a Beethoven symphony, just knocking your head on the ground with admiration and respect for the way he can build.

I can only imagine what the spaces we inhabit will look and sound like once society starts listening to deaf people.

Shapelessness

While I wait for society to start listening to deaf people, I have found that it has been essential for me to listen to myself. Instead of ignoring my feelings or concerns, I write.

It's said a writer lives twice: once in the moment, then once again in the retelling. Perhaps a deaf person lives many more times? First in the anticipation of a conversation, then physically alert, ready to latch onto each sentence, phrase, word—a short life in every syllable. Then reliving the aftershock of conversations, replaying them, wondering: did I hear that correctly?

But, for me, continually asking for clarity would have meant revealing my deafness. Letting go of my secret always felt too exposing. For years, I imagined it would lead to terrible things. So often, and with such force, I couldn't foresee anything welcoming. My fears felt factual, as visceral and obvious to me as the blue of my eyes and the length of each second toe.

Looking back now, I can see the cost of keeping my secret. The quiet exertion it took to carry it with me all the time. The apartness I always felt—knowing that if I were to relax, lower my guard, the truth would somehow seep out of me. In my twenties, I sought quick relief by changing jobs, living arrangements, suburbs and cities. It all kept me busy and distracted. I avoided lazy midafternoons, empty weekends, long, hammock-bound holidays. If alone, I read. If left unoccupied, I risked hearing myself.

'There are two kinds of silence; silence with oneself and silence with others. Both kinds make us suffer equally,' wrote Natalia Ginzburg. It wasn't until I began to write about my deafness that I realised my secret had always kept me small, suspicious and self-contained.

It has taken me years to think about deafness in ways that are not medical, to re-energise my vocabulary with words such as pride and culture, instead of deficit and malfunction. In large part, I've been helped by the writing of other deaf people—Cece Bell, Raymond Antrobus, Donna MacDonald, Judith Wright, Sara Nović, Jessica White, Brenda Jo Brueggemann, Ilya Kaminsky, Dorothy Miles.

I started writing about deafness with the intention of containing my thoughts in sentences with crisp resolve, hoping to construct a truthful story. But as the words came together—framing small, ordinary moments—I couldn't ignore the swell and sink of my emotions about living in a deaf body.

Until I was thirty-one years old, I had thought that my body was hewn in two: half-hearing, half-deaf. It was only when I began to consider deafness as a complete state—a vast and complex continuum without borders and hard edges—that I could embrace its shapelessness.

To find a community and language that accentuates rather than exhausts my body has been thrilling. To gain any degree of fluency will take years. But as my ear bones harden, so too does my resolve. I keep practising even though I have the opportunity to have a hearing device drilled into my skull. I know that the surgery isn't going to cure me. I will always be Deaf.

'Deaf identity is not a static concept but a complex ongoing quest for belonging, a quest bound up with the acceptance of being deaf while "finding one's voice" in a hearing-dominant society,' writes academic Guy McIlroy.

Sign language allows my deafness to sprawl. Reaching beyond my ears, it runs through my blood, encircling my heart and mind. I tried to cage off my deafness, starve it of attention. I fractured with the stress of self-containment.

Since disclosing my deafness, some of my fears have been realised—just like when I was a child, my hearing loss is often tested. But instead of screaming into my ear, adults tend to ask a series of insistent and condescending questions. As someone who likes to please, I feel compelled to answer each question fully and truthfully. But it often feels as if there is little I can do to appease a stranger's curiosity or suspicion.

I continue to hold my deafness close. Though now, without shame. It is precious and mine to delight in. Now, instead of considering it a secret or a lie, I accept that I have the right to choose when to disclose my deafness. While some people tell stories in order to live, some of us hide our stories in order to survive.

It is not easy being deaf. It never has been. Our lives are shorter. We experience mental ill-health at far greater rates than the general population. Our brains and bodies are continually stressed by the demands of having to live in a hearing world. Our access to language, education, healthcare and secure work continues to be curtailed both by legislation and by ignorance. We are simultaneously held to extraordinarily high and frustratingly low expectations. It is exhausting.

As a white woman, my life is not threatened like it is for Indigenous people, Black people or people of colour. Racism compounds the stress and danger of being deaf in a hearing-centric world. A landmark study conducted in Darwin and Alice Springs revealed that more than ninety per cent of Indigenous people who were incarnated had hearing loss ranging from mild to severe. It is possible that some might not have known they were deaf. In 2018–19, the Australian Bureau of Statistics found that forty-three per cent of Aboriginal and Torres Strait Islander people aged over seven years old had hearing loss in one or both ears. Of those with hearing loss, seventy-nine per cent had been unaware of their diagnosis.

In *A Treatise of Human Nature*, Scottish philosopher David Hume proposed that people only really understand things, ideas, if they have experienced them.

The majority of literature I've read about deafness, be it scientific or recreational, has been written by hearing people. Perhaps this is why I've struggled to understand and then apply those ideas to my body. They simply don't fit.

There are times, however, said Hume, when the difference between a first-hand and second-hand experience becomes blurred: 'Thus in sleep, in a fever, in madness, or in any very violent emotions of soul, our ideas may approach to our impressions: As on the other hand it sometimes happens, that our impressions are so faint and low, that we cannot distinguish them from our ideas.'

The grappling and anguish described by Hume is exactly what I have experienced in the years since my hearing-aid trial. When I had hearing aids on, I experienced a sudden, violent rush of new sensory impressions. I immediately disliked 'normal' hearing. As

I began to question how I perceived my body, it became clear that most of my ideas about deafness had come from others—science, medicine, society. In turn, my concept of silence had been shaded by second-hand experiences and taken on a sustained, sinister register—I learned to diminish it, wish it away.

But now, by writing, alone and at length, I am trying to clear my head of those ideas and embrace and expand the experience of silence, my silence. And while I have yet to decide whether I want to have a bolt screwed into my skull, my hands stay busy—hooking, stretching, flexing—conversing.

Works cited

ATTACK

In words

N. Wolters, H.E. Knoors, A.H. Cillessen & L. Verhoeven, 'Predicting acceptance and popularity in early adolescence as a function of hearing status, gender, and educational setting', *Research in Developmental Disabilities*, vol. 32, no. 6, 2011, pp. 2553–65

In secret

M.L. Slepian, J.S. Chun & M.F. Mason, 'The experience of secrecy', *Journal of Personality and Social Psychology*, vol. 113, no. 1, 2017, pp. 1–33

Michael Slepian, 'The problem with keeping a secret', Society for Personality and Social Psychology, 1 July 2019, www.spsp.org/news-center/blog/slepian-keeping-secrets

M.L. Slepian, E.J. Masicampo, N. Ambady, 'Relieving the burdens of secrecy: Revealing secrets influences judgments of hill slant and distance', *Social Psychological and Personality Science*, vol. 5, no. 3, 2014, pp. 293–300

Wegner, D. M. (1994). Ironic processes of mental control. *Psychological Review, 101,* 34–52.

In corners

UK Hansard, 'House of Commons Rebuilding', *House of Commons Debates*, vol. 393, cc. 403–73, 28 October 1943, https://api.parliament.uk/historic-hansard/commons/1943/oct/28/house-of-commons-rebuilding

UK Parliament, 'Churchill and the Commons Chamber', www.parliament.uk/about/living-heritage/building/palace/architecture/palacestructure/churchill

Eric Taylor, *The House of Commons at Work*, Penguin Books, United Kingdom, 1951

Sara Nović, 'Between the lines: Disability invisibility in literature', *Signature Reads*, May 2018, quoted in 'Ethics in publishing: Our bodies, and whose gazes?', *Portland Review*, 30 January 2019, http://portlandreview.org/ethics-in-publishing-our-bodies-and-whose-gazes

Gaston Bachelard, *The Poetics of Space*, Penguin Classics, 2014

L.G. Moseley & D.S. Butler, 'Fifteen years of explaining pain: The past, present, and future', *The Journal of Pain*, vol. 16, no. 9, 2015, pp. 807–13

Wayne Stabb, 'Churchill's Hearing Loss', Hearing Health Matters, 24 February 2014, https://hearinghealthmatters.org/waynesworld/2014/churchills-hearing-loss

On lips

Michael Strauss, 'Hearing psychology: Both ears were not created equally', Audicus, 25 March 2015, www.audicus.com/hearing-psychology-both-ears-were-not-created-equally

Simone Weil, *Gravity and Grace*, Routledge & Kegan Paul, 1952

V. Best, E. Roverud, L. Baltzell, J. Rennies & M. Lavandier, 'The importance of a broad bandwidth for understanding "glimpsed" speech', *The Journal of the Acoustical Society of America*, vol. 146, 2019, pp. 3215–21

Daniele Marzoli & Luca Tommasi, 'Side biases in humans (*Homo sapiens*): Three ecological studies on hemispheric asymmetries', *Naturwissenschaften*, vol. 96, 2009, pp. 1099–1106

A.D. Alzahrani & M.A. Almuhammadi, 'Left ear advantages in detecting emotional tones using dichotic listening task in an Arabic sample', *Laterality*, vol. 18, no. 6, 2013, pp. 730–47

G. Malatesta, D. Marzoli, M. Rapino & L. Tommasi, 'The left-cradling bias and its relationship with empathy and depression', *Scientific Reports*, vol. 9, article 6141, 2019, www.nature.com/articles/s41598-019-42539-6

Michael D. Seidman, Bianca Siegel, Priyanka Shah & Susan M. Bowyer, 'Hemispheric dominance and cell phone use', *JAMA Otolaryngology Head & Neck Surgery*, vol. 139, no. 5, 2013, pp. 466–70

In sound

Larissa Faw, 'Lyric campaign promotes hearing aid's invisibility', Media Post, 22 March 2017, www.mediapost.com/publications/article/297665/lyric-campaign-promotes-hearing-aids-invisibility.html

P. Avan, F. Giraudet & B. Büki, 'Importance of Binaural Hearing', *Audiology and Neurotology*, vol. 20, suppl. 1, 2015, pp. 3–6

Charles Duhigg, *The Power of Habit: Why we do what we do in life and business*, Random House, 2012

Access Economics, 'Listen Hear! The economic impact and cost of hearing loss in Australia', Access Economics, February 2006, https://apo.org.au/sites/default/files/resource-files/2006-02/apo-nid2755.pdf

DECAY

On scars

L.G. Moseley & D.S. Butler, 'Fifteen years of explaining pain: The past, present, and future', *The Journal of Pain*, vol. 16, no. 9, 2015, pp. 807–13

In jest

S. Lacey, R. Stilla & K. Sathian, 'Metaphorically feeling: Comprehending textural metaphors activates somatosensory cortex', *Brain and Language*, vol. 120, no. 1, 2012, pp. 416–21

Deaf Australia Inc., 'Terminology', version 1.1, August 2010, https://deafaustralia.org.au/wp-content/uploads/Terminology-policy-approved-Nov-2010.pdf

Emergency Management Victoria, 'Increasing accessibility during summer', 11 January 2017, www.expression.com.au/newsasp?aid=1049&t=increasing-accessibility-during-summer

Handshape

Auslan Signbank, www.auslan.org.au

Longform Podcast, '#361: Ken Burns', 25 September 2019

M. Hegarty & D. Waller, 'A dissociation between mental rotation and perspective-taking spatial abilities', *Intelligence*, vol. 32, no. 2, 2004, pp. 175–191

M.P. Walker, T. Brakefield, J. Seidman et al., 'Sleep and the time course of motor skill learning', *Learning & Memory*, vol. 10, no. 4, 2003, pp. 275–84

Masterclass, 'Helen Mirren teaches acting: Official trailer', YouTube, 16 November 2017, www.youtube.com/watch?v=-hYDmRq_PHY

S.L. Rogers, C.P. Speelman, O. Guidetti & M. Longmuir, 'Using dual eye tracking to uncover personal gaze patterns during social interaction', *Scientific Reports*, vol. 8, art. no. 4271, 2018

Orientation

Trevor Johnston & Adam Schembri, *Australian Sign Language (Auslan): An introduction to sign language linguistics*, Cambridge University Press, 2007

Oliver Sacks, *Seeing Voices: A journey into the world of the deaf*, University of California Press, 1989

Mother tongue

Oliver Sacks, *Seeing Voices: A journey into the world of the deaf*, University of California Press, 1989

Trevor Johnston & Adam Schembri, *Australian Sign Language (Auslan): An introduction to sign language linguistics*, Cambridge University Press, 2007

J.J. Murray, W.C. Hall & K. Snoddon, 'Education and health of children with hearing loss: The necessity of signed languages', *Bulletin of the World Health Organization*, vol. 97, 2019, pp. 711–16

Brenda Jo Brueggemann, *Deaf Subjects: Between identities and places*, New York University Press, 2009

M. MacSweeney & V. Cardin, 'What is the function of auditory cortex without auditory input?' *Brain*, vol. 138, no. 9, 2015, pp. 2468–70

Stephanie Dalzell, 'Auslan national curriculum for Australian schools hailed as "huge step" for deaf community', ABC News, 19 December 2016, www.abc.net.au/news/2016-12-19/deaf-community-hails-school-rollout-of-auslan-curriculum/8132474

World Federation of the Deaf, 'Advancing human rights and sign language worldwide', August 2016, https://wfdeaf.org/our-work/human-rights-of-the-deaf

L.F. Halliday, O. Tuomainen & S. Rosen, 'Language development and impairment in children with mild to moderate sensorineural hearing loss', *Speech, Language, and Hearing Research*, vol. 60, no. 6, 2017, pp. 1551–67

T. Humphries, P. Kushalnagar, G. Mathur et al., 'Language acquisition for deaf children: Reducing the harms of zero tolerance to the use of alternative approaches', *Harm Reduction Journal*, vol. 9, art. no. 16, 2012

A. van Wieringen, A. Boudewyns, A. Sangen et al., 'Unilateral congenital hearing loss in children: Challenges and potentials', *Hearing Research*, vol. 372, 2019, pp. 29–41

R.E. Mitchell & M.A. Karchmer, 'Chasing the mythical 10 percent: Parental hearing status of deaf and hard of hearing students in the United States', *Sign Language Studies*, vol. 4, 2004, pp. 138–63

Discover Ireland, 'Kerry international dark-sky reserve', www. discoverireland.ie/kerry/kerry-international-dark-sky-reserve

Pain points

Dan Shewan, 'Pain points: A guide to finding & solving your customers' problems', The WordStream Blog, 1 May 2020, www.wordstream. com/blog/ws/2018/02/28/pain-points

Miranda Ward, 'Victorian Hearing apologises for "Hearing aids can be ugly" campaign following online backlash', Mumbrella, 25 May 2015, https://mumbrella.com.au/victorian-hearing-apologies-for-hearingaids-can-be-ugly-campaign-following-online-backlash-295849

L.R.M. Hallberg & M.L. Barrenäs, 'Living with a male with noise-induced hearing loss: Experiences from the perspective of spouses', *British Journal of Audiology*, vol. 27, no. 4, 1993, pp 255–61

P. Dawes, M. Maslin & K. Munro, 'Getting used to hearing aids from the perspective of adult hearing-aid users', *International Journal of Audiology*, vol. 53, no. 12, 2014, pp. 861–70

L. Hickson & L. Worrall, 'Beyond hearing aid fitting: Improving communication for older adults', *International Journal of Audiology*, vol. 42, suppl. 2, 2003, pp. S84–S91

Donna McDonald, 'The reluctant memoirist', *Griffith Review 33: Such is Life*, August 2011, www.griffithreview.com/articles/ the-reluctant-memoirist

Donna McDonald, *The Art of Being Deaf*, Gallaudet University Press (2014)

Australian Competition and Consumer Commission, 'ACCC takes action against hearing aid retailers for misleading pensioners', media release number MR175/18, 6 September 2018, www.accc.gov.au/media-release/accc-takes-action-against-hearing-aid-retailersfor-misleading-pensioners

Australian Competition and Consumer Commission, 'Issues around the sale of hearing aids: Consumer and clinician perspectives', 3 March 2017

G. Scambler, 'Heaping blame on shame: "Weaponising stigma" for neoliberal times', *The Sociological Review*, vol. 66, no. 4, 2018, pp. 766–82

House of Representatives Standing Committee on Health, Aged Care and Sport, 'Still waiting to be heard…: Report on the Inquiry into the Hearing Health and Wellbeing of Australia', Parliament of the Commonwealth of Australia, Canberra, September 2017

O.L. Habaneca & R. Kelly-Campbella, 'Outcomes of group audiological rehabilitation for unaided adults with hearing impairment and their significant others', *American Journal of Audiology*, vol. 24, no. 2, 2015, pp. 40–52

A. Kral, W.G. Kronenberger, D.B. Pisoni & G.M. O'Donoghue, 'Neurocognitive factors in sensory restoration of early deafness: a connectome model', *Lancet Neurology*, vol. 15, 2016, pp. 610–21

My News Desk, 'Hearing aids market will grow by $13.54 bn during 2020 to 2027', press release, 29 June 2020, www.mynewsdesk.com/us/wired-herald/pressreleases/hearing-aids-market-size-will-grow-by-dollars-13-dot-54-bn-during-2020-to-2027-3018053

SUSTAIN

On topics of conversation

Mary Roach, *Grunt: The curious science of humans at war*, W.W. Norton & Company, 2017

99% Invisible (podcast), 'Combat hearing loss', episode 222, 26 July 2016

Reasonable adjustments

Annie Dillard, *The Writing Life*, Harper & Row, 1989

S. Darcy, T. Taylor & J. Green, '"But I can do the job": Examining disability employment practice through human rights complaint cases', *Disability & Society*, vol. 31, no. 9, 2016, pp.1242-74

T. Shakespeare, L.I. Iezzoni & N.E. Groce, 'Disability and the training of health professionals', *The Lancet*, vol. 374, no. 9704, 2009, pp. 1815-16

Productivity Commission, 'Review of Disability Discrimination Act (Cth) 1992', report, 14 July 2004, Law Institute of Victoria (Submission 81), www.pc.gov.au/inquiries/completed/disability-discrimination/submissions/law_institute_of_victoria/sub081.pdf

Andrew Solomon, *Far from the Tree: Parents, Children and the Search for Identity*, Penguin, 2012

Andrew Byrnes, Alex Conte, Jean-Pierre Gonnot et al., 'Chapter One: Overview: The relationship between disability and development', in United Nations Enable, *Handbook for Parliamentarians on the Convention on the Rights of Persons with Disabilities*, www.un.org/development/desa/disabilities/resources/handbookfor-parliamentarians-on-the-convention-on-the-rights-of-personswith-disabilities/chapter-one-overview-5.html

Hearing Care Industry Association, 'Hearing for life: The value of hearing services for vulnerable Australians', report prepared with assistance from Deloitte Access Economics, Canberra, 2020

B. Engdahla, M. Idstada & V. Skirbekka, 'Hearing loss, family status and mortality: Findings from the HUNT study, Norway', *Social Science & Medicine*, vol. 220, 2019, pp. 219–25

D.C. Baldridge & M.L. Swift, 'Age and assessments of disability accommodation request normative appropriateness', *Human Resource Management*, vol. 55, no. 3, 2016, pp. 385–400

D.C. Baldridge & M.L. Swift, 'Withholding requests for disability accommodation: The role of individual differences and disability attributes', *Journal of Management*, vol. 39, no. 3, 2013, pp. 743–62

Australian Institute of Health and Welfare, 'People with disability in Australia 2020: In brief', 2 October 2020, www.aihw.gov.au/reports/disability/people-with-disability-in-australia/contents/employment/unemployment

Australian Network on Disability, '2017 Disability Confidence Survey Report', www.and.org.au/data/Disability_Confidence_Survey/Disability_Confidence_Survey_Report_2017_FINAL.pdf

M.L. Slepian, J.S. Chun & M.F. Mason, 'The experience of secrecy', *Journal of Personality and Social Psychology*, vol. 113, no. 1, 2017, pp. 1–33

World Health Organization, 'World report on disability', 13 December 2011, www.who.int/teams/noncommunicable-diseases/disability-and-rehabilitation/world-report-on-disability

Kate Kelly, 'Understanding invisible disabilities in the workplace', Understood, n.d., www.understood.org/en/workplace/disability -inclusion-work/understanding-invisible-disabilities-in-the-workplace

Care work

S.C.E Batterbury Magil, 'Legal status for BSL and ISL: Discussion paper', British Deaf Association, March 2014

K. Wolfgang, 'Hearing loss and dementia: Breakthrough research seeks causal link', *The Hearing Journal*, vol. 72, no. 9, 2019, pp. 22–26

M. Osler, T.C. Gunhild, E.L. Mortensen et al., 'Hearing loss, cognitive ability, and dementia in men age 19-78 years', *European Journal of Epidemiology*, vol. 34, no. 2, 2019, pp. 125–30

In circles

R.I.M. Dunbar, 'The anatomy of friendship', *Trends in Cognitive Sciences*, vol. 22, no. 1, 2018, pp. 32–51

L.R.M. Hallberg & S.G. Carlsson, 'A qualitative study of strategies for managing a hearing impairment', *British Journal of Audiology*, vol. 25, no. 3, 1991, pp. 201–11

E.H. Bart, 'Finding deaf gain: Changing languages, changing lenses, changing society', M.A. thesis, University of Texas, 2015

Wayne Stabb, 'Churchill's Hearing Loss', Hearing Health Matters, 24 February 2014, https://hearinghealthmatters.org/waynesworld/2014/churchills-hearing-loss

A. Novotney, 'The risks of social isolation', *Monitor on Psychology*, vol. 50, no. 5, 2019, p. 32, www.apa.org/monitor/2019/05/ce-corner-isolation

J. Holt-Lunstad, T.F. Robles & D.A. Sbarra, 'Advancing social connection as a public health priority in the United States', *American Psychologist*, vol. 72, no. 6, 2017, pp. 517–30

F.H. Bess & B.W. Hornsby, 'Commentary: listening can be exhausting—fatigue in children and adults with hearing loss', *Ear and Hearing*, vol. 35, no. 6, 2014, pp. 592–99

J. Yanguas, S. Pinazo-Henandis & F.J. Tarazona-Santabalbina, 'The complexity of loneliness', *Acta Biomedica*, vol. 89, no. 2, 2018, pp. 302–14

On learning

Rosemarie Garland-Thomson, 'Becoming disabled, *New York Times*, 19 August 2016, www.nytimes.com/2016/08/21/opinion/sunday/becoming-disabled.html

RELEASE

The smallest bone to pick

O.J. Ungar, O. Handzel, O. Cavel & Y. Oron, 'Superior semicircular canal dehiscence with concomitant otosclerosis: A literature review and case discussion', *Clinical Case Reports*, vol. 6, no. 12, 2018, pp. 2364–70

Judith Wright, 'South of my Days', *Collected Poems*, Fourth Estate, 2016, p. 19

Judith Wright, 'Northern River', *Collected Poems*, Fourth Estate, 2016, p. 6

Robin Wallace, *Hearing Beethoven: A story of musical loss and discovery*, University of Chicago Press, 2018

S.K. Swain, S. Nyak, J.R. Ravan & M.C. Sahu, 'Tinnitus and its current treatment: Still an enigma in medicine', *Journal of the Formosan Medical Association*, vol. 115, 2016, pp. 139–44

In company

N. Dauman & S.I. Erlandsson, 'Learning from tinnitus patients' narratives: A case study in the psychodynamic approach', *International Journal of Qualitative Studies on Health and Well-being*, vol. 7, no. 1, 2012, art. no. 19540

C. Weise, M. Kleinstäuber, H. Hesser, V. Zetterqvist & W. Andersson, 'Acceptance of tinnitus: Validation of the Tinnitus Acceptance Questionnaire', *Cognitive Behaviour Therapy*, vol. 42, no. 2, 2013, pp. 100–15

Location

Trevor Johnston & Adam Schembri, *Australian Sign Language (Auslan): An introduction to sign language linguistics*, Cambridge University Press, 2007

Andrew Trouson, 'Speaking my language: Indigenous Deaf sign', *Pursuit*, University of Melbourne, 27 October 2017, https://pursuit.unimelb.edu.au/articles/speaking-my-language-indigenous-deaf-sign

In marginalia

B.N. Beckner & D.W. Helme, 'Deaf or hearing: A hard of hearing individual's navigation between two worlds', *American Annals of the Deaf*, vol. 163, no. 3, 2018, pp. 394–412

Donna McDonald, 'The reluctant memoirist', *Griffith Review 33: Such is Life*, August 2011, www.griffithreview.com/articles/the-reluctant-memoirist

Oliver Sacks, 'Mishearings', *New York Times*, 5 June 2015, www.nytimes.com/2015/06/07/opinion/oliver-sacks-mishearings.html

Dirksen Bauman & Joseph J. Murray, 'An introduction to deaf gain', *Psychology Today*, 12 November 2014, www.psychologytoday.com/au/blog/deaf-gain/201411/introduction-deaf-gain

M. Leonard, M. Baud, M. Sjerps & E.F. Chang, 'Perceptual restoration of masked speech in human cortex', Nature Communications, vol. 7, 2016, art. no. 13619

Expression

Trevor Johnston & Adam Schembri, *Australian Sign Language (Auslan): An introduction to sign language linguistics*, Cambridge University Press, 2007

Different sounds of blue

C.D. Lunberry, 'Suspicious silence: Walking out on John Cage', *Current Musicology*, no. 94, 2014, pp. 127–42

Frank Scheffer, *How to Get Out of the Cage: One year with John Cage*, Silk Road Film Salon in coproduction with EuroArts, 2012

Ian Maleney, *Minor Monuments: Essays*, Tamp Press, 2019

Robert Sirvage, 'An insight from DeafSpace', TEDxGallaudet, YouTube, 6 March 2015, www.youtube.com/watch?v=EPTrOO6EYCY

E. Ndopu, Tweet, 22 August 2020, https://twitter.com/eddiendopu/status/1296826252775632903

World Health Organization, 'Burden of disease from environmental noise: Quantification of healthy life years lost in Europe', WHO, 2011

H-Dirksen L. Bauman & Joseph J. Murray, *Deaf Gain: Raising the stakes for human diversity*, University of Minnesota, 2014

Hansel Bauman, 'Ethics and DeafSpace architecture',CreativeMornings HQ, YouTube, 11 April 2016, www.youtube.com/watch?v=V488A9J5eP0

Hansel Bauman, 'A new architecture for a more livable and sustainable world', TEDxGallaudet, YouTube, 6 March 2015, www.youtube.com/watch?v=nBBdQnni9Go

Frank Lloyd Wright, *Frank Lloyd Wright: An autobiography*, Pomegranate Communications, 1943

Laura Kuhn (ed.), *The Selected Letters of John Cage*, Wesleyan University Press, 2016

BBC Press Office, 'BBC orchestra silenced at the Barbican and on Radio 3', press release, 12 January 2004, www.bbc.co.uk/pressoffice/pressreleases/stories/2004/01_january/12/john_cage.shtml

In Our Time, 'Beethoven', Originally broadcast 21 December 2017 on BBC Radio 4, https://www.bbc.co.uk/programmes/b09jbsjc

Jim Robbins, *The Wonder of Birds: What they tell us about ourselves, the world, and a better future*, Black Inc., 2017

V.O. Knudsen, 'Noise, the bane of hearing', *Noise Control*, vol. 1, no. 3, 1955, p. 11

United Nations, Department of Economic and Social Affairs, Population Division, The world's cities in 2018: Data booklet', 2018, www.un.org/en/events/citiesday/assets/pdf/the_worlds_cities_in_2018_data_booklet.pdf

J. Quinan, 'Frank Lloyd Wright's intuitive sound modernity', *The Journal of Architecture*, vol. 23, no. 6, 2018, pp. 961–85

Shapelessness

Natalia Ginzburg, *The Little Virtues*, Faber Factory, 2018

David Hume, *A Treatise of Human Nature*, 1739

G. McIlory & C. Storbeck, 'Development of deaf identity: An ethnographic study', *The Journal of Deaf Studies and Deaf Education*, vol. 16, no. 4, 2011, pp. 494–511

Belinda Lopez, 'Is hearing the biggest Aboriginal justice issue in the Top End?', ABC Radio National, 1 July 2017, www.abc.net.au/news/2017-07-01/is-hearing-loss-the-biggest-aboriginal-justice-issue-in-top-end/8663102

T. Vanderpoll & D. Howard, 'Massive prevalence of hearing loss among Aboriginal inmates in the Northern Territory', *Indigenous Law Bulletin*, vol. 7, no. 28, 2020, pp. 3–7

Australian Bureau of Statistics, 'National Aboriginal and Torres Strait Islander Health Survey: Statistics about long-term health conditions, disability, lifestyle factors, physical harm and use of health services', 2019, www.abs.gov.au/statistics/people/aboriginal-and-torres-strait-islanderpeoples/national-aboriginal-and-torres-strait-islander-health-survey/latest-release

Acknowledgements

I was extremely fortunate to receive an immense amount of support while writing this memoir, including a WestWords Emerging Writer Fellowship; a Wheeler Centre Hot Desk Fellowship; a Writers Victoria Publishability fellowship; a Neilma Sidney Literary Travel grant; a Griffith Review Contributors Circle Residency; and an RMIT Writers Immersion and Cultural Exchange (WrICE) fellowship to Indonesia. Studying for the Associate Degree of Professional Writing and Editing at RMIT was also invaluable; it has been a pleasure belonging to a creative and wholehearted community.

Some passages in the book have been previously published in a different form in *Kill Your Darlings*, *Overland*, *The Lifted Brow*, *The Wheeler Centre*, *The Near and the Far: Volume 2* (Scribe) and *Growing Up Disabled in Australia* (Black Inc.).

To Penny Hueston and the entire team at Text Publishing, you've been an absolute dream.

Kathy, thank you for your patience, kindness and good humour.

Jax Jacki Brown, I'm grateful that you were my Write-ability mentor. You continue to teach me so much about disability equality. This has given me tremendous courage and confidence. Thank you.

Fiona Wright and Jessica White, this book wouldn't exist without your endless insights, encouragement, mentorship and friendship.

Ben Law, thank you for your enthusiasm and practical advice.

Suzy Garcia, I wouldn't have got through 2020 without you. The next round of drinks is on me.

Jam, Ellie and Rose; Nathania; Kirby and Neve; Zena; An; Kate; Frances Ha; and the Bright Sparks—you're all such good eggs, I'm so very lucky to count you as friends.

Finally, thank you to my family. You are simply the best.